Psychology for the Classroom

Johanna Turner

Methuen
London

First published in 1977
by Methuen & Co Ltd
11 New Fetter Lane, London EC4P 4EE
© 1977 Johanna Turner
Printed in Great Britain
at the University Printing House
Cambridge
ISBN 0 416 76790 7 (hardbound)
ISBN 0 416 76800 8 (paperback)

To my parents
Winifred Mary and Edward Harold Thompson

Contents

Acknowledgements

I would particularly like to thank Professor H. J. Butcher for reading and commenting on the manuscript and also my colleagues at the University of Sussex for their helpful suggestions and criticisms. I am very grateful to Mrs Peggy Paine for typing the manuscript. The publishers and I would like to thank all authors, publishers, journals and other copyright holders for their permission to quote tables, diagrams and passages in the text namely:

Addison-Wesley Publishing Company for Fig. 6.2, from J. H. Davis, *Group Performance*, 1969; and Fig. 7.2, from N. A. Flanders, *Analyzing Teaching Behavior*, 1970.

American Council on Education for Table 7.1, from D. G. Ryans, *Characteristics of Teachers*, 1960.

American Psychological Association for Table 6.1, from B. W. Tuckman, 'Developmental Sequences in Small Groups', *Psychological Bulletin 63*, 1965, pp. 384–99 (© 1965 by the APA); Table 6.2, from S. Milgram, 'Behavioural Study of Obedience', *Journal of Abnormal and Social Psychology 67*, 1963, pp. 371–8 (© 1963 by the APA); and Fig. 6.7, from S. Milgram, 'Group Pressure and Action against a Person', *Journal of Abnormal and Social Psychology 69(2)*, 1964, pp. 137–43 (© 1964 by the APA).

O. Banks and D. S. Finlayson for Tables 10.4, 10.10 and 10.11, and Fig. 10.1, from *Success and Failure in the Secondary Schools*, 1973.

Basic Books, Inc., for Tables 8.1, 8.2, 8.3 and 8.4, from L. J. Yarrow, 'Infancy Experiences and Cognitive and Personality Development at Ten Years', in L. J. Stone, H. T. Smith and L. B. Murphy (eds) *The Competent Infant: Research and Commentary*, 1973 (© 1973 by Basic Books, Inc., Publishers, New York).

Classroom Interaction Newsletter in co-operation with Research for Better Schools for Tables 7.3 and 7.4, from A. Simon and E. G. Boyer (eds) *Mirrors for Behaviour II. An Anthology of Observation Instruments* (2 Vols), 1970.

Duke University Press for Table 3.1, from P. S. Jackson and S. Messick, 'The Person, the Product and the Response: Conceptual Problems in Assessment of Creativity', *Journal of Personality 33*, 1965, pp. 309–29 (© 1965 by Duke University Press).

Harper & Row, Publishers, Inc., for Tables 2.1, 2.2, 2.3, 2.4 and 2.5, from *Productive Thinking*, rev. ed. by Max Wertheimer, ed. by Michael Wertheimer, pp. 14–16 (© 1945, 1959 by Valentin Wertheimer).

Institute for the Study and Treatment of Delinquency for Table 10.5, from M. J. Power, R. T. Benn and J. N. Morris, 'Neighbourhood, School and Juveniles before the Courts', *British Journal of Criminology 12*(2), 1972, pp. 113–31.

The Journal Press for Figs 3.1, 3.2 and 3.3, from R. Dreistadt, 'The Use of Analogies and Incubation in Obtaining Insights in Creative Problem Solving', *Journal of Psychology 1*, 1969, pp. 434–40.

S. Karger AG, Basel, for the excerpt on pp. 200–2, from L. Kohlberg, 'The Development of Children's Orientation towards a Moral Order. 1 Sequence in the Development of Moral Thought', *Vita Humana 6*, 1963, pp. 11–33.

Longman Group Limited for Tables 10.1 and 10.2, from E. M. Hitchfield, *In Search of Promise. Studies in Child Development*, 1973.

D. C. McClelland for Fig. 9.1, from *The Achieving Society*, 1961.

McGraw-Hill Book Company for Fig. 6.4, from F. E. Fiedler, *A Theory of Leadership Effectiveness*, 1967 (© 1967 by F. E. Fiedler).

National Society for the Study of Education for Fig. 6.6, from J. W. Getzels and H. A. Thelen, 'The Classroom Group as a Unique Social System', in N. B. Henry (ed.) *59th Yearbook of the National Society for the Study of Education Part 2*, 1960, pp. 53–82.

NFER Publishing Company Ltd for Tables 10.3 and 10.6 and Fig. 10.2, from D. Pidgeon, *Expectation and Pupil Performance*, 1970.

Penguin Books Ltd for Table 8.5, from D. W. Brierley, 'The Use of Personal Constructs by Children of Three Different Ages', in D. Bannister and F. Fransella, *Inquiring Man*, 1971.

Pergamon Press Ltd for Table 4.2, from J. R. Gibb, 'Managing for Creativity in the Organization', in C. W. Taylor (ed.) *Climate for Creativity*, 1972.

Personnel Press, Inc., for Figs 3.4 and 3.5, adapted from E. P. Torrance, *The Torrance Tests of Creative Thinking: Verbal A Booklet*, 1966.

Plenum Publishing Corporation for Table 6.3, from M. Jahoda, 'Conformity and Independence', *Human Relations 12*, 1959, pp. 99–120; and Table 7.6, from B. Sugarman, 'Social Norms in Teenage Boys Peer Groups', *Human Relations 21*, 1968, pp. 41–58.

Routledge & Kegan Paul Ltd for Tables 10.7, 10.8 and 10.9, from B. Jackson, *Streaming: An Education System in Miniature*, 1964.

Scottish Academic Press Limited for Table 4.1, from F. A. Haddon and H. Lytton, 'Teaching Approach and the Development of Divergent Thinking Abilities in Primary Schools', *British Journal of Educational Psychology 38*, 1968, pp. 171–80; and Table 9.2, from P. Sutton, 'Correlation between Streaming and Season of Birth', *British Journal of Educational Psychology 37*, 1967, pp. 300–4.

The Society for the Study of Social Problems for Table 9.1, from R. J. Simon, S. M. Clark and K. Galway, 'The Woman Ph.D.: A Recent Profile', *Social Problems 15*, 1967, p. 2.

Stanford University Press for Fig. 6.3, from L. Festinger, S. Schachter and K. Back, *Social Pressures and Informal Groups*, 1950 (© 1950 by Leon Festinger, Stanley Schachter and Kurt Back).

Tavistock Publications Ltd for Table 5.1, abridged from R. D. Laing and A. Esterson, *Sanity, Madness and the Family*, 1964.

Teachers College Press for Fig. 7.1, from J. Herbert, *A System for Analyzing Lessons*, 1967 (© 1967 by Teachers College, Columbia University).

The University of Chicago Press for Fig. 6.5, from R. F. Bales, *Process Analysis*, 1951 (© 1951 by R. F. Bales).

John Wiley & Sons, Inc., for Figs. 2.6, from R. M. Gagné, 'Human Problem Solving: Internal and External Events', in B. Kleinmuntz (ed.) *Problem Solving: Research, Method and*

Theory, 1966; Fig. 2.9, from J. S. Bruner, J. J. Goodnow and G. A. Austin, *A Study of Thinking*, 1956; and Fig. 6.1, from R. L. Kahn, *Organizational Stress. Studies in Role Conflict and Ambiguity*, 1964.

Introduction

This book is offered as an aid, and no more than that, to people who are learning themselves, and helping other people to learn, that is to parents, students, and particularly, teachers. The activity of teaching is essentially interpersonal in that, to be successful, it requires the teacher to understand the behaviour of the learner as fully as possible. Psychology attempts to gain insights into the behaviour of human beings and some of these insights may prove helpful to others in complementing their own experience and intuitive understanding. The topics covered have been chosen with the aim of summarizing relevant information which psychologists have gained and are, therefore, together with the research findings reported, highly selective since there has been no attempt to provide either an overview of the whole of psychological knowledge or total coverage of any one aspect. Specialist texts have done this better and they are referred to in the text or under 'Further reading'. Certain studies and aspects of psychology have been highlighted which are thought to be of particular relevance to the teacher who is attempting to understand the behaviour of his pupils in order to make his teaching more effective.

Section One is concerned with cognitive aspects, an understanding of which is essential since cognitive processes are the means by which individuals are able to make sense of their environment. They are the central core of our human understanding. Man is able to use symbols to mediate between the environmental input and his response. It is this skill which the child rapidly develops during infancy, middle childhood and adolescence. The facts a child learns in school are undoubtedly important but his education will only be of value if he learns how to learn through developing his immense latent cognitive powers. As Bronowski (1973) argues so eloquently:

In man, before the brain is an instrument for action, it has to
be an instrument of preparation. For that, quite specific areas
are involved; for example, the frontal lobes have to be un-
damaged. But, far more deeply, it depends on the long preparation of human childhood ... Think of the investment that
evolution has made in the child's brain. My brain weighs three
pounds, my body weighs fifty times as much as that. But when
I was born, my body was a mere appendage to the head; it
weighed only five or six times as much as my brain. For most
of history, civilisations have crudely ignored that enormous
potential. In fact the longest childhood has been that of
civilisation, learning to understand that.

Section Two considers the social situation in which knowledge
and understanding develop. Man is, above all, a social creature
who influences, and is influenced by, his peers. We do not, nor
can we, live in isolation. When a number of people are brought
together in a school or a classroom they are affected by the composition of the group and adapt their behaviour accordingly. The aim
of understanding some elements of social interaction is not to
enable a person to manipulate others but to become more aware
of the fact, obvious in itself but often overlooked, that one person's
perception of a situation may be markedly different from another's,
and that one person's mode of interaction may have developed
in a culture which makes it strange to one from another culture.
Such diversity can divide man from man whereas knowledge can
bring tolerance and flexibility.

Section Three focuses on the individual with special reference
to academic achievement. It underlines the view that success
may not just depend on hard work but is intimately related to
an individual's personal development and personality. Academic
success and failure are interactive in the sense that the cause is
likely to lie in the combination of pupil, school, teacher, subject
and peers. Nobody can succeed in everything but surely everybody
has the right, through their long years in school, to succeed in
some areas. If they do not action is necessary, but the basis for
such action should be a subtle diagnosis of the needs of the
individual and the setting in which he will be able to flourish.

Educational policy and provision are a political matter but
psychological insights can be one type of information to be taken

into account when decisions are made, so that the inevitably inadequate resources are used as wisely as possible. It is to be hoped that individuals will use psychology not as a body of facts but as the basis for forming hypotheses which they can then test for themselves, not necessarily as researchers but in a mood of personal exploration.

This book offers an introduction to certain aspects of psychology of relevance to those who spend much time trying to understand other people's children or their own. The individuality of another will always be mysterious simply because he is 'other', but the search for some understanding is, in the author's view, 'the proper study of mankind'.

We are all afraid – for our confidence, for the future, for the world. That is the nature of the human imagination. Yet every man, every civilisation, has gone forward because of its engagement with what it has set itself to do. The personal commitment of a man to his skill, the intellectual commitment and the emotional commitment working together as one, has made the Ascent of Man.

(Bronowski, 1973)

Section I

Focus:

Cognitive aspects

[1]
Intelligence

Intelligence is often confused with learning, thinking, problem solving, concept formation, attainment and achievement. It is none of these but it affects them all in a positive way, i.e. it improves performance. This concept has caused considerable controversy in recent years and there are two main reasons for this: firstly intelligence is thought to be connected with achievement and is therefore of importance in our society and educational system; and, secondly, some people are thought to be more intelligent than others. Such an, apparently, unequally distributed yet desirable attribute is naturally of interest to people concerned with individual development.

---
1 *The concept of intelligence*

There are many definitions of intelligence which do not say what it is but point to the results of having it. Thus a certain level of performance is taken as evidence of a person possessing this quality to a greater or lesser extent than others. Such an approach was characterized by Karl Popper (1945) as methodological nominalism:

> Instead of aiming at finding out what a thing really is, and at defining its true nature, methodological nominalism aims at describing how a thing behaves in various circumstances, and especially, whether there are any regularities in its behaviour. In other words, methodological nominalism sees the aim of science in the description of the things and events of our experience, and in an 'explanation' of these events, i.e. their description with the help of universal laws. The methodological nominalist will never think that a question like '*what is* energy?' or '*what is* movement?' or '*what is* an atom?' is an important

question for physics; but he will attach importance to a question like: 'How can the energy of the sun be made useful?' or 'How does a planet move?' or 'Under what conditions does an atom radiate light?'

Popper contrasted this with methodological essentialism: '... the view, held by Plato and many of his followers, that it is the task of pure knowledge or "science" to discover and describe the true nature of things, i.e. their hidden reality or essence ... and a description of the essence of a thing they all called a "definition".'

Considerable confusion has been caused by nominalist descriptions of intelligence masquerading as essentialist definitions. However, views of intelligence can be divided roughly into three: first, 'intelligence as product'; second, 'intelligence as process'; and third, 'intelligence as judgement'.

1.1 *Intelligence as product* (F. Galton, A. Binet, C. Burt)

To see 'intelligence' as a name given to the product of an intelligence test is, historically, the most accurate view, as Cyril Burt (1968) reminds us: '"Intelligence" was from the very outset a technical term used by erudite specialists; and it is only during the last 60 years or so, since its adoption by a small group of psychologists that it has filtered through into everyday parlance.' Three early specialists who were particularly significant for the development of the psychometric concept of intelligence were Francis Galton, Alfred Binet and Cyril Burt.

Although it is often said today that all children are born with the same intelligence, this idea is relatively recent as Galton's (1870) original thinking was based on the statistical assumption that mental capacity would be 'normally distributed'. In 1849 an English translation of Quetelet's *Letters on Probability* was published in which Quetelet showed that the height of 100,000 French conscripts was normally distributed, i.e. a few were very short, a few very tall, and the majority fell between these two extremes. Diagrammatically this normal distribution can be expressed by the bell-shaped Gaussian Curve (Fig. 1.1).

Galton (1870) therefore argued that:

... if this is the case with stature, then it will be true as regards

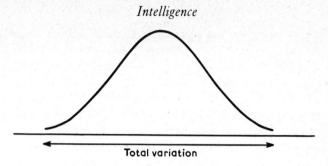

Fig. 1.1 *A normal curve*

every other physical feature – as circumference of head, size of brain, weight of grey matter, number of brain fibres, etc. and thence, by a step on which no physiologist will hesitate, as regards mental capacity.

Thus the notion of inequality between individuals was built into the original formulation of the concept of 'mental capacity'.

Galton next became concerned with the mental resources of the nation. Writing to a friend, he said: 'You are wondering what amount of coal the nation possesses and where it lies; I am wondering what mental abilities we possess and where it is to be found.' In 1902 he persuaded the anthropological section of the British Association to finance a survey of Britain which would include mental as well as physical characteristics and be carried out through the schools. Burt was one of those who were asked to devise a set of tests to be used in this survey. Therefore the first intelligence tests arose in a context in which mental ability was thought of as something which was normally distributed, like height and weight, and the function of the tests was to measure individual variations in this trait.

Meanwhile, in France, Alfred Binet was also concerned with individual differences. Having studied his own two daughters, he was particularly interested in the nature of thought. Indeed his idea of intelligence, particularly in his early work, was closely linked with thought. Reeves (1965) points out that Binet had taken the term 'intelligence' directly from Taine's *D'Intelligence*: '... for Taine "l'intelligence" meant thinking, but explained in terms of the patterning and re-patterning of images derived from sensory experience.'

Binet however was not so much concerned with intelligence in the normal population as with separating out those who were educationally retarded, and then subdividing this retarded group into the subnormal and the educationally deprived. In 1905 Binet, together with his co-worker, Simon, published the results of the testing which they had been doing in the schools since, in Binet's case, 1894. They had used many types of tests but ultimately retained only those items which discriminated between bright and dull children. These tests were entirely empirical in that Binet watched the children and used their behaviour as his guide in item selection. It is largely due to the context within which Binet worked that 'intelligence' is now thought of as being exhibited in certain characteristic situations. Since in the Parisian schools in 1900 the instruction was academic and authoritarian, Binet's primary criterion for item selection was whether the children who passed certain items were seen to be successful in this rather narrow context.

The 1905 scale arranged all the items in order of difficulty and the child worked through until he could do no more, but in the 1908 revision the items were grouped according to age. In any group 60 to 75 per cent of the mental age group were expected to be able to perform the tasks. Binet then compared the child's mental age with his chronological age and if the latter was more than two years behind the former this was regarded as 'a serious deficiency'. This original scale has since been revised and improved, notably by the Americans, Termain and Merrill. Today, the revised scale, called the Stanford–Binet Intelligence Scale, is one of the best known measures of intelligence.

Sir Cyril Burt has been one of the most influential figures in Britain in the area of intelligence testing and, it is worth considering how views on the nature of psychology and on the concept of intelligence have changed since the time of his early work. When he submitted his first article to the new *British Journal of Psychology*, the editor, Ward, did not wish to print, 'so lengthy an article based merely on experimental or statistical research' and wrote to Burt regretting that he had, 'devoted so much time and industry to a transient problem, like mental testing, which holds so little promise for the future'. Today psychologists attempt to express their findings in quantitative terms but at that time Burt's statistics, which accompanied the article, were initially relegated to an appendix and subsequently left out of the published version.

Burt studied classics at Oxford but took psychology as a special subject in finals after which he did postgraduate work and set up an informal child guidance centre where he and Keating tested backward and delinquent children. In 1907 he went to Liverpool where he started a new course of psychology for medical students and prospective teachers. In order to get more information on the children he had to deal with he lived in the Nile Street settlement. At this time there was growing dissatisfaction with the way in which doctors were certifying mentally defective school children. Burt quotes the following description as being typical of the methods used: 'The pupils are drawn up in ranks, in standards, i.e. class or grade at a time ... The trained observer can then read off the physiognomy of the individual's features and other bodily parts, as quickly as a printed book' (Warner, 1890). As a result of this dissatisfaction, and of pressure from professional bodies, the London County Council decided to employ an education psychologist for an experimental three-year period. Burt was chosen and he tells how the Scottish Sir Robert Blair, chief education officer, gave him his blessing with the words: 'Young man, ye're the fust official psychologist in the wurrld, and ye've all London at yer feet! Now come back in a week and tell me what ye're going to do.'

What Burt did was to instigate the large scale testing of pupils and open the schools to research students. He carried out over thirty extensive investigations in the next fifteen years. Once again he sought field experience by living in a settlement near Euston and staying with 'a docker in Stepney, a coster in Kennington, and a burglar in a back street off the Seven Sisters Road' (Burt, 1952) in order to learn more of the background of his pupils. Later he managed to infiltrate a criminal gang to follow up delinquents he had studied. He felt this field work to be especially important, remarking: 'Nowadays it is so often forgotten that to appreciate the cultural outlook of the child you are studying you must yourself have shared it.' As early as 1910 he had started to prepare a revision of the Binet–Simon Intelligence Scale and after the war he concentrated on constructing standardized age norms and developing group and performance tests. At this time he combined the case study and statistical approach, working on the assumption that intelligence was 'an innate, general, cognitive ability'.

One result of the researches of these early workers was to establish the psychometric concept of intelligence, i.e. intelligence was seen as something which could be *measured*. This gave rise to the operational definition of intelligence as 'what the tests test'. An operational definition is akin to Popper's nominalist description in that it defines scientific concepts in terms of physical operations (thus acid is any substance that turns blue litmus paper red). The fact that Galton, Binet and Burt all worked within an educational setting of a particular kind has meant that their tests are tests of a specific set of behaviours and it is therefore unwise to extrapolate from such findings to more general behaviour.

1.2 *Intelligence as possession* (C. E. Spearman, L. L. Thurstone, J. P. Guilford)

It is perhaps unfortunate that the notion of intelligence as a 'product' became transformed into that of a 'possession'. Intelligence is often spoken of as if it were similar to height or weight, not just a quality which can be measured in the same way. People are therefore thought to have a fixed intelligence waiting to be assessed, as if it were a mental secretion or something the brain 'had' in the way blood has red corpuscles.

If this approach is accepted too uncritically it is very easy to confuse intelligence with attainment, achievement, or even, ability. Although it can affect all of these it should not be thought to be interchangeable with any. An example may make this clearer: Two pupils sit 'A' levels, both have identical motivation, John has an IQ of 130 and gets an A in Chemistry, an A in Physics and a C in German. Jane has an IQ of 110 and gets a C in French, a C in German and an E in Physics. Both pupils have *attained* 'A' level standard, both pupils have *achieved* the level they required. John appears to have more scientific than linguistic *ability*, Jane the reverse. But John is more *intelligent* than Jane and therefore, as they have equal motivation, his final scores exceed hers.

How has this confusion of intelligence with ability, in particular, arisen? To answer this it is necessary to take a brief look at the statistical background. The statistical technique of factor analysis

is often applied to test scores. This is a technique based on
correlation. Two scores, or sets of scores, are said to be correlated
if they co-vary, i.e. if A increases when B increases or A decreases
when B increases; in the former case the correlation would be
positive in the latter negative (Table 1.1).

Table 1.1 *Correlation patterns*

	Perfect positive		Perfect negative	
	test A	*test B*	*test A*	*test B*
Child 1	70	70	70	30
Child 2	65	65	60	40
Child 3	60	60	50	50
Child 4	55	55	40	60
Child 5	50	50	30	70

The correlation obtained expresses the closeness of fit between
two sets of measures. A high correlation can be illustrated if we
think of scores as two dancers who may either move side by side
(positive correlation) or, as in ballroom dancing, face to face, so
that one advances whilst the other retreats (negative correlation).
The important point is that they move together and it is this
mutual relationship which a correlation expresses. A correlation
of 'o' means that there is no correlation; a correlation of +0.1
to +1.00 expresses varying degrees of positive correlation and
a correlation of −0.1 to −1.00 expresses varying degrees of negative correlation; in both cases the higher the figure the closer the
correlation.

If we have an array of test scores some tests in the battery
correlate more highly with each other than with other tests; i.e.
more people who score high on test B score high on tests E, F
and G. If we ask what does test B have in common with tests
E, F and G to result in this similarity an answer can be arrived
at by the technique of factor analysis. This breaks down the
components which compose the final score, and shows if any of
these components are common to several tests. These components
are called factors. Therefore a factor is something which both

accounts for part of the score in an individual test and links this
individual test with others which have this same factor as part
of their score.

If scores on tests of mathematics, physics and chemistry were
seen to correlate one might, by factor analysis get out a 'factor'
which contributed a high proportion of the score within a particular
test and was common to the three tests. However, a factor is a statistical construct, it need have no psychological reality. To show
that these tests have a high 'x' loading is one thing, it is another
to say that 'x' is numerical ability or reasoning. It could have
happened that the tests in question had a certain format, were
given at a certain time of day or were given to a certain group
of children; factor 'x' could then be the interactions amongst these
variables.

Spearman (1904, 1927) was the first to use factor analysis and
came to the conclusion that every test score represents a combination of general ability, 'g', which will be common and consistent
across all the tasks an individual performs, plus an ability specific
to that test. The consistency between an individual's scores is thus
accounted for by 'g', and the specific factors, together with 'g',
account for the scores within a particular test. This two-factor
theory was challenged in Britain and America for it was noticed
that although people did show consistency of performance there
was also a tendency for people to be better at certain related tasks
than at others. In other words, the two-factor theory assumed that
the most important factor that was common between tests was
the ability of the person doing them whereas it could be argued
that there was an inter-relationship between a person and the type
of test being done, so similarity of test task could contribute to
the correlation between tests.

This led Thurstone (1938) to introduce the notion of correlated
factors and to distinguish the primary mental abilities of

S – Spatial ability
P – Perceptual speed
N – Numerical ability
V – Verbal meaning
M – Memory
W – Verbal fluency
I or R – Inductive reasoning

It was also seen that test variances could be further split into even more specific factors. In America this multi-factor approach, strengthened by the work of J. P. Guilford has been particularly popular. Guilford (1956) produced a model of the structure of the intellect (Fig. 1.2) in which he distinguished between the *operations* which the intellect can perform, the *contents* of these operations and the resulting *products*. Taken together 120 cells were generated, each of which Guilford argued represented a different mental ability. Although Thurstone's method made the existence

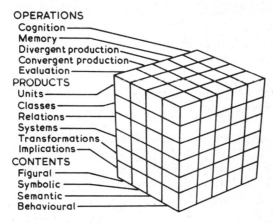

Fig. 1.2 *Guilford's model of the structure of the intellect*
(Butcher, 1968)

of a general factor impossible, hierarchical models usually have a general factor at the top and it is this factor 'g' which is often equated with intelligence. To equate 'g' with intelligence has led to the mistaken assumption that intelligence is an ability. The problem is that Spearman's general factor 'g' is *not* an ability in the same sense as Thurstone's primary mental abilities or Guilford's specific ones are. But because both 'g' and the others are factors there is a tendency to view them as similar in kind.

It must be appreciated that for the primary and specific factors it is possible to think of specific tasks which would test them and hence there are 'verbal', 'numerical' and 'spatial' tests. But one cannot specifically test 'g' since it, by definition, has a general effect across all the tests. Its only function is to express the fact that the correlation between tests means that they have something in common. Thus it is allowable to equate 'g' with intelligence but not to say that 'g' is an ability, and therefore intelligence is an ability – neither are abilities.

1.3 *Intelligence as process* (G. Ryle, J. Piaget, M. Wertheimer)

Since a misunderstanding of intelligence as product led to its being considered a possession, psychologists have attempted to stress the fact that intelligence should be thought of as an adverb rather than as a noun. It indicates *how* a man behaves, not some specific ability he possesses. Neither does it represent any end state that can be approached by time and effort (one cannot conceive of 'O' or 'A' level intelligence papers); rather it delimits a *standard* of performance which can be exhibited in tasks at all levels, whether primary mathematics, CSE geography, or postgraduate studies in high temperature physics.

The philosopher Gilbert Ryle (1949) referred to intelligence as a disposition. He argued that intelligence was not the same as knowledge, just as stupidity was not ignorance, and he was at pains to show that when a person behaves intelligently he cannot be said to be thinking what to do and then doing it, as this would mean that the prior thinking would, in turn, have to be thought about and there would be an infinite regress. To behave intelligently is to do one thing, i.e. perform an action in a certain way, not to go through some previous mental operation. But this does not mean that intelligence is the same as habit. An intelligent person has not developed a wide repertoire of good habits, rather there are a wide variety of situations in which he could be expected to respond in a certain way; that is he is *disposed* to behave intelligently just as, to use Ryle's examples, glass is disposed to break and sugar to dissolve.

What, then, does it mean to behave intelligently? What is characteristic of the behaviour of those who score high on intelligence tests? For Ryle the intelligent man

... conducts his operations efficiently, and to operate efficiently is not to perform two operations. It is to perform one operation in a certain manner or with a certain style or procedure, and the description of this *modus operandi* has to be in terms of such semi-dispositional, semi-episodic epithets as 'alert', 'careful', 'critical', 'ingenious', 'logical', etc.

This approach draws attention to the relationship between intelligence and a given task. In the previous section the fact that intelligence implied a comparison between people was stressed, here it is the way a person performs a certain task that shows whether he is intelligent or not, without reference to other people. However, if everybody were to perform a task in the same intelligent fashion this manner of performance would be called the 'correct' way, not an intelligent way. It would seem then, that it is only when a person adds something to the accepted pattern and improves the performance in a particular way, that he is said to be intelligent. If a person were to have a computer-like brain so that he could calculate at high speeds, using rather laborious methods, he could not be said to be intelligent; but if he could order the numbers in such a way that he saved time and therefore calculated quickly, he would be behaving intelligently. Intelligent behaviour would seem to imply parsimony and the conservation of mental energy.

So far the emphasis has been on what it makes sense to say about intelligence viewed as process, but psychologists such as Piaget and Wertheimer have approached the process question in a more empirical manner. These cognitive psychologists should be distinguished from the psychometricians Galton, Binet, Burt, Spearman, Thurstone and Guilford in that they have concentrated on the thinking and reasoning process, thus focusing on one part of cognitive psychology which studies '... all the processes by which the sensory input is transformed, reduced, elaborated, stored, recovered and used' (Neisser, 1966). The significance of cognitive studies for those interested in intelligence is that if it is known how people think and reason and how their methods vary, the intelligent person will be characterized by using the most appropriate method for the task before him. That is if a logical, convergent, analytic approach is required he will adopt this, if on the other hand a more divergent strategy is necessary, he will adapt his thinking accordingly. The major question of whether the 'intelligent' man will be as successful in a more divergent context will be discussed later (see p. 70) but we need to note that the inclusion of 'creativity' within the list of dispositional properties is still in dispute.

The indications are that an intelligent person may achieve a quantitatively higher score or do quantitatively more items on a test, but this is because his thinking is qualitatively different from others. Piaget has always been concerned with qualitative differences in intelligence and for him 'intelligence' is the process of intellectual functioning. He (1950) calls it: 'essentially a system of living and acting operations; i.e. a state of balance, or equilibrium achieved by the person when he is able to deal adequately with the data before him. But it is not a static state, it is dynamic in that it continually adapts itself to new environmental stimuli.' He equates intelligence with intellectual functioning in general, having its genesis through the manner in which humans interact with the environment, and becoming most fully developed when it gives rise to 'formal' adult thinking. Wertheimer (1945) (see p. 33) claims to have a constructive approach to thinking as he is concerned with 'productive' thinking by means of which a solution is arrived at by the *direct* apprehension of the structure of a problem, which echoes Ryle's 'one process, not two'.

Thus to view intelligence as process is to see it as part of the complex of processes which mediate between the organism and the environment, giving rise to higher mental activities. It is dynamically linked with thinking and reasoning although it is not interchangeable with either.

1.4 *Intelligence as judgement* (A. Jensen, L. Hudson)

It seems that intelligence, viewed as a product of testing, implies a certain process or manner of behaviour, although no particular process can be denoted. Therefore intelligence is a 'polymorphous' or 'open' concept, i.e. there are, possibly, an infinite number of activities which can be indicative of intelligent behaviour. But what is significant is that intelligence implies an *appropriate* process. When a person is called 'intelligent' a judgement is made about the level of his performance. In other words, it is being stated that he has done something *well*, not necessarily correctly. Although we would assume that an intelligent process would usually result in correct performance, one does not entail the other. Intelligence is thus an evaluative term and it is this fact which generates a great deal of the heat in debate. In this it can be compared with bravery: to say a person is not brave, i.e. cowardly, is not simply to make a statement of fact but to make a perjorative statement. Equally, to say that a child is not musical is neutral, to say is he unintelligent is derogatory. This is because to be musical means to have a specific ability; to be intelligent is to be judged to have the disposition to do a wide range of things well. The position is further complicated because it is often said that we differ from animals by having reason; intelligence is seen to be linked to reason and therefore, by a fallacious chain of reasoning, it is thought that to be called less intelligent means that a person is less human, less worthy, etc.

Once this evaluative dimension is understood its social consequences become apparent. Jensen (1969) (acknowledging a debt to Professor Otis Dudley Duncan, 1968) has brought together three sets of figures to make a point of some substance. The passage is worth quoting in full:

> Let us consider three sets of numbers. First, the Barr scale of occupations, devised in the early 1920s, provides one set of data. Lists of 120 representative occupations, each definitely and concretely described, were given to 30 psychological judges who were asked to rate the occupations on a scale from 0 to 100 according to the grade of intelligence each occupation was believed to require for ordinary success. Second, in 1964, the National Opinion Research Centre (NORC) by taking a large public opinion poll, obtained ratings of the *prestige* of a great number of occupations; these prestige ratings represent the average standing of each occupation relative to all others in the eyes of the general public. Third, a rating of socio-economic status (SES) is provided by the 1960 *Census of Population: Classified Index of Occupations and Industries,* which assigns to each of the hundreds of listed occupations a score ranging from 0 to 96 as a composite index of the average income and educational level prevailing in the occupation.
>
> The interesting point is the set of correlations among these three independently derived occupational ratings:
>
> The Barr scale and the NORC ratings are correlated .91
> The Barr scale and the SES index are correlated .81
> The NORC ratings and the SES index are correlated .90

In other words, psychologists' concept of the 'intelligence demands' of an occupation (Barr scale) is very much like the general public's concept of the prestige or 'social standing' of an occupation (NORC ratings) and both are closely related to an independent measure of the educational and economic status of the persons pursuing an occupation (SES index).

Intelligence, then, should be viewed as a normally, i.e. unequally, distributed quality, which indicates a superior level of performance on a range of tasks and which correlates with social status. Hudson (1971) ironically outlines this sequence of events:

> Many psychologists ... still make assumptions about the IQ that date from our earliest thinking on the matter – originally from Galton and then from Spearman and Thorndike. Such psychologists assume that the IQ serves as the core, or code, or blue-print, of intelligent behaviour as we normally understand it. On this argument, the man who excels at the simple puzzles an IQ test contains will excel in every other skill, whether simple or complex. He is superior, and his superiority is homogeneous: the man is a natural aristocrat. This view transposes into the field of behavioural science an older model of aristocracy, founded on birth or blood. In practice, like most myths, the model of the natural, biological, aristocrat accords rather poorly with the empirical evidence; but its grip over the minds of psychologists has been compelling.

The point, however, is not that the empirical evidence is lacking but that there is no clear relationship between the evidence and the phenomenon it is meant to support. The statistical construct, IQ, relates to intelligence as product, and this does not provide sufficient information to judge intelligence as process. The superman myth arises out of viewing intelligence as judgement. One can move freely within each of these views of intelligence but not from one to the other at will. To associate the product with the judgement without clearly specifying the sequence of moves whereby the one becomes the other is to see 'homogeneous superiority'. However, all that has in fact been shown is superiority in a range of tasks which are characterized by having had their genesis in the schools of Britain and France at the turn of the century and have been shown to correlate with occupational success.

---

2 *The development of intelligence*

Psychometric concepts of intelligence are based on a study of groups – an approach which needs to be complemented by the investigation of the growth of cognitive capacity in the individual. Psychometricians make predictions concerning individual performance from their understanding of population norms, whereas developmentalists extrapolate from individual, or small group, studies to the general population. Whenever a person responds to an environmental stimulus some mediating process is posited whereby the environmental stimulus is recognized and reacted to. There are three main centres of research concerning the development of this central process, in Russia, in Europe and in America, all of which have a useful contribution to make, although the European research is perhaps the most extensive.

2.1 *Russian studies* (I. R. Pavlov, A. P. Luria, N. P. Paramanova, A. V. Zaporozhets)

Although, ideologically, the Russians are committed to an environmentalist view of intelligence as such, seeing it purely as the product of the environment and denying the validity of intelligence testing, they have shown considerable interest in higher mental processes. Such interest stems from the work of Pavlov who is perhaps best known for his conditioning studies, but to see these as his only contribution to psychology is to take too narrow a view. Initially, he was a physiologically-orientated experimental psychologist but later he argued that man's behaviour was qualitatively different from that of animals. He found, during his experiments with dogs, that it was possible to induce experimental neurosis by requiring the dogs to make finer and finer discriminations until they failed to discriminate at all, at which point their behaviour became neurotic. He was stimulated by this to study neurosis in human beings and began to appreciate the significance of language as a regulator of behaviour. He initiated (1941) the notion of language as a 'second signal system' although later psychologists have done most of the experimental work.

When Pavlov (1927) studied dogs he distinguished between 'inborn' and 'conditional' reflexes, being more interested in the latter which he saw as the 'first signal system'. The paradigm was that of a dog who was exposed to two unrelated stimuli; firstly the sound of a tuning fork to which its only response was to turn its head and cock its ears and, secondly, meat powder which caused salivation. The tuning fork was then sounded at the same time as meat powder was blown into the mouth of the dog. Finally the fork was sounded alone and the dog responded by salivating. That is, initially, it automatically salivated in response to the meat powder, but during training built up a link between the sound of the tuning fork and the meat powder so that finally the tuning fork alone elicited the meat powder salivary response. Without training, salivation to the sound of a tuning fork would not occur. This is known as classical conditioning.

Pavlov then extended this paradigm to include a second signal system which he explained (1941) by saying that in man the first mechanism for dealing with the environment is the subcortex which controls 'unconditioned reflexes' of the inborn 'instincts, urges, affections and emotions'; the second mechanism requires the cerebral hemispheres, but without the frontal lobes, and this makes possible the first signal system of 'conditioned connexions and associations'. To this he then added a 'second signal system' – speech – which 'signals the first system'. By means of this system words can become a stimulus, thus the word 'food' can cause salivation in the absence of the absolute stimulus (real food). 'Speech is a real conditional stimulus to human beings as real as the others which are common to animals as well.' The 'second signal system' was seen as having a regulatory function. In hypnosis

> instead of the usually predominant (in the waking state) function of the second signalizing system, there arises the activity of the first system, primarily and more stably as fantasies and day dreaming, but further and more definitely as sleep, dreaming, and drowsiness, freed from the regulating influence of the second system. Hence the chaotic character of this activity depending chiefly upon the emotional influence of the sub-cortices.

Luria (1961) has taken up this question of the regulatory role of speech showing how speech influences behaviour firstly by initiating or impelling responses, secondly by inhibiting inappropriate responses, thirdly by regulating behaviour (for example a child will press a bulb when he or the experimenter says 'press'); and, finally, as instrumental in self-regulation when internal speech develops through the internalizing of the previously overt commands.

An experimental study, the results of which were interpreted in terms of a second signal system, was done by Paramanova (1956). In this experiment the task was for children to learn to press a bulb when a red light appeared and not to press when a green light did so. Older children, of five or six, learnt this very quickly and could reverse the procedure almost as quickly; younger children had considerable difficulty. The explanation offered was that the older child was using the second signalling system. That is he had an internal mediating response between seeing the light and pressing whereas the younger child was responding *directly* to the light and building up a classically conditioned response to the light. Obviously in this situation the older child would show much greater flexibility and be able to generalize his response to a greater extent through the use of words as a mediator.

Pavlov was also concerned with the 'what-is-it reflex' or 'orientation reflex' and this aspect of his work has been continued by Zaporozhets (1965) who investigated those higher processes which seem to obey different laws from the simpler conditioned reflex. This orientating response enables the subject to be selective when bombarded with environmental stimuli and Zaporozhets saw this response as part of the definition of voluntary behaviour. A second important aspect of such behaviour is the subject's ability to monitor his actions whilst performing them by a kind of continuous feedback. The young child, or animal gets feedback at the end of a task whereas the older one can adapt and readapt his behaviour whilst performing the task in response to the feedback he is receiving. Therefore Zaporozhets argued that a child will learn faster if his orienting responses are taken into account and he is specifically told what to attend to and to seek, and to use continuous feedback. It would seem that the older child is able to use the internal, mediating, second signal system to plan his behaviour in advance.

In summary, Russian studies have described the development

of four mechanisms, all of which are necessary for intelligent behaviour; the inborn reflex, the conditional response, the orientating reflex and the verbal second signal system. This last is seen as a mediating response which regulates behaviour and which needs to be fully developed for mature thinking. The orienting response is also considered to be of importance together with the use of continuous feedback, which in turn requires verbal mediation.

2.2 *European studies* (J. Piaget)

European research is also concerned with the development of internal mediators, although the terminology is different, and here the most influential figure is that of Jean Piaget. Piaget came to psychology by way of zoology and philosophy, and as early as eighteen had formulated two of the ideas which were to influence much of his later thinking. The first was that 'Action in itself admits of logic ... and that, therefore, logic stems from a sort of spontaneous organisation of acts' (1952). The second was concerned with the relation between the whole and its parts; he argued that 'In all fields of life (organic, mental, social) there exist "totalities" qualitatively distinct from their parts and imposing on them an organization' (ibid).

In 1919 Piaget met Simon in Paris and Simon suggested that he should check Burt's tests with Parisian children. Thus Piaget was initially concerned with psychometric notions of intelligence but because of his background and interest in parts and wholes, he soon extended the concept of intelligence beyond that of its being a product of testing.

Now from the very first question I noticed that though Burt's tests certainly had their diagnostic merits, based on the number of successes and failures, it was much more interesting to try to find the reasons for the failures. Thus I engaged my subjects in conversations patterned after psychiatric questioning, with the aim of discovering something about the reasoning process underlying their right, but especially their wrong answers. I noticed with amazement that the simplest reasoning task involving the inclusion of a part in the whole, of the co-ordination of relations, or the 'multiplication of classes' (finding the part common to two wholes), presented for normal children up to the age of eleven or twelve difficulties unsuspected by the adult ... At last I had found my field of research. First of all it became clear to me that the theory of the relations between the whole or the part can be studied experimentally through the analysis of the psychological processes underlying logical operations.

Piaget has spent the rest of his life studying these psychological processes and the result has been a view of intelligence which is as illuminating as it is unique. He is, above all, concerned with the *qualitative* changes which take place in a person's thinking between infancy and maturity. These changes show, not that a child thinks like an adult but knows less, rather that a child's thinking is different in kind from that of an adult. He distinguishes four developmental stages through which children pass; sensori-motor (from birth to two years), pre-operational (from two to seven), concrete operations (from seven to eleven) and formal operations (from eleven to adulthood). Each stage is characterized by particular behaviours and a descriptive sketch is necessary before Piaget's explanatory theory can be considered.

Like Binet, Piaget began by observing his own children and most of his empirical data for the sensori-motor stage was gained from observing his three children. He found that at birth the infant exhibits a limited range of unco-ordinated reflexes which are a necessary condition for any subsequent development. During the first four months these reflexes are modified and co-ordinated into simple *schemes* (i.e. fixed behavioural routines); these are further elaborated so that by eight months the infant is also able to react to objects outside himself and show some signs of intentionality.

By the end of the first year the child becomes interested in strange objects and, provided he has not been frightened, will seek novelty for its own sake. Throughout the sensori-motor stage all the child's actions are overt physical ones and his organization of the environment is in terms of these physical actions, thus this stage is overwhelmingly one of intelligence in action. Subsequently the child internalizes these actions and thinks about doing 'x' rather than actually performing the physical manipulations. He is therefore able to 'symbolize' these actions and such symbols are called 'operations' or internalized actions. It is the development of operations which characterizes later cognitive development. Therefore, for Piaget, the mediating response is the internalized *gesture* rather than the *verbal* mediator of the Russians.

From two to seven the child is in the period of pre-operational thought and it is the end of this period, the 'intuitive stage' (four to seven), which Piaget has studied thoroughly. During this time the symbolic function is developed, overt actions and imitations are internalized and the child can represent events to himself within his own mind. These 'symbols' are to be distinguished from 'signs', i.e. words and mathematical notations, which bear no intrinsic reference to the object signified. Symbols are thought to precede signs and therefore it is a mistake to equate the development of symbolic function with the development of language. It would appear that Piaget is distinguishing two internalized processes, the symbolic, and the sign, where Pavlov saw only one – the 'second signal system'.

Pre-operational thinking has several distinguishing characteristics: it is fluid, unstable, intensely realistic, irreversible and egocentric. The fluidity and instability of pre-operational thought can best be illustrated by the child's difficulties with classification and conservation. During this stage the child cannot classify in the true sense although he is able to make pseudo-classes. He can divide flowers into roses and tulips but if he is shown a bunch consisting of six roses and two tulips and asked 'Are there more roses or more flowers?' he will not reply 'more flowers' since he does not understand that the subordinate classes, tulips and roses, are included in the superordinate class of flowers. Conservation requires the child to realize that certain aspects of a situation are invariant despite changes in other aspects; for example, the amount of matter in an object will remain constant if nothing is added and nothing taken away even though, perceptually, the shape of the object may have changed. When an experimenter shows a child two balls of dough and the child agrees that they contain the same amount he will no longer agree that the amount is the same if the experimenter changes the shape of one of the balls by flattening it out into a pancake shape or rolling it into a sausage. The child has been misled by the observable perceptual change because of his tendency to concentrate on one aspect of a situation to the exclusion of others. This concentration, or *centration*, is illustrated by the experiment on one to one correspondence. Here if the child lays out five counters and matches them with five sweets he will agree that there are the same number of sweets and counters but if the sweets are then bunched together the child will say that there are more counters, or an older child may recount them showing that he has not grasped the principle of conservation. Bryant (1974) argues that, in this situation, children can conserve but are showing a failure to understand *which* method of estimating 'how many' is the correct one and are using incorrectly, the method 'longer means more'. Obviously young children have problems in this area although the precise nature of their problem may be unclear.

The child's thinking at this time is ego-centric in that although he realizes that other people have a separate existence he is not able to comprehend that their point of view may be different from his own, so that he cannot tell a story to another if doing so requires him to make allowance for what the other does not know or cannot see. His verbal schemes are also still closely tied to actions so that names of objects are thought to be properties of the object and not arbitrary labels. Finally pre-operational thinking is irreversible in that having worked through a sequence A, B, C, the child cannot go backwards and return to point A through C and B. If $2 + 2 = 4$ he does not see it as necessarily true that $4 - 2 = 2$. Similarly it is not clear to children of this age that if the French are foreigners to the Swiss then the Swiss are foreigners to the French.

The development of operation lasts from, approximately, seven to sixteen and has two sub-stages; 'concrete operations' from seven to eleven or twelve and 'formal operations' from twelve onwards. During the concrete period the child's thought becomes less ego-centric, less fluid and more reversible, so that he is now able to take several aspects of a situation into account. He begins to develop coherent cognitive systems, schemes, for dealing with environmental stimuli – these systems being initially sequences of actions. Piaget, as we have seen, believed that 'action in itself admits of logic' and, for the first time at the concrete period, he is able to describe cognitive functioning in terms of logico-mathematical structures.

Nine different groupings are thought to underlie concrete thinking and the first has been thoroughly studied by Piaget and Inhelder (1958). This describes the inclusion of one class within another which is in turn part of another until the largest class is reached which includes all the members of the set. Piaget and Inhelder describe empirical studies designed to test a child's understanding of this additive classification system. Children were given objects which varied along the dimensions of shape, colour and material so that the child when asked to 'put together the things that are alike' could use any of these attributes as criteria for classification. The youngest children showed fluid, chaining collections; a red circle followed by a blue square, etc., or they made graphic collections which had recognizable figural properties – they looked like a train or a house. Next the children made many small collections based on a mixture of criteria, and finally were able to classify correctly. But even then, if they had chosen shape, for example, as the basis of their classificatory system children of seven or eight would find difficulty in reclassifying using colour as the criterion.

The change from concrete to formal operations marks a change in attitude. Concrete operations deal directly with objects but formal operations extend concrete systems to include ideas of combination and possibility due to the child becoming aware of the *interdependence* of variables such as weight, speed, time, etc., which had previously been considered in isolation. The child, having formed the discrete concrete structures, begins, once he has realized their interdependence, to unite them in various ways and it is the integrated structure of formal thought which makes it unique: '... Thinking becomes formal as soon as it undertakes the co-ordination of concrete groupings into a single system (of the second degree) because it deals with possible combinations and no longer with objects directly.'

The child is now able to distinguish and order all the possible combinations of units of data so that if he has four variables he can generate the sixteen possible combinations of them. Piaget (1964) names eight cognitive schemes which he claims are not present before the formal period; they are combinatorial operations, proportions, co-ordination of two systems of reference and the relativity of motion or acceleration, the concept of mechanical equilibrium, the notion of probability, the notion of correlation, multiplicative compensations and the forms of conservation which go beyond direct empirical investigation. He says: 'These operational schemata consist of concepts or special operations, the need for which may be felt by the subject when he tries to solve certain problems. When the need is felt he manages to work them out spontaneously ... before the formal level he is not able to do this.'

Piagetian theory begins from the notion that 'intelligence is adaptation' (Piaget, 1953). Using a biological model Piaget distinguishes 'variant structures' and 'invariant functions'. The variant cognitive structures are to be seen in the differences between child and adult thought (thus the above description of the characteristics of the stages was a description of the variant structures). These variant structures are brought about by the invariant functions of *organization* and *adaptation*. *Adaptation* can be subdivided into *accommodation* and *assimilation* and refers to the fact that biologically, and Piaget would argue intellectually as well, an organism takes in to itself substances from the environment and in doing so changes them, that is they are assimilated. However as a result of taking in these substances the organism is, itself, changed and therefore accommodates its structure in response to the newly assimilated substances. Intellectually every time there is a meeting between the thinking organism and the external environment, the organism has to interpret the object in accordance with its existing structures and then modify those structures, if necessary, to take account of the properties of the object. This 'taking account' or accommodation leads to the *adaptation* of the variant cognitive structures.

Organization refers to the total integration of the various adaptations. Piaget, having argued that these functional invariants – not the changing structures – are the essence of intelligence, is particularly concerned with the *process* of 'equilibration' whereby initially a child is in a state of equilibrium with a series of mental techniques, or schemes, capable of dealing with the environment as he knows it. Then an environmental stimulus proves that the present schemes are inadequate and the child is thrown into 'disequilibrium'. The child modifies, that is accommodates, its present schemes by assimilating the novel stimulus. The child then adapts his cognitive structures and equilibrium is restored.

Piaget (1971) explains the passage from one stage to another by saying that once the structures of one stage are in operation they necessitate the emergence of those of the next:

... once he is able to manipulate the classification, sooner or later he will construct a classification of all the classifications, and thus he will end up by producing the combinatorial, which is a necessary form of formal thought ... But nothing is given in an 'a priori' or innate fashion; nothing is performed or pre-determined in the activity of the baby.

Piaget, therefore, began from the work of the psychometricians but extended his interests to cover the genesis and development of intelligence.

2.3 *American studies* (J. Bruner)

American research, especially that of Jerome Bruner and his associates combines, to a certain extent, the views of the Russians and the Europeans. Bruner (1966) emphasizes more strongly than Piaget the influence of the environment:

> We believe that intellectual growth can be understood only in terms of the psychological mechanisms that mediate it and that the explanation of growth cannot be effected by involving the nature of language, the inherent logic of child thought, or the nature of man's evolutionary history. One finds no internal push to growth without a corresponding external pull, for, given the nature of man as a species, growth is as dependent upon a link with external amplifiers of man's powers as it is upon those powers themselves.

This approach is, according to Neisser (1966) representative of 'dynamic' psychology, which he distinguishes from 'cognitive' psychology:

> Dynamic psychology begins with motives rather than with sensory input ... Instead of asking how a man's actions and experiences result from what he saw, remembered, or believed, the dynamic psychologist asks how they follow from the subject's goals, needs, or instincts. Asked why I did a certain thing I may answer in dynamic terms, 'Because I wanted ...' or, from a cognitive point of view, 'Because it seemed to me ...' The distinction is not clear cut because a subject will only act if the situation 'seems' to him to be appropriate for such action.

Bruner calls the mediators between the organism and the environment 'representations', saying that the child represents the world in three different ways; initially by *enactive* representation when he copes with the world by 'habitual actions' (knowing something through doing it); secondly by representation through imagery, *iconic* representation (knowing something by means of a picture or image); and, finally, by *symbolic* representation when action and image are translated into language (knowing by means of this symbolic agency). For Bruner (1973) the intellect is defined as 'man's capacity to achieve, retain and transform knowledge to his own uses' and he argues that the idea of representation is the most fruitful way of describing its development.

At the enactive stage the child cannot distinguish between a percept and an action so that if a baby drops its rattle it tries to retrieve it by shaking its hand as if it, once more, was holding the rattle and as if it believed that the action of shaking and the presence of the rattle were one and the same. In other words events are literally defined in terms of the actions they evoke.

Iconic representation appears when a child can replace an actual object with an image of the object when an image is, literally, a 'mental picture'. Bruner (1966) says of this:

> When he 'matches' something in his mind to something he is encountering, he does so by pointing to some particular sensory correspondence between the two ... It is only when he can go beyond this 'match by direct correspondence' that he comes to deal with such 'nonsensory' ideas as the relation between quantities, invariance across transformations, and substitutability within a conceptual category.

Regarding symbolic representation Bruner (1966) says: 'We take the view that symbolic representation stems from a form of primitive and innate symbolic activity that, through acculturation, gradually becomes specialized into different systems.' Thus the child is born with a basic capacity or latent power but he requires external stimuli to actualize it.

A particularly neat series of experiments which illustrate Bruner's views of development through representation were done by Olson (1966) on conceptual strategies. He maintained that the child would use different strategies depending on his mode of representation. The experiment had several variations but essentially the method was to show the child a bulb board some of whose bulbs would light up when pressed. These bulbs formed a pattern which was 'hidden' until they were pressed. The child was also given two cards with printed patterns one of which corresponded to the pattern 'hidden' in the bulb board. On the cards bright red circular dots corresponded to the bulbs that would light up, while dark grey spots represented those which would remain unlighted. The child had to decide, by pressing the bulbs, which card corresponded to the pattern 'hidden' in the bulb board.

The youngest children, aged three, used a *search strategy*. They did not press at random but their searches were not related to the diagrams. Five-year-olds used a *successive pattern matching strategy* in which they tried out the *whole* pattern against the bulb board to see which matched. At about the age of seven the *information selection strategy* began to develop, and the child concentrated on the *one* bulb which would tell which alternative was correct. By age nine this was the most popular strategy. There the child is being asked to use a diagram to guide his action, that is to 'abstract a model of a thing from the real thing'. He must then reproduce the pattern he has recognized to move from *search* to *pattern matching*. *Information selection* requires the combined use of several pieces of information. One could hypothesize that at the enactive stage the child merely responds in a non-random, but non-systematic manner; imagery allows matching, and symbolizing the hierarchical organization necessary for information selection. Bruner puts forward the hypothesis that there is a greater push towards hierarchical connections in technical cultures than in less technical ones. (If he is correct this might explain the figures quoted by Jensen (see p. 15), in that if certain cultures require a differential use of cognitive skills and people have differential abilities, one would expect the reported correlations.)

Bruner (1966) concludes: 'In so far as man's powers are expressed and amplified through the instruments of culture, the limits to which he can attain excellence of intellect must surely be as wide as are the culture's combined capabilities.'

A developmental approach to intelligence would indicate that all men are born with a repertoire of reflexes and modes of functioning. Initially, the child's behaviour is in terms of overt actions, and simple links, like those made by animals, are all that are available to him. Soon (the exact timing is in dispute) he develops 'plans' or 'conceptions' or 'images' so that they are no longer tied to overt manipulation. These cognitive mediators are gradually elaborated into a *second signal system* (Pavlov), or *concrete* and *formal operations* (Piaget), or *symbolic representations* (Bruner) at which point adult thinking is reached. It is this elaborated cognition which is characteristic of intelligent thought and a person is more or less intelligent to the extent that he exhibits such elaborated thinking. Since this is the result of development, and hence open to environmental influences, it is not surprising that people vary in their ability. However, whether the 'innate' components are unequally distributed cannot be answered. All that can be said is that no normal people have *no* inborn reflexes or modes of functioning, which would seem to suggest that it is the use made of the biological basis which determines adult levels of intelligence. This differential use could be due to environmental influences or to some internal mechanism which cannot *be* intelligence, since it results in intelligence, but must be a factor contributed by the unique interaction of heredity and environment which leads to what we call an 'individual'.

Further reading

Anglin, J. M. and Bruner, J. (eds) (1973) *Beyond the Information Given.* London: George Allen and Unwin.

Bruner, J. S., Olver, R. R. and Greenfield, P. M. (1966) *Studies in Cognitive Growth.* New York: John Wiley.

Bryant, P. (1974) *Perception and Understanding in Young Children.* London: Methuen.

Butcher, H. J. (1968) *Human Intelligence. Its Nature and Assessment.* London: Methuen.

Furth, H. G. (1970) *Piaget for Teachers.* Englewood Cliffs, New Jersey: Prentice-Hall.

Miller, S. (1975) *Experimental Design and Statistics.* London: Methuen.

Turner, J. (1975) *Cognitive Development.* London: Methuen.

[2]
Thinking,
problem solving
and concept learning

In schools teachers often claim that they are encouraged to teach children to think; their aim is to teach the structure and main concepts of a subject rather than the facts. But, in these situations, teachers may wonder what exactly it is they are being asked to do: Doesn't everybody think? What is a concept? What is involved in problem solving?

The discipline of psychology was originally primarily concerned with the study of thinking – the activity of the conscious mind. Psychologists today are particularly interested in the cognitive processes by means of which man makes sense of his environment, both material and social. Thinking, problem solving and concept learning, all of which children use in school, are three basic cognitive processes whose psychological theory is introduced in the work reviewed in this chapter. In particular, the findings of Furth and Wachs, Wertheimer, and Klausermeier and his associates, may help teachers to design lessons which will deliberately aid their pupils to develop these processes and hence be able to apply them more effectively.

1 Thinking

1.1 *Ways of thinking*

Like 'intelligence', 'thinking' is a polymorphous term in that it can be applied to many different sorts of activity, from rigorous logical analysis to free floating daydreaming. However, in the school situation, six types of thinking are likely to be most commonly used, these are: everyday thinking, artistic thinking, logical and mathematical thinking, explanatory thinking, productive thinking and directed thinking.

Everyday thinking.   Bartlett (1958) saw thinking as an advanced form of skilled behaviour and described it as: 'Not simply the description, either by perception or recall, of something which is there, it is the use of information about something present to get somewhere else.' He defined everyday thinking as 'those activities by which most people, when they are not making any particular attempt to be logical or scientific, try to fill up gaps in information available to them in which for some reason they are specially interested'. Everyday thinking was seen by him to be mainly related to social matters and is characterized by the thinker's tendency to favour certain points of view and reject others. In it an argument is clinched not by the strength of the evidence adduced but by the manner in which the statement is made, together with an appeal to group consensus. When a teacher asks a pupil to express his own view it is likely that it will originally appear in this form. Everyday thinking does provide a basis from which more rigorous forms of thought can be developed, for once the pupil becomes willing to express an opinion the teacher can further refine his thought.

Artistic thinking.   In this form of thinking the artist, through intuitive leaps, fills one gap but thereby opens others until he bridges them all and arrives at the finished work. To illustrate the special nature of this process Bartlett quotes Clive Bell's (1956) comments on Virginia Woolf and Picasso:

> Virginia and Picasso belong to another order of beings: they were of a species different from the common; their mental processes were different from ours; they arrived at conclusions by ways to us unknown. Also their conclusions or comments or judgements or flights of fancy or witticisms, or little jokes even, were true or convincing or effective or delightful for reasons that are not the reasons of logic nor yet of our well tried common sense ...
>
> Their conclusions were as satisfying as the conclusions of mathematics though reached by quite other roads ...

Peel (1960), when writing of children's modes of thinking delimits
artistic thinking more simply as 'imaginative' or 'traumatic'. The
'thinking' here is fairly free in that the writer is bound by no
particular practical problem which he has to solve. However
although it is relatively free such thinking has to be consistent
as a whole with the theme of the essay, painting or piece of music.

Logical and mathematical thinking.   This is probably the most
structured form and requires the thinker to proceed from start
to finish as parsimoniously and as accurately as possible. Bartlett
points out that a characteristic feature is that 'as the number of
steps taken towards filling up a gap increases the number of
probable next steps decreases, until a stage in the sequence is
reached beyond which all thinking must proceed through the same
number and order of steps to the same terminus'.

In one of his experiments the subjects were given the words,
'A, By, ... Horrible' and told to 'look at the terminus words and
then fill up the gap in any way you think to be indicated'. After
trying to complete this the subjects were given another piece of
information, namely that the third word could be 'Cow'. Using
this clue it becomes clear that the sequence required the first letter
of each to be determined by alphabetical order and the number
of letters in each word to increase by one each time giving final
sequences, like 'By, Car, Dive, Eager, Fright, Gaskets, Horrible'
or 'A, By, Can, Door, Every, Floods, Gunners, Horrible'.

Explanatory thinking.   Peel (1960) sees this as having four features:
'(1) The control of associations by practical criteria; (2) the testing
of hypotheses against the facts; (3) the acceptance of some event
or theory as being reasonably probable; and (4) the formation of
language that deals with concepts and classes of objects.'

Explanatory thinking relies on the thinker making use of what
he already knows to explain or describe actions and events which
initially puzzle him. One form of explanatory thinking is Bartlett's
'experimental thinking' which, he says, 'comes as a relatively late
development in the search for knowledge of the world, since it
has to be based upon much prior accumulation, description and
classification of observed facts, and upon the invention of special
methods and usually special instruments for establishing controlled
sequence among these facts.'

Productive thinking. Productive thinking requires the pupil to go beyond what he has absorbed and restructure a problem in order to reach a solution. It does not simply reproduce but creates new schemes of thought. Wertheimer (1880–1943) was an important member of the 'Gestalt' school of psychology which originated in Germany early in the century. Its members held that the whole was greater than the sum of its parts and good or effective thinking required the thinker to grasp the total structure of the problem. Thus development in thinking was essentially a restructuring process.

Wertheimer (1945) became concerned with 'productive thinking' as a result of the following reflections on teaching. 'A teacher teaches a class the usual proof for the theorem that the area of a parallelogram is equal to the base by the altitude by using the usual figure' (Fig. 2.1).

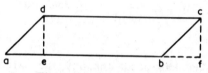

Fig. 2.1 *Traditional figure*
(Wertheimer, 1945)

The next day the teacher tests the pupils and they respond by giving the correct answers. Wertheimer comments, 'What have they learned? ... Have they grasped the issue at all? How can I clarify it? What can I *do*?' He then drew the following figure (Fig. 2.2) and describes the ensuing few minutes:

Some are obviously taken aback. One pupil raises his hand:

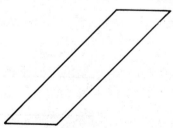

Fig. 2.2 *Wertheimer's figure*
(Wertheimer, 1945)

'Teacher, we haven't had that yet.' Others are busy. They have copied the figure on paper, they draw the auxiliary lines as they were taught, dropping perpendiculars from the two upper corners and extending the base line [Fig. 2.3]. They look bewildered, perplexed.

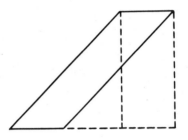

Fig. 2.3 *Alternative solution*
(Wertheimer, 1945)

Some do not look at all unhappy; they write firmly below their drawing: 'The area is equal to the base times the altitude' – a correct subsumption, but perhaps an entirely blind one ...
With still others it is entirely different. Their faces brighten,

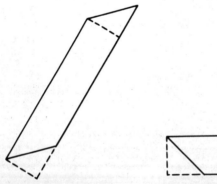

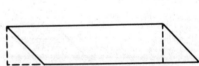

Fig. 2.4 *Rotated solution 1*   Fig. 2.5 *Rotated solution 2*
(Wertheimer, 1945)   (Wertheimer, 1945)

they smile and draw the following lines in the figure, or they turn papers through 45°, and do it [Figs. 2.4, 2.5].

The teacher, observing that only a minority of the pupils has mastered the problem, says to me with some indignation: 'You certainly gave them a queer figure. Naturally they are unable to deal with it.'

The above example is all too familiar, showing that the children failed to really grasp the nature of the problem and hence reach pseudo-solutions. Wertheimer suggested that to teach a child the relationship between a parallelogram and a rectangle and hence the meaning of the theorem, they should be introduced to it by playing with cardboard shapes or shown relevant figures. The aim was that the child should see the relationship for himself so that his thinking would be 'productive' not reproductive. He argued (1945) that such thinking was characterized by a regrouping of the information in accordance with the structure of the problem, by being related to an understanding of the problem as a whole and by having a consistent, not piecemeal, development during the process of problem solving. 'When one grasps a problem situation its structural features and requirements set up certain strains, stresses, tensions in the thinker. What happens in real thinking is that these strains and stresses are followed up, yield vectors in the direction of improvement of the situation, and change it accordingly.'

1.2 Helping children to think

Arousing curiosity.   Berlyne (1965) suggested that 'epistemic curiosity' or 'a will to know' will be aroused by 'conceptual conflict, that is when two symbolic response patterns appear to be incompatible'. He distinguished six special types of conflict which could lead to 'epistemic curiosity'. First 'doubt', when the subject is torn between belief and disbelief; second 'perplexity', when two sets of belief seem equally tenable but are mutually exclusive; third 'contradiction', in which the subject is virtually forced to accept two incompatible beliefs; fourth 'conceptual incongruity', when the subject has to accept that two properties occur together which he has not previously expected to occur together (for example the mudskipper fish which walks on dry land is confusing if one believes that fish will die out of water); fifth 'confusion', when the subject has incomplete information; and, sixth 'irrelevance', in which apparently irrelevant ideas occur and interfere in the subject's search for a solution which is eluding him.

When a person experiences conceptual conflict he will attempt to reduce it and this will motivate him to think about the topic. Berlyne therefore suggested that information is only valued and sought after when there has been a previous period of uncertainty during which the person's need for this new information has become clear, since it will reduce the conceptual conflict. In an early experiment (1954) secondary-school children were given questions about invertebrate animals. They were then asked to choose twelve questions to which they would most like to be given the answers. The children were most curious about questions which they found surprising or when the questions suggested that animals had characteristics which were unexpected.

Developing thinking skills.   It is often assumed that at school children will increase their knowledge and understanding of the world, but it is less common for children to be specifically *taught how to think*. Furth and Wachs (1974) in a research project in Charleston USA set out to do just this. The aim of the project was 'to aid and nourish the normal developing process of thinking in the primary school age child, subordinating all school activities to this first goal'. Therefore they set up a 'thinking school' for kindergarten and first-grade children. In discussing the rationale for the classroom activities six characteristics were listed:

1. It was maintained that the activity of thinking was intrinsically worth while. The child was encouraged to think as fully and accurately as possible but not to compare his thinking with that of others. Furth comments that most children enjoy running as fast as they can but 'this healthy asset attitude – running fast is fun – can easily be transformed into an unhealthy comparative attitude – fun is running faster than another'.

2. The activities were structured to give 'freedom within structure' as a means of developing the child's intelligence in a coherent manner. The importance of structure has been stressed by Gestalt thinkers and Berlyne, in addition to Piaget, and it is difficult to see how directed thinking could be expected to occur if the structure of the situation is not apparent to the thinker.

3. Each item or activity was intended to challenge the child's thinking but was not made difficult enough to make failure likely. To challenge a child's thinking is to raise the possibility of restructuring the situation or of restoring the equilibrium which has been disturbed by the child's attempting to apply previously developed schemes to the new piece of information and finding them to be inadequate. Both Piaget and Berlyne consider such a process essential for intellectual development, although Berlyne would interpret it in terms of cognitive conflict.

4. The children were encouraged to focus on the activity and not on the teacher. The teacher was there to help but the child's knowledge was his own and could only be developed by himself.

5. The children were expected to work together with a small group of peers so that their thinking could influence each other and also enable the children to develop socially.

6. This last characteristic is interesting in that although the child was to gain knowledge from the activities, the teacher was expected to provide a model of a *thinking* person and not be a storehouse of knowledge.

Within the school there were nine types of activities, from body and sense thinking games through the more familiar-sounding 'reading' and 'science', to music and physical activities. The 'body games' were designed to help the child form a mental map of his body. In one ('crossed-legged walk') a straight line was drawn on the floor of the classroom and the child had to put his right foot on the left side of the line and his left foot on the right side. He then had to walk the length of the line alternating his feet. Once this was accomplished he would try to do the same thing going backwards. There were sixty games in all related to thinking about, and with, all parts of the body. There were then many more obviously 'cognitive' games relating to copying block designs, for example a design drawn on the vertical board which the child would reconstruct on his horizontal desk. Class discovery games could be simple or difficult depending on the number of attributes; in one form the children were given nine geometrical cut-outs, three triangles, three circles, three squares, which were of three colours – blue, yellow and red. They then had to sort them into groups. If they started with colour they would then be praised and asked to find another method of sorting. This game could be made more complex by adding the further dimension of size: 'seriation' can be encouraged by the apparently simple game 'lining up' when the children have to form a line in order of height, alphabetical order of first names, by hair colours or by chronological order of their birthdays. One hundred and seventy-nine different games were used and each child's progress was monitored.

Furth and Wachs were convinced that: 'a school must intentionally and purposefully emphasize the development of thinking in the child. Otherwise it will not be able to avoid learning failures and, in addition, an even greater number of children will loose their creative curiosity that is part of all children's natural equipment.'

---

2 *Problem solving*

A prisoner sits in the condemned cell. Before him are two doors. If he goes through one he will be killed, if through the other he will be free; but he does not know which door is which. In the cell with him are two jailors one of whom always tells the truth while the other always lies; again he does not know which is which. The prisoner is allowed to ask one question of one jailor in order to find out which door leads to freedom. What should the question be?

The question is: If you were the other jailor which door would you say was the one that led to freedom?' Thus if we imagine we have two doors, Life (L) and Death (D), and two jailors, False (F) and True (T), if the prisoner (P) asks F, F will know that T would say L but since F always lies F will say that T would say D. Alternatively if P asks T, T will know that F should say L, but, since F always lies, he would answer D and therefore T will answer D. Thus whichever jailor the prisoner chooses the answer will be the same (D) and to be free he must choose the door they do not name (i.e. L). To solve this problem requires intelligence plus other specific cognitive processes such as directed thinking, insight and hypothesis testing. In school pupils are often asked to solve problems and they can be helped if their teachers are aware of the nature of these processes of problem solving.

2.1 *What is a problem?*

A person can be said to have a problem if he has a target, for example a puzzle to be solved, a house to be designed as economically as possible, or an explanation to be found, and therefore knows what should be achieved but does not know how to achieve it. Sometimes the formulation of the problem, or asking the right questions, is, itself, a problem. At other times when, for example, a person is asked the distance between the Earth and Uranus, he lacks information but he does not have a problem unless he does not know how to go about obtaining this information. Alternatively, a person may have all the necessary information but fail to order this information correctly and therefore miss the solution; for example, if John is taller than Bill and shorter than Peter, the fact that Peter is the tallest of the three may not be obvious to a young child. There can, therefore, be many types of problems, the main criterion being that there is a gap between the initial formulation of the target and the achievement of the solution which must be bridged by the person 'solving' the problem. Information retrieval does not fall within this definition although determining where the information is to be found does. Once a problem situation has been defined the complex nature of the process of solution becomes apparent if the range of requirements for success is considered. A solution requires the correct formulation of the problem, the necessary information and cognitive abilities, the employment of the relevant strategy, and the evaluation and verification of the solution.

Gagné (1966) emphasized that problem solving is a change in individual performance leading to a change in human capability. He argued that the problem solver must develop a new rule, not recall an old one. This definition makes problem solving sound like a form of learning (i.e. learning the new rule). However Gagné (1964) stresses a crucial difference when he says that in trial and error learning (for example when a rat learns the way through a maze), the act to be learned (running through a maze), is part of the learning situation, whereas in problem solving the solution is not part of the learning situation. Therefore he calls problem solving a 'non-reproductive' type of learning. Greeno (1973) represented the problem solving process by a relational network showing how a problem is composed initially of both 'givens' and 'unknowns'. These elements must then be connected before the solution can be reached.

2.2 Theoretical approaches to the problem solving process

The Gestalt approach.   Most of the earliest research on problem solving was carried out by the Gestalt school of psychology (see p. 33) which stressed the importance of seeing problems as a whole, and hence problem solving was seen to require the subject to grasp the nature of the total situation after which the solution would suddenly appear and fit in like a piece in a jigsaw. That is, the material must be restructured according to the requirements of the problems. Such a restructuring or 'recentring' of the material then becomes a sufficient condition for solving the problem. Wertheimer called it 'seeing the light' and others saw it as 'insight'; it can mean a sudden realization 'ah ha', or a grasp of the structure, often opposed to trial and error behaviour. (However, it does not follow that an absence of overt trial and error implies no such covert behaviour. It would seem that 'insight' may be a useful description of a form of behaviour but cannot be explanatory, as an explanation would require greater clarity concerning the internal mechanism of such a phenomenon.)

Kohler (1927), a member of the Gestalt school, described a series of experiments designed to show that chimpanzees behave with 'intelligence and insight under conditions which require such behaviour'. In the first of three experiments a chimpanzee in a cage could see a banana which was just out of reach outside. In his cage was a stick. Suddenly the chimp grasped the stick and using this pulled the banana towards him until he could reach it. The chimps were also found to join two sticks to make one long enough to reach the banana, to push fruit away from themselves until it was near a place where the netting surrounding them was lower so that they could reach over and get it, and stack boxes to reach hanging fruit. However, Schiller (1952) reported that when he gave chimps sticks and boxes to play with, in the absence of fruit, they joined them, from which it could be concluded that many of Kohler's results can be explained by the association of common habits, e.g. stick joining, with a situation in which fruit is desired but out of reach.

Dunker, another member of this school, concentrated on

rational, abstract problems and required his subjects to 'talk aloud' while solving them in an attempt to externalize their thought processes. He claimed (1945) that problem solving could either be seen as the process of 'arriving at a solution' or the process of 'developing the problem' in so far as 'the finding of a general property of a solution means each time a reformulation of the original problem'. He dwelt on the importance of 'recentring' the material as shown in his famous 'tumour' problem. This problem is: 'Given a human being with an inoperable stomach tumour, and rays which destroy organic tissue at sufficient intensity, by what procedure can one free him from the tumour by these rays and at the same time avoid destroying the healthy tissue which surrounds it?' A correct solution requires the subject to abandon attempts to get at the tumour in a linear way and realize that if the tumour is irradiated from all angles the rays coming together at the tumour will be strong enough to destroy it but no single ray will be enough to destroy the healthy tissue.

The behaviourist approach. The Gestalt 'insightful' approach is essentially cognitive, i.e. its exponents are primarily concerned with the internal processes whereby subjects perceive, process, store and reproduce information. The behaviourist, S/R (stimulus response) approach concentrates on external behaviour as exemplified by the building up of associations between stimuli and responses while stressing the central role of reinforcement. This approach maintains that the laws established as operating in simple learning situations apply to even the most complex forms of human behaviour, including problem solving. Thus the process becomes some form of conditioning, chaining of responses, or discrimination learning. The behaviourist approach, however, is not a single monolithic one but can be divided into 'mediation' theorists who posit covert responses which mediate between the 'given' and the 'solution' and theorists who, following Skinner, see problem solving as a special form of conditioning.

The Kendlers, two mediation theorists, argued (1962) that the study of problem solving required the experimenters to formulate tasks which would 'isolate and magnify the basic mechanisms' operating in the more complex problems of daily life and which are therefore necessary conditions for their solution. Having adopted this analytic aim they represented the behaviour studied in S/R terms, not, as they said, because this is how we find behaviour but because they thought it was a clear way of representing it. Starting from the thinking of the Gestalt school they accepted the importance of insight but accounted for it by hypothesizing that independent levels of behaviour could occur simultaneously in independent chains so that sometimes a stimulus in one chain would be linked to a response in another. The resultant 'sparking across' could then be called 'insightful' behaviour.

B. F. Skinner (1966) offered an 'operant' analysis of problem solving which he said is often 'mistakenly identified with S/R theories'. In operant analysis a correct response is rewarded and hence strengthened, but the reward is dependent on the subject *initially* making the correct response. For example, if a rat is put in a cage it will move around and may, accidentally, push a bar. When this happens a food pellet is dropped into the cage. Gradually the rat will learn that bar pushing will bring food, *but* the important point is that no food came until the rat first pressed the bar. This operant analysis presupposes trial and error behaviour as the subject has to try several responses before he hits upon the one which will be rewarded.

Problem solving as a form of learning.   Davis, in a useful review paper (1966), summarized current approaches to problem solving, and argued that 'insightful' solutions to problems are the result of *covert* trial and error learning whereas all other solutions rely on *overt* trial and error learning. He was thus able to characterize all problem solving behaviour as falling into one or other of these categories. 'Covert' problems are characterized by being in the Gestalt tradition; concrete tasks are used, possible outcomes to the various responses are known and the behaviour sequence is unobservable. In the 'overt' category are problems springing from the behaviourist tradition of simple laboratory based tasks, the outcomes are unknown and the behaviour is therefore, necessarily overt.

Gagné (1964) argued that although it is true that learning must precede problem solving (i.e. the ability to manipulate letters and symbols is a precondition for being able to use them as tools in the solution of verbal and numerical problems), nevertheless problem solving is in itself an additional form of learning and shares many characteristics with other forms. To see problem solving in this way is to stress the importance of the subject's previous learning which would result in individual differences in expertise. But once the experimenter has established the subject's capabilities the second main independent variable will be the instructions given as stimuli. After this the process becomes internal, and Gagné (1966) depicts the process so as to show the mixture of internal processes, external processes and individual differences (Fig. 2.6).

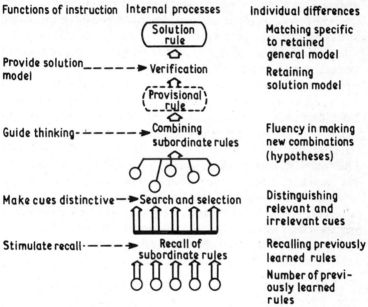

Fig. 2.6 *Gagné: Factors in problem solving*
(Kleinmuntz, 1966)

Problem solving as information processing. The behaviourist approach, which sees problem solving as a form of learning, will represent it by an S/R model whereas the information processing approach will represent it by means of a computer analogy whereby information originally stored in the memory, is retrieved and used in the new problem situation. Information processing theorists argue that human problem solving can be 'simulated' by a computer and hence it becomes possible to make 'overt' that which was previously 'covert'. To 'simulate' means that the computer goes through a series of actions which essentially resemble the actions of a human subject. In order to simulate, the computer's performance must offer a *one to one correspondence* with the human subject's actions. For example, if a child has a clockwork train set this is a 'model' of a real train but if the child's train is an exact replication and works on the same principle, i.e. by diesel oil or steam, using an exact mechanical replication, then this can be said to be isomorphic or a 'true' model. It is this second model which is intended when the term 'simulation' is used, unlike 'artificial intelligence' which means that the computer may solve the same problems as the human subject but by a different strategy and using different processes.

Information processing, by means of simulation, is primarily concerned with process. Newell, Shaw and Simon (1958) put this interest succinctly by saying: 'If one considers the organism to consist of effectors, receptors, and a control system for joining these, then this theory is mostly a theory of the control system.' One of the earliest attempts to model process was that of Miller, Galanter and Pribram (1960) who spoke of 'images' and 'plans'. The 'plan' was most like a computer program as it controlled 'the order in which a sequence of operations is to be performed'. They posited a TOTE unit as a model of cognitive functioning (Test – Operate – Test – Exit). This emphasis on process results in a level of explanation which is distinctly different from physiological explanations and which cannot, at present, be reduced to them. Fiegenbaum and Feldman (1963) remarked:

we have not yet been able to develop an integrated theory of thinking which will simultaneously account for all that takes place in the way of electrical, chemical, organizational and informational processes. Hopefully one day all these levels of explanation will be integrated, and the relationships between them will be established.

Another problem has been the immense difficulty in simulating human thinking. Having reviewed many attempts Hunt (1968) came to the conclusion that 'of this date, no programme has been shown to simulate human problem solving, although there are several programmes which solve problems'.

Information processing makes a distinction between *algorithms* and *heuristics*, the second of which is more relevant for problem solving. An algorithm is no more than a series of steps or moves which will inevitably lead to the solution of a problem as every possibility is tried. This method is particularly applicable to computer programs and can be used by humans to solve problems, especially mathematical ones, more accurately and speedily than they could do themselves. However, there are many problems for which there is no algorithm and therefore heuristics are used. Heuristics are orientating procedures which indicate some possible strategies for reaching a solution by trying schemes which have been useful before, rather than trying them all. (When Dunker spoke of 'resonance' as the use of previous strategies in a present situation which appears similar, he was in fact describing the heuristic method. However, computer programs have the advantage of being explicit.) Many years ago Polya (1945) described four stages in an heuristic process and they are still relevant; first, understanding the structure or nature of the problem; second, devising a strategy for solving it; third, applying the plan; and fourth, evaluating the solution.

One of the best known programs is the GPS (General Problem Solver) of Newell, Shaw and Simon (1959) and Newell and Simon (1961) which deals with problems in mathematics and logic. Newell and Simon's investigation (1963) is particularly interesting in that there was an attempt to bridge the gap between artificial intelligence and computer simulation and to some extent also the gap between the simple associationism of the behaviourists and the Gestalt notion that the task affects the form of the subject's thinking. Initially Newell and Simon had a subject talk aloud while he was working on a problem and they then attempted to write a program which would manipulate symbols in the same way as the human subject did, so that, if the end result of the program fitted the human subject's overt behaviour, an analysis of the computer's behaviour at decision points could form the basis for a theory of problem solving. When they compared the computer with the human they found that the program did provide an explanation of the subject's behaviour with some exceptions – one of which was that the human subject used parallel processing while the computer dealt with items singly. (The significance of this difference is apparent if we remember the Kendlers' work (see p. 42) and their theory of 'insightful' behaviour, which relies on sparking across between parallel chains.) There are certain limitations to the information processing approach as it tends to concentrate on Polya's stage two, whereas the first stage of representing the problem has been seen to be important. If the programmer gives this prior information the task is considerably simplified.

---

3   *Concept learning*

3.1   *What is a concept?*

What is it that a person has when he has a concept? And what is it that he has to do to get one? These two questions are fundamental to understanding one of the most fascinating yet murky areas of human cognitive behaviour, namely the learning of concepts. If Amanda has a concept and Adrian does not, Amanda will be able to do things that Adrian can not. If, for example, she has the abstract concept of sadism she will be able to recognize new instances of sadistic behaviour, and not merely associate the word 'sadism' with certain behaviours which she has heard others call sadistic. She will also be able to distinguish sadistic acts from ignorant mishandling which unintentionally causes pain. If, on the other hand, she has the relatively simple concept of 'blue squares' she will be able to pick out, or put together, all the exemplars of the concept from an array that includes many colours and shapes in various combinations.

Once a concept has been formed or attained the person will be able to do two distinct things: firstly he will recognize its relevant attributes and, secondly, he will know how they are related to one another. There can be three forms of relationship between attributes: a conjunctive relationship when the concept requires all the relevant attributes to be present; for example if the concept is 'yellow squares with a green circle in the centre', exemplars of this concept would have to be yellow, square, and have a green circle in the centre. Secondly there can be a disjunctive relationship when, if either one or other attribute or both are present, the concept exists; for example a disjunctive concept could be one in which anything which is yellow, square, or both is an exemplar. In this abstract form disjunctive concepts appear strange and are difficult to learn but in everyday life there are many concepts such as 'ill' 'drunk' 'sexy' or 'intelligent' all of which exist if some or all of a list of attributes are present. The third form of relationship is the relational one when it is the relationship between two attributes which defines the concept, for example 'all school classes with equal numbers of boys and girls', or 'I/Q' which refers to the relationship between mental and chronological age.

3.2 *How are concepts learned?*

An important distinction in learning concepts is that between concept formation and concept attainment made by Bruner, Goodnow and Austin (1956). 'Concept formation' is an initial creative action which results in the formation of superordinate classes or abstract categories: it means to see how things are alike and to provide a name to express this similarity. Notions such as 'overkill', 'education priority areas' or 'alienation' are all the result of some person having formed the concept initially. However, 'concept attainment' is more often of interest to teachers and this means the activity of finding exemplars of a concept which is already in mind, or attempting to reconstruct the concept that is already in someone else's mind. Concept formation is the more fundamental process; concept attainment the more familiar.

Psychologists interested in studying the processes by which people learn concepts usually employ either the 'reception' or the 'selection' method of study. In the first the experimenter shows the subject a single object, or stimulus (e.g. a red circle) and the subject has to respond by classifying it as an exemplar, or not, of the concept, or categorizing it in some way. In other words the experimenter has pre-arranged the order in which he will present instances of the concept and these instances are therefore 'received' by the subject. In the 'selection' method the subject is presented with the whole array of stimuli (e.g. red circles, red squares, yellow squares, blue circles etc.) and he has to select one which he then shows to the experimenter asking whether it is a positive or negative instance of the concept. The subject then continues to select stimuli until he learns the concept.

Associative versus mediational theories of concept learning. Perhaps the simplest theory is the associative one which sees concept learning as a matter of *associating* positive or negative instances of stimuli, with reward or punishment, so that if, for example, the concept is 'birds' the subject will associate pictures of birds with a positive response from the experimenter and pictures of everything else with a negative one and will thus learn, himself, to respond positively to birds. Mediational theory says that the subject uses covert cues with which he organizes his behaviour. Thus the single initial stimulus 'three yellow squares' can be subdivided into three separate mediational responses, referring to relevant dimensions (number, colour, shape), each of which can be checked against the criterion, i.e. the concept in the experimenter's mind (Fig. 2.7).

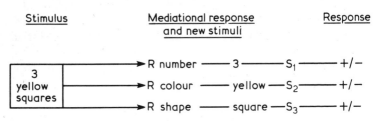

Fig. 2.7 *Mediational model*

The relative power of these two theories – the associative and the mediational – can be clearly compared by observing the subject's behaviour when faced with making 'reversal' or 'non-reversal' shifts. This experimental design was pioneered by the Kendlers (1962) and has considerable elegance. Imagine that in the first phase of the experiment the subject is presented with an array consisting of a yellow circle, a yellow square, a red circle and a red square. He learns at this stage that red is positive and yellow negative, irrespective of shape. If the experimenter wishes to 'shift' the subject's response he can do it in one of two ways. If in the second phase the experimenter makes red negative and yellow positive, still irrespective of shape, the subject has to make a 'reversal' shift, i.e. he has to reverse the values of the colours he has been using. However, if the experimenter decides that in the second phase squares will be positive and circles negative the subject has to make a 'non-reversal' shift – i.e. he has to learn a new method of discriminating (rather than 'reverse' the old one) and realize that this time it is shape and not colour which is significant (Fig. 2.8).

Associative and mediational theories make different predictions as to which of these shifts the subject will find most difficult.

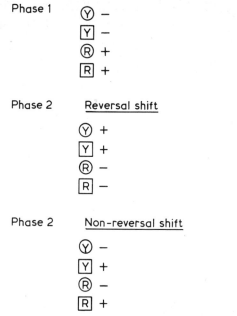

Fig. 2.8 *Reversal v. non-reversal shift*

Associative theory says that in phase one the subject associates red with a positive response and yellow with a negative one. In a reversal shift *all* the previous associations have to be changed whereas in a non-reversal only *some* of them have to be, since all the red squares will still be positive and all the yellow circles negative. Thus this theory predicts that non-reversal shifts would be easier. On the other hand if the subject is using mediational responses in the first phase and uses the mediator 'colour' all he has to do, in the second phase, is to swop the actual colours but the dimension (i.e. colour) remains the same. With a non-reversal shift he has to *change* dimensions from colour to shape and then learn which shape is positive. Thus this theory would predict that reversal shifts would be easier. In practice subjects younger than four and rats find non-reversal shifts easier and older subjects prefer reversal shifts, which seem to suggest that mediational theories are more powerful as predictors of older children's and adults' behaviour. Therefore it could be hypothesized that by age four people have developed the capacity to make mediated responses.

Concept learning and hypothesis testing. An entirely different theory is that when a person is attempting to learn a concept what he does is to set up a series of hypotheses, e.g. 'it's red circles' or 'it's yellow squares with green dots', and tests each of these

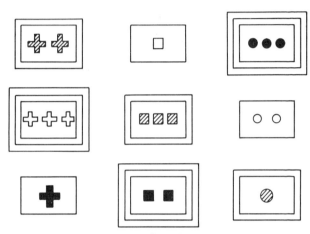

Fig. 2.9 *Sample cards*
(Bruner, Goodnow and Austin, 1956)

until he arrives at a correct solution. A hypothesis will be rejected as soon as the first error is made and a different hypothesis will be tried. Bruner, Goodnow and Austin (1956) produced some seminal data on the strategies a person uses when attempting to attain a concept. For their experiment, they presented subjects with an array of cards which varied with respect to the shape of figures on them (crosses, squares or circles), the number of figures (from one to three), the number of borders (from one to three) and the colour of the figures (red, black, or green) (Fig. 2.9). The subjects, having been given a positive instance, had to discover the correct concept by asking the experimenter if other cards represented positive or negative instances of the concept. The experimenters distinguished four types of strategy: (1) 'simul-taneous scanning' in which the subject would consider all the in-formation at one and the same time and work out a logical solution. This strategy, in fact, puts a great load on memory and is therefore highly unusual; (2) 'part-scanning' in which the subject starts with a hypothesis and then only has to scan the parts of the cards relevant to his hypothesis. This is easier for the subject but not very efficient since he will not learn very much while pursuing a hypothesis that turns out to be incorrect; (3) 'conservative focusing' in which the subject, once he has found a positive instance (which in this experiment was given to begin with), tests each attribute of it in turn to find out which ones are significant. If the subject is prepared to take more of a risk he will engage in (4) 'focus gambling' and vary two attributes at a time. If his guess is right he will gain but if wrong he will have to start again.

3.3 *Facilitating concept learning*

Klausmeier, Ghatala and Frayer (1974) distinguish three categories of factors which can affect concept learning: (1) characteristics of the learner, (2) characteristics of the instructional situation and (3) characteristics of the concept. Obviously the child's age and ability will affect concept learning, but Klausmeier and his associates give reasons for ability being important. They quote Wiviott's (1970) results that children who scored highly on mathematics tests scored more highly on a test of concept mastery. The high achievers were more aware of the dimensions of the concept and therefore the authors conclude 'it appears that one reason for the superior concept mastery shown by high achieving children is the fact that they are more likely to have discriminated and named attributes than low achieving children of the same age'. Related to this are these writers' findings on cognitive style in that individuals with an 'analytic' cognitive style (those who break the stimuli up into parts) were superior in concept learning to those which had a 'global' style (those who categorize without differentiating). This too is related to identifying attributes since 'analytic' subjects were more able to recognize attributes than 'global' subjects.

Of particular importance for the teacher are Klausmeier and his colleagues' findings concerned with the instructional situation. Klausmeier and Meinke (1968) listed six functions of instruction in concept learning: (1) to acquaint the subject with the stimulus material; (2) to acquaint the subject with the response desired; (3) to inform the subject of a strategy or method to apply for the solution of the task; (4) to provide substantive information; (5) to provide a set to recall relevant information; and (6) to change the level of motivation of the subject. The extent to which teachers use instructions which fulfil these purposes will determine, to an extent, the success of their pupils in attaining the concepts.

The more complex the concept, i.e. the more relevant dimensions there are, the more difficult it is to attain. So too is a concept more difficult if it has a large number of irrelevant dimensions. However Bourne, Ekstrand and Dominowski (1971) point out the significance of redundancy as a facilitator in accordance with the general principle 'the more cues to the same response, the more likely is that response, at least up to a point', by taking the example of traffic lights saying that:

> the stop signal appears at the top and is always red; the 'go' signal is always at the bottom and green. Colour and position of light are completely redundant in informational content. The values – red, green, yellow, and top, bottom, middle, occur together in perfect correlation, and either alone provides a fully sufficient source of information.

In any stimuli for concept-attainment tasks, some attributes are more salient than others, and if these are the distinguishing attributes the subjects will learn the concept more readily. Colour is particularly significant. It would appear that it is important to attract the subject's attention to the dimensions which are relevant for attaining a particular concept. On the other hand if a salient dimension is irrelevant then concept learning will be slower (Archer, 1962; Trabasso, 1963). However, when there are only a few irrelevant features which are salient these are quickly checked and discounted by the subject whose learning is then quicker than that of the subjects who are given irrelevant dimensions which are less salient (Fischbein, Haygood and Frieson, 1970).

Abstract concepts are more difficult to learn than concrete ones, even if they are equally familiar, possibly because they have less perceptible instances and less perceptible common attributes. For example, Reed and Dick (1968) found that college students had greater difficulty learning the abstract concepts (punishment, distance and travel) than they had learning the concrete concepts (food, furniture and plant).

This section has shown that it is the interaction of the learner, the instructional situation and the nature of the concept itself which affects concept learning. Therefore, when a person wishes to enable others to attain a concept, it is necessary to consider these factors as well as objectives, teaching materials and methods of assessment. Thinking about thinking is a complex task, but it is fundamental to the educational process.

Further reading

Bartlett, Sir Frederick (1958) *Thinking: An Experimental Social Study*. London: George Allen and Unwin.
Berlyne, D. E. (1965) *Structure and Direction in Thinking*. New York: John Wiley.
Bolton, N. (1972) *The Psychology of Thinking*. London: Methuen.
Bourne, L. E., Ekstrand, B. R. and Dominowski, R. L. (1971) *The Psychology of Thinking*. Englewood Cliffs, New Jersey: Prentice-Hall.
Bruner, J. S., Goodnow, J. L. and Austin, G. A. (1956) *A Study of Thinking*. New York: John Wiley.
Bruner, J. S., Oliver, R. R. and Greenfield, P. M. (1966) *Studies in Cognitive Growth*. New York: John Wiley.
Furth, H. G. and Wachs, H. (1974) *Thinking goes to School. Piaget's Theory in Practice*. New York: Oxford University Press.
Klausmeier, H. J., Ghatala, E. S. and Frayer, D. A. (1974) *Conceptual Learning and Development: A Cognitive View*. New York: Academic Press.
Kleinmuntz, B. (1966) *Problem Solving: Research Method and Theory*. New York: John Wiley.
Melton, A. W. (ed.) (1964) *Categories of Human Learning*. New York: Academic Press.
Peel, E. A. (1960) *The Pupil's Thinking*. London: Oldbourne.
Radford, J. and Burton, A. (1974) *Thinking: Its Nature and Development*. London: John Wiley.
Reeves, J. W. (1965) *Thinking about Thinking*. London: Secker and Warburg.
Shouksmith, G. (1970) *Intelligence, Creativity and Cognitive Style*. London: Batsford.
Wertheimer, M. (1945) *Productive Thinking*. Enlarged Edition (1959). New York: Harper Bros.

[3]
The concept
of creativity

Psychologists, until the middle of this century, seemed considerably more interested in reproductive than in productive thinking and the curriculum of many schools today still appears to be based on the more convergent processes of concept attainment and problem solving than on the divergent ones of concept formation and creative production. The distinction between creativity and intelligence, however, may not be an altogether helpful one unless creativity is carefully defined and value judgements are not implied. Since one form of thinking may be more appropriate to one situation and the other to another, the task of the teacher would seem to be to foster all types of thinking.

---

1 *What is meant by creativity?*

1.1 *Some views of creativity*

A famous account of the creative process is that given by Poincaré (1924):

> For fifteen days I strove to prove that there could not be any functions like those I have since called Fuchsian functions. I was then very ignorant, every day I seated myself at my work table, stayed an hour or two, tried a great number of combinations and reached no results. One evening, contrary to my custom, I drank black coffee and could not sleep. Ideas rose in clouds; I felt them collide until parts interlocked, so to speak, to make a stable combination. By the next morning I had established the existence of a class of Fuchsian functions, those which come from the hypergeometric series; I had only to write out the results, which took but a few hours.

The inspirational view of creativity is a popular one and has led to the related definition of it as a quality possessed by the few men who have made an outstanding contribution in the Arts or Sciences, e.g. Beethoven, Shakespeare, Botticelli, Einstein or Freud. Ausubel (1963) defines it as 'a rare and unique talent in a particular field of endeavour'. If this is the case it is indeed rare since even the few unique individuals who have given evidence of possessing this talent are only creative at certain times of their lives or are honoured for specific contributions. J. P. White (1968) maintained that 'creative' is not the name of an activity or process at all but rather 'a medal we pin on public products', for by calling certain years a person's 'creative' years, we are drawing attention to the fact that he produced certain products in those years and are not justified in implying that his mental processes differed. Parsons (1971) disagreed and argued that the term 'creative' can be applied to 'works, persons, and processes', although it is primarily connected with persons (a creative person being one who has produced valuable work and one who is capable of so doing).

It is obviously true that 'creative' is an honorific term but it can be applied to both products and their producers. To say this does not however rule out the possibility that everybody is capable of behaving creatively in their everyday lives. The fact that a person cannot climb Everest does not mean that he cannot climb the hill to the shops or the stairs to bed. The two forms of climbing are different in degree but not in kind, and although it could be argued that it is precisely the difference in degree which is being marked by the adjective 'creative', this is not necessarily so. Bruner (1962) takes a less elitist view when he defines the creative process as one which results in 'an act that produces *effective surprise*'.

Linking creativity to surprise or novelty leads to another popular definition (Guilford, 1950, 1959, 1962) which sees creativity as representing 'divergent' rather than 'convergent' thinking. According to this definition creativity is an ability possessed in varying degrees by all people and is exemplified by certain responses to open-ended 'creativity' tests. For example when Guilford asked his subjects how many uses they could think of for a brick, responses which merely listed things that could be built with it were assessed as 'convergent' whereas 'divergent' thinkers gave responses in different categories, for example: 'make a door stop;

make a red powder; throw at a dog; make a paper weight; make a bookcase; drown a cat; drive a nail; use for baseball bases.' For Guilford the divergent thinker shows more flexibility, originality, and fluidity than the convergent. This definition makes creativity a particular form of thinking and while it has a certain precision, care should be taken that creativity is not too unthinkingly associated with divergence. There are examples of thinking which is divergent, as in thought disordered patients, which is in no sense creative. Alternatively convergent lines of thought can, when juxtaposed, lead to a creative outcome.

1.2 *The creative act*

Shouksmith (1970) suggests that creativity should not be thought of as a single unitary trait, seeing that the 'creative act' is a complex affair: 'a creative cognitive act may well occur in more than one way, the circumstances and the material involved determining in part which thinking mode will lead to discovery or creation.' Jackson and Messick (1965) suggest that a creative act can be conceptualized as having four 'response properties', which can be assessed by four 'judgmental standards' and which will give rise to four 'aesthetic responses' (Table 3.1). They argue that unusualness is often taken as the defining characteristic of creativity yet

Table 3.1   *The creative product*

Response properties	Judgmental standards	Aesthetic responses
Unusualness	Norms	Surprise
Appropriateness	Context	Satisfaction
Transformation	Constraints	Stimulation
Condensation	Summary power	Savouring

(Jackson and Messick, 1965)

it is necessary to compare the creative product against a norm in order to decide whether it is indeed unusual enough to constitute a novel object. The aesthetic response of surprise in the observer is central to Bruner's (1962) definition, although Jackson and

Messick as well as Bruner point out that such unusualness must be 'appropriate' and such surprise 'effective'. Products that are merely odd or exceptional in a statistical sense cannot be counted as creative for those reasons alone. A product must, it is argued, be appropriate to its context or, if it is a complex product, then its constituent elements must be 'appropriate to each other'. When Prufrock exclaims 'I have measured out my life in coffee spoons' (T. S. Eliot, 1917), the image is novel since 'coffee spoons' are unexpected measures of time; yet the usage is contextually appropriate for here it is a relevant way of measuring a life which has had the qualities of Prufrock's own. Similarly Dylan Thomas' 'a grief ago' is a novel yet evocative way of describing a portion of time. The recognition of such contextual appropriateness leads to satisfaction.

In addition to being unusual and appropriate a creative product needs to be the result of the 'transformation' of old ways of thinking or methods of approach, leading to a new solution while still mindful of the constraints which operated previously. Such a transformation is thought to be likely to stimulate the observer who, realizing the significance of the change, will be inspired to reassess the original idea or situation. Jackson and Messick's fourth criteria is 'condensation' by which they mean 'the unity and coherence of meaning derived from the condensation as compared with the unrelated and irrelevant meanings derived from disorder'. It is this intensity of meaning which makes the creative product capable of revealing new facets of itself as time goes on and therefore have an enduring appeal. In other words the work represents a 'summary' which will be interpreted variously by different observers or by the same observer at different times. These discrete interpretations and responses, however, will all be genuinely based on the product the appeal of which is precisely that 'custom cannot stale' its 'infinite variety'. Hence the observer is able to 'savour' the work in all its aspects.

1.3 *The creative process* (Wallas' four stages)

This description of the creative product and the aesthetic response it evokes does seem to provide a concise summary of the nature of creative works. Nevertheless psychologists are also interested in the process whereby these products are made. Wallas (1926)

quoted Helmholtz's description, in 1891, of how new ideas came
to him. Having attempted to investigate the question, 'in all direc-
tions ... happy ideas come unexpectedly without effort, like an
inspiration. So far as I am concerned, they have never come to
me when my mind was fatigued, or when I was at my working
table ... They came particularly readily during the slow ascent
of wooded hills on a sunny day'. This account led Wallas to
identify four stages in the creative process: preparation, incubation,
illumination and verification. During the preparatory phase the
thinker is trying in a systematic and logical way, to understand
the problem before him and gathers as much information as he
can. It is possible that during this phase some kind of cognitive
'set', or blindness caused by rigidly viewing the problem in one
particular way will occur, which will make it difficult for the thinker
to consider the problem objectively and he may therefore be
baffled. If he then lays the problem aside, the phase of 'incubation'
will commence. What actually happens during this period is
obscure although, in theory, the unconscious mind is thought to

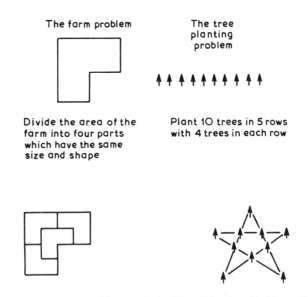

Fig. 3.1 *The Farm Problem and the Tree Planting Problem with their
instructions and solutions*
(Dreistadt, 1969)

take over and to continue to work upon the problem while the conscious mind is no longer actively considering it. Since the unconscious mind appears to work while the conscious mind is asleep it is possible that it also works, in an underground way, while the conscious mind is awake. We do, however, know very little about this process although most people will have experienced the phenomenon of forgetting a name or a book title and then suddenly remembering it a few hours later when they had stopped trying consciously to recall it. Here Wallas speaks of 'fringe consciousness', a term which he says he took from William James (1890) who said: 'Let us use the words *psychic overtone, suffusion* or *fringe* to designate the influence of a faint brain process upon our thoughts, as it makes it aware of relations and objects but dimly perceived.'

Dreistadt (1969) studied experimentally the effects of the use of analogies (clues) and incubation on creative problem solving and found that incubation alone was insufficient whereas incubation together with pictures which contained material analogous to the solution was significantly related to reaching a correct solution. In his experiment half of the subjects were given the Farm Problem and half the Tree Planting Problem to solve (Fig. 3.1). Each group was then subdivided into four experimental conditions: (1) control subjects; (2) those with pictorial analogies but no incubation; (3) those with incubation but no pictorial analogies; and (4) those with both incubation and pictorial analogies. (There were eight groups in all, of ten subjects each.) The control subjects worked on the problem for twenty minutes. Those with analogies worked for twenty minutes but had the pictures on a board before them throughout (Figs. 3.2, 3.3). The incubation subjects worked on the problem for five minutes, then had eight minutes off when they played a simple guessing game and then returned to the problem for seven minutes. The combined subjects worked on the same schedule as the incubation group but also had the pictures before them all the time. The results demonstrated the significance of combining incubation and analogies (Table 3.2). Dreistadt suggested that the value of incubation here was that it allowed the subjects more time to take in the pictorial analogies, especially for the farm problem. This suggests that in real life the incubation phase, as well as providing a rest and hence reducing fatigue or giving time for cognitive sets to be broken down (Woodworth and

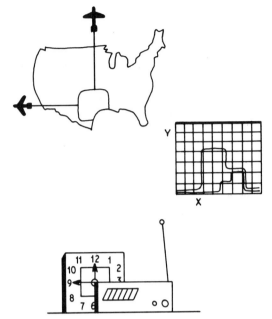

Fig. 3.2 *The visual pictorial analogies for the Farm Problem*
(Dreistadt, 1969)

Fig. 3.3 *The visual pictorial analogies for the Tree Planting Problem*
(Dreistadt, 1969)

Schlosberg, 1954), is also 'generally helpful because it brings a person back into contact with the larger more enriched behavioural environment with its manifold and varied patterns of stimulation where he may find a pattern of stimulation – which was not in the immediate environment while he worked on the problem – that he can use as an analogy for solving the problem.'

Table 3.2 *Solution scores of all subjects*

	No analogies		Analogies	
	No incubation	*Incubation*	*No incubation*	*Incubation*
Farm Problem	28	24	33	45
Tree Planting Problem	26	28	42	47

(Adapted from Dreistadt, 1969)

Incubation ends when illumination occurs and the pieces fall into place, the right word is found, or the solution is apparent. In the final stage the term 'verification' is perhaps more appropriate to scientific or mathematical enterprises, but, nevertheless, artists too have to check that their illumination was indeed a true revelation and not just another false start. Spender (1954), for instance, speaking of the creative process says: 'Beethoven wrote fragments of themes in note books which he kept beside him, working on and developing them over the years. Often his first ideas were of a clumsiness which makes scholars marvel how he could, at the end, have developed from them such miraculous results.' He also remarks that: 'For every poem that I begin to write, I think of at least ten which I do not write down at all. For every poem which I do write down, there are seven or eight which I never complete.'

The four phases, however, may not always appear in Wallas' sequence. Spender's view is that: 'Inspiration is the beginning of a poem and it is also its final goal. It is the first idea which drops into the poet's mind and it is the final idea which he at last achieves in words. In between this start and this winning post there is the hard race, the sweat and toil.' This seems, intuitively, to be as likely to be a correct description of the creative process as Wallas' stages.

---

2 Theoretical approaches to the study of creativity

To a large extent a person's view of the nature of the creative process will be determined by his theoretical predelictions. Five main approaches can be discerned when reading accounts of creativity: the psychoanalytic; the associationist; the psychometric; the cognitive; and the holistic.

2.1 *The psychoanalytic approach* (S. Freud, E. Kris)

The psychoanalytic, or unconscious, theory of creativity has an intuitive appeal, and yet repels.

> The underground theory always bears with it an ethic of dark gods, proposing to lend an aura of scientific respectability to an atavistic mystique that, one fears, has only too sure an appeal in every time, ours being no exception. If human culture is indeed created in a pitchblack cave below the functions of perception, imagination, thought and reason that empower our conscious life, then our incalculable gratitude and respect for the creative abilities of a Shakespeare, a von Kekulé, a Molière, a Poincaré, are properly owed to primitive, chthonic forces.

Here Williams (1967) seems to have captured the ambivalent attitude often held towards this particular theory. Yet is it either as plausible or implausible as its supporters or opponents would have us believe?

Freud (1908) clearly identified the creative writer with one who conjures up phantasies and then presents them in a way which is acceptable to others since they satisfy the others' unconscious wishes.

> The creative writer does the same as the child at play. He creates a world of phantasy which he takes very seriously – that is, which he invests with large amounts of emotion – while separating it sharply from reality . . . The motive forces of phan-

tasies are unsatisfied wishes, and every single phantasy is the fulfilment of a wish, a correction of unsatisfying reality. These motivating wishes vary according to sex, character and circumstances of the person who is having the phantasy ... A strong experience in the present awakes in the creative writer a memory of an earlier experience (usually belonging to his childhood) from which there now proceeds a wish which finds its fulfilment in the creative work.

This view equates the creative writer with one who dreams while awake – the account of his dreams subsequently giving vicarious satisfaction to others.

Although the source of creative thoughts may be the unconscious it is necessary for these thoughts to become conscious otherwise they would remain unrecognized and incommunicable. In order to explain this it is necessary to consider Freud's theory of Primary and Secondary processes. The Primary process is the dream process in which ideas are combined to fulfil some wish. It is characterized by the bringing together of disparate elements by 'condensation' as in the composite landscapes, buildings or people that occur in dreams, and by 'displacement' when something is referred to obliquely or by symbol. The Secondary process relates to the real world and is governed by the 'ego', or reality-testing principle. Kris (1953) uses this Freudian distinction to describe creative thinking as 'regression in the service of the ego'; by which he means that the creative person is able to conjure up the Primary processes and yet control them, unlike the mentally ill person who is overwhelmed by them. It is, of course, possible that the same person will be overwhelmed at one time and show symptoms of disturbance, yet be in control at another and produce creative works. There are several difficulties with this view since it implies a very strong ego, capable of breaking down defences in order to regress, and then selecting from the Primary process 'le mot juste', being motivated here by artistic, and not the usual reality-maintaining criteria. Nevertheless 'condensation' and 'displacement' do seem to be prerequisites for many intuitive, or creative productions, and the free floating nature of dream thought may be more conducive to creative responses than more controlled, directed, fully conscious thinking.

If the unconscious does have a part to play it is likely to be during the phase of incubation and indeed it is difficult to see where else this process could be taking place since, by definition, it is a phase in which the individual is not consciously thinking about the problem. There is, however, a considerable difference between saying that much creative activity is 'unconscious', and saying that the unconscious activity has the characteristics attributed to it by Freud, particularly in respect of wish fulfilment and phantasy.

2.2 *The associationist approach* (S. A. Mednick)

Lowes (1930), writing of Coleridge, said: 'We have to do, in a word, with one of the most extraordinary memories of which there is a record, stored with the spoils of an omnivorous reading, and endowed into the bargain with an almost uncanny power of association.'

This power of association may be more related to creativity than is often thought and forms the basis of Mednick's (1962) influential theory. Starting from Poincaré's statement that 'to create consists of making new combinations of associative elements which are useful', Mednick described three ways of arriving at creative solutions: (1) serendipity, when associations occur by chance; (2) contiguity between similar associative elements, and (3) by association being evoked through the mediation of common elements. Individual differences in creativeness were therefore accounted for by the individual's ability to associate. In order to do this he needs to have a wide range of potentially associable elements to hand (gathering these could be the purpose of the preparation phase), to be flexible in his associative hierarchies so that, for example, 'table' can relate to both 'periodic' and 'mountain', and be willing to abandon cognitive 'sets', which restrict thinking.

In order to test his hypothesis Mednick devised a Remote Association Test (RAT) in which the subject was given three stimulus words and asked to 'draw a spark from their juxtaposition'; in other words to think of an association which would link all three (Table 3.3). When this test was given to architecture students their scores on it were found to correlate highly with faculty members' assessment of their creativity. Since Mednick devised this test there have been several studies aimed at analysing exactly what it is

Table 3.3 *RAT stimuli*

			Possible solution
rat	blue	cottage	(cheese)
railroad	girl	class	(working)
surprise	line	birthday	(party)
wheel	electric	high	(chair or wire)
out	dog	cat	(house)

(Mednick, 1962)

testing. For example Mendelsohn and Griswold (1964), having given the RAT test to a group of students asked them to memorize a list of twenty-five words. The task was made more complex by the experimenters playing another list of twenty-five words to the subjects while they were attempting to learn the first list. The subjects were then asked to solve thirty anagrams; ten of the solution words had actually occurred in the list of twenty-five words which they had been asked to memorize (focal exposure), ten had occurred in the list they had heard played (peripheral exposure) and ten were new. The high RAT scorers solved more anagrams than the low scorers when the solution words had been exposed, which suggested that they were more able to pay attention to more aspects of a situation, and use what they had picked up, than were the low scorers. Koestler (1964) rejected the term 'association' as suggesting no more than the extension of a single line of thought and used the word 'bisociation' to draw attention to the significance for creative activity of the association of two or more previously separate systems of thought.

2.3 *The psychometric approach* (J. P. Guilford, E. P. Torrance)

The psychometric concept of creativity is perhaps the best known since to approach creativity through testing is likely to appeal to academic psychologists. It should be remembered, however, that creativity tests are primarily concerned with identifying creativity and not with explaining its nature. Guilford (1950) in his inaugural lecture realized that to test creativity needed a distinctly different approach from that applied to intelligence testing: 'What

I am saying is that the quest for easily objectifiable testing and scoring has directed us away from the attempt to measure some of the most precious qualities of individuals and hence to ignore those qualities.' This new approach was also a response to the frustration felt by many because of the unsatisfactory nature of psychoanalytic explanations.

> The belief that the process of incubation is carried on in a region of the mind called the unconscious is of no help. It merely chases the problem out of sight and thereby the chaser feels excused from the necessity of continuing the chase further. It is not incubation itself that we find of great interest. It is the nature of the processes that occur during the latent period of incubation, as well as before it and after it. It is individual differences in the efficiency of those processes that will be found important for identifying the potentially creative.

Faced with the problem of identifying creativity, Guilford started with certain hypotheses which he then planned to test to see if items in the sub-tests of each ability correlated with each other and, further, to see if together the sub-tests identified a trait exhibited to a varying degree by different people. He suggested that creative people might be more sensitive to problems, more fluent, and more flexible. In addition they would need to be able to synthesize, to analyse, to deal with complexity and reorganize familiar data in unfamiliar ways. Having performed these operations the creative person would also be able to evaluate realistically the results of his labours. He proposed that the way to test these hypotheses was through a research design based on the statistical technique called 'factor analysis' (see p. 8).

Guilford was one of the earliest to devise sub-tests a high score on which would lead to the person's total score being heavily weighted with an 'originality' factor. The test 'Plot Titles' gave subjects a summary of a story and asked them to make up as many titles for it as they could. In one story a missionary is captured by cannibals and is given the choice of marrying their princess or being eaten. He refuses and is boiled alive. Examples of unoriginal responses are: 'Eaten by savages', or 'The Princess', and of original ones: 'Pot's plot', 'Pot luck dinner', 'Stewed parson', 'A mate worse than death', 'He left a dish for a pot' and 'Hot price for freedom'. The test 'Unusual Uses' required the subject to think of as many uses as he could for the common object and a high score was given for the more unusual uses mentioned.

Once Guilford's approach was adopted 'creativity' became something capable of being tested and, like intelligence before it, could be defined as a product of testing, while remaining a criterion for constructing the original tests. Guilford's initial assumption that creativity could be distinguished from intelligence has led to several attempts to see if this distinction is valid (see p. 70), but this is a specific problem and the psychometric approach has a wider relevance.

Torrance (1962a and b, 1965) has concentrated on the educational aspects of creativity testing and has produced tests which can be used by teachers in classroom settings. His study of teachers' concepts of the ideal pupil indicated that teachers have mixed feelings about the highly creative child. They appeared to undervalue courage in thought and action in comparison with courtesy, obedience and punctuality. Torrance therefore decided to direct his efforts both towards alerting teachers to the needs of creative children and to their identification. His tests allow the children to manipulate any objects used and require them to think, for example, of ways of improving objects such as their own toys (Product Improvement Test, Fig. 3.4), to suggest causes and results related to a stimulus picture (Ask and Guess Test) or give solutions to an unusual situation (Just Suppose Test, Fig. 3.5).

Above is a sketch of a stuffed toy rabbit of the kind you can buy in most dime stores for about one to two dollars. It is about six inches tall and weighs about six ounces. In the spaces on this page and the next one, list the cleverest, most interesting and unusual ways you can think of for changing this toy rabbit so that children will have more fun playing with it. Do not worry about how much the change would cost. Think only about what would make it more fun to play with as a toy.

Fig. 3.4 *Product Improvement Test*
(Torrance, 1966)

You will now be given an improbable situation – one that will probably never happen. You will have to *just suppose* that it has happened. This will give you a chance to use your imagination to think out all of the other exciting things that would happen IF this improbable situation were to come true.

In your imagination, *just suppose* that the situation described were to happen THEN think of all of the other things that would happen because of it. In other words, what would be the consequences? Make as many guesses as you can.

The improbable situation – JUST SUPPOSE *all wheels suddenly turned square, like in the tricycle and wheelbarrow below.* What would happen? How would this change life on the earth?

Fig. 3.5 *Just Suppose Test*
(Torrance, 1966)

2.4 *The cognitive approach*

The cognitive approach sees creative productions as the result of using a certain 'cognitive style'. Cognitive theorists are concerned with how an individual processes the information he obtains from the environment and argue that individual differences in ways of processing give rise to different forms of thinking about, or conceptualizing, the world. Although cognitive tests are administered they are very different from tests in which creativity is measured by the psychometricians. Three well known cognitive tests are the 'Embedded Figures Test', the 'Rod and Frame Test' and the 'Body Adjustment Test'. In the first the subject has to find a simple figure hidden in a complex design. The second requires a subject in a dark room to place a luminous rod in an upright position, when it has already been placed in a tilted luminous frame. For the third test the subject is placed in a small room, which can be tilted, on a chair, which can also be tilted and he has to make his body upright while the room is tilted. Witkin and his co-workers (1954, 1962) used these tests to assess a subject's degree of 'field dependence' or 'field independence'; the 'independent' being the person who can deal with components in a field separately from their background, or keep their bodies upright despite the tilt of the room. They claimed that field dependence/independence is an enduring characteristic of a person's thinking, although people vary in the extent to which they display either characteristic.

The relationship between these cognitive styles and creativity is not clear, since studies relating scores on psychometric creativity measures to Witkin dimensions have found that high scorers may be either field dependent or independent (McWhinnie, 1967, 1969; Bloomberg, 1967, 1971). Gardner (1961) has also assessed the scanning procedures used by subjects when carrying out these tests and it does appear that the ability to take note of many features in the environment is related to creativity. Ward (1969) also found that his 'creative' group of nursery school subjects made more use of environmental cues than did a matched 'uncreative' group. The cognitive approach is most useful in identifying people who make best use of the 'preparation phase', and hence gather the relevant associations, but it throws little light on the phase of incubation or illumination.

2.5 The 'holistic' approach

Rogers and Maslow take a holistic approach since they see the creative product as the result of an interaction between the creative person and his situation. Rogers (1954) defined the creative process as 'the emergence in action of a novel, relational product, growing out of the uniqueness of the individual on the one hand, and the materials, events, people or circumstances of his life on the other'. The creative act was seen by him as motivated by the individual's desire to expand and grow and hence, 'form new relationships to the environment'. The creative individual therefore needs to be open and receptive to experience, not to think in pre-determined categories nor be finally influenced by the evaluations of others. He needs to be autonomous, adventurous, and accepting of life. This individual sounds very unlike Freud's (1920) characterization of the artist as 'an incipient introvert who is not far from being a neurotic'.

Maslow's (1972) formulation is closer to Rogers' since he is inclined to equate creativity with mental health. He quotes a study (Craig, 1966) in which the author listed the characteristics Torrance had found to correlate with creative talent, and matched them with a list of characteristics which Maslow had used to describe self-actualizing people and took to correlate with mental health. Craig found the overlap to be virtually perfect. Maslow's contention then is that the 'problem of creativeness is the problem of the creative person, rather than of creative products, creative behaviours etc'. That is that the mentally healthy, self-actualizing person is more likely to be creative.

These five approaches would appear to be complementary rather than contradictory since they can be applied in part to different phases of the creative process as defined by Wallas.

---

3 Intelligence and creativity

Since Guilford first drew psychologists' attention to their neglect of creativity a question which has generated a considerable amount of debate is that of the relationship between 'creativity' and 'intelligence' when 'intelligence' is defined as 'what the tests test'.

The very earliest studies suggested a close
Terman's (1947) study of genius he quotes Cox
which she assessed the IQs of 300 men out of C
1,000 most eminent men in history. Her metho
biographical data on the interests, reading, writi
ments of these people as children, paying partic
any documentary evidence. This data was then studied independently by three psychologists who were experts in the study of
what one would expect of a child at a certain age. They then
made an estimate of the subject's childhood IQ, for example, if
a mental age of six is required for reading and John Stuart Mill
read at three, then dividing mental age by chronological ages gives
an IQ of 200. The results of Cox's work suggested that the
average IQ of these eminent men was 155: the mean of the
philosophers was 170, poets, novelists, dramatists, and revolution-
ary statesmen 160, scientists 155, musicians 145, artists 140, and
soldiers 125.

If a person has completed a set of creativity tests (for example
Guilford's 'Plot Titles', Mednick's RAT or Torrance's 'Just Suppose') as well as conventional intelligence tests, the obvious question is the extent to which the two sets of scores are related. If
there is a high correlation between the person's scores on the
various creativity tests, as well as on the intelligence tests, but
a low correlation between his 'creativity' and his 'intelligence'
scores, then it is reasonable to conclude that each set of tests is
measuring a distinct quality or trait. Indeed virtually all the discussion concerning the relationship between creativity and intelligence centres around this point.

Thorndike (1963) however, was one of the earliest to point out
that even if a low correlation is found between the two sets of
tests this merely tells us *that* they are measuring different things.
It does not tell us *what* the 'creativity' tests are measuring.
Although these tests require the subject to produce an answer
rather than select one from our array, the answers produced may
represent fluency, originality or flexibility and it is an open question whether these can be thought of as different behaviours linked
to a single trait.

Guilford (1959) defined a trait as 'any distinguishable, relatively
enduring way in which one individual differs from another' and
argued that they were best identified by the statistical technique

ctor analysis. He identified the three primary traits of 'fluency', flexibility' and 'originality' as being related to creativity. Fluency was subdivided into 'word fluency' or the ability to think of words containing a certain number, or a certain combination, of letters; 'associational fluency' or the ability to give synonyms; 'expressional fluency' which requires not the production of single words but of phrases or sentences; and, finally, 'ideational fluency' or the production of ideas in tests such as 'Unusual Uses' or 'Plot Titles'. He subdivided 'flexibility' into 'spontaneous flexibility' which enables a person's mind to move from idea to idea; and 'adaptive flexibility', apparent when a person is trying to solve a problem which appears to be soluble by one method but which in fact requires an adaptation of thinking and a change of method. 'Originality' appeared in Remote Association Tests (see p. 64) and in 'clever', rather than ideationally fluent responses to 'Plot Titles'.

Probably the best known study which suggested that creativity and intelligence were discrete, independent traits was that of Getzels and Jackson (1962). Their original interest was in gifted children and they were concerned that: 'For all practical purposes, the term "gifted child" has become synonymous with the expression "child with a high IQ", thus blinding us to other forms of excellence.' They therefore took as their subjects children from a private school whose parents were mainly either professional or managerial. The mean IQ of the children was 132. They gave the children a standard IQ test and five creativity measures, and on the basis of the scores they composed two contrasting groups: a 'high creativity group', which consisted of the twenty-six children who were in the top 20 per cent for creativity scores but not for IQ, and a 'high IQ group' who were in the top 20 per cent for IQ but not for creativity. Getzels and Jackson then attempted to explore other facets of the two groups and found that the high creativity group achieved in the school as highly as the high IQ group, and were thus 'overachieving' since their average IQ was considerably lower. They did not, however, express any greater need for achievement (see p. 235) than did the high IQ group. The teachers appeared to prefer the high IQ children to both the high creativity group and the sample as a whole. The high creativity group ranked 'a sense of humour' as an important personal quality whereas the high IQ group placed it last. The high IQ children were found to desire the qualities for themselves which they thought made for adult success and were favoured by teachers (diligence, tidiness), whereas the high creatives wished for qualities which had no connection with adult success and were not just unrelated, but negatively related, to those favoured by teachers. With respect to career aspirations 18 per cent of the high IQs gave unconventional choices, (inventor, artist, space man, disc jockey) whereas 62 per cent of the high creativity group did so.

The nature of the phantasies of the two groups also differed, which is illustrated by two responses to the picture of a man sitting in a reclining seat on a plane:

High IQ subject: Mr Smith is on his way home from a successful business trip. He is very happy and he is thinking about his wonderful family and how glad he will be to see them again. He can picture it, about an hour from now, his plane landing at the airport and Mrs Smith and their three children all there welcoming him home again.

High creative subject: This man is flying back from Rome where he has just won a divorce from his wife. He couldn't stand to live with her any more, he told the judge, because she wore so much cold cream on her face at night that her head would skid across the pillow and hit him in the head. He is now contemplating a new skid-proof face cream.

In summary Getzels and Jackson say:

The high IQs tend to converge upon stereotyped meanings, to perceive personal success by conventional standards, to move towards the model provided by teachers, to seek out careers that conform to what is expected of them. The high creatives tend to diverge from stereotyped meanings, to produce original fantasies, to perceive personal success by unconventional standards to seek out careers that do not conform to what is expected of them.

This research has been severely, and probably justifiably, criticized as badly designed, since it ignored children who were both highly creative and highly intelligent. More seriously there is only a low correlation between the creativity measures themselves, and the difference between the children's scores on the creativity measures and the intelligence tests taken over all, is not large enough to justify the researchers seeing the groups as distinct in the first place. Their work did, however, generate a great deal of interest and subsequent research. Since their findings seem to have become a part of educational folklore it is important to see to what extent they are defensible.

One of the first studies to be stimulated by Getzels and Jackson's was Ripple and May's (1962) in which they selected four groups, three were homogeneous with respect to intelligence (one being high, one medium, and one low) and the fourth was heterogeneous. They then compared the groups' intelligence scores with their creativity scores. Correlations were found to vary between the groups, being lower in the homogeneous groups and relatively high in the heterogeneous group, which suggests that Getzels and Jackson's lower correlation was merely the result of their having a highly selected homogeneous group in the first place.

In 1965, Edwards and Tyler investigated the relationship between creativity and school achievement and found that, for their subjects, creativity scores were not related to school achievement, whereas scores on the School and College Ability Test (SCAT) were. Their results are not in agreement with Getzels and Jackson's and they hypothesize that this was because the general level of ability in their subjects was much lower than in Getzels and Jackson's sample. A 'threshold effect' might therefore be involved whereby in the lower ability ranges, IQ does predict scholastic achievement whereas for children with high IQs a high creativity score may be more important for school achievement than having an even higher IQ with a low creativity score. They therefore compared a third group of subjects, who scored high on both SCAT and the creativity tests, with the original high SCAT group but once again found no evidence to favour the creative group. Both groups had almost identical attainment scores related to their high ability.

In the same year Yamamoto (1965) studied two groups of primary school children and found that the overall correlation between intelligence and creativity was not high but it became increasingly smaller as the intelligence level of the children rose. In other words it was possible to find some kind of distinction between creativity and intelligence in highly intelligent children, but at a lower level the two were related and he concludes, 'we should regard creativity tests as complementary components in new and more inclusive measures of human intellectual behaviour, and not as a measure wholly independent and exclusive of the general factor of intelligence.'

It therefore appeared that Getzels and Jackson's findings were incorrect and this view was supported by Wallach and Kogan (1965) who, having reviewed previous studies, could find no evidence in them for separating creativity and intelligence, since the measures of creativity used seemed to be as closely related to general intelligence as they were to each other. They suggested, however, that a 'creative' trait might be more apparent if the tests were limited to the generation of associations and given in a more relaxed atmosphere which would be more conducive to abundant and unique responses.

They therefore introduced the tests to their 151 primary school subjects as 'games' and ensured, by individual testing, that the children did not associate the tasks with academic evaluation. They used five procedures, aimed at generating five kinds of associations, both visual and verbal. Two variables were scored in each of the five procedures – uniqueness of association and total number of associations. For example 'life savers' (a type of sweet) was scored as a unique response to 'round things' whereas 'buttons' was not. In the visual procedures the child had to think of meanings for various abstract patterns. They therefore obtained a total of ten 'creativity indicators' which they compared with ten 'general intelligence indicators' obtained independently. Their results showed high correlations within the creativity indicators (0.4), and within the intelligence indicators (0.5), but low ones between the sets (0.1). They concluded that they had demonstrated the existence of two independent traits.

Wallach and Kogan then composed four groups of children all of the same sex:

1 High creativity, high intelligence (Hi/Hi)
2 Low creativity, low intelligence (Lo/Lo)
3 High intelligence, low creativity (HiI/LoC)
4 Low intelligence, high creativity (LoI/HiC)

They looked in more detail at the children's behaviour in the school environment; their ways of conceptualizing as exemplified in the basis used for grouping objects; sensitivity and willingness to consider divergent suggestions; and levels of anxiety. In the school environment there was a sex difference in that the boys' response to school life was affected by IQ rather than creativity whereas for the girls the Hi/Hi group were the most popular with their peers and the most self-confident, although they were inclined, through over enthusiasm, to be disruptive in class. The HiC/LoI group appeared to be the least happy in school: they were isolated and unsure, with their disruptive behaviour stemming from distress rather than over-eagerness. The HiI/LoC group seemed assured, and although reserved and not inclined to seek friends for themselves, they were popular and sought after by others. The Lo/Lo group were more assured than the HiC/LoI and compensated for their low academic achievement by taking an active part in social activities.

When asked to group objects the findings for the boys showed clear differences between the groups. The HiI/LoC used common conceptual elements and avoided a thematic or relational approach, for example they would be likely to group a fork, a spoon, a cup and a glass as 'for eating' and avoid labelling a group consisting of a comb, a lipstick, a match, a pocket book, and a door as 'getting ready to go out'. The other three groups were prepared to thematize. When, on another task, the children were specifically required to thematize, the HiI/LoC group were able to do as well as the others, so their low usage was due to unwillingness rather than inability. The creative children appeared to be able to switch between conceptual and thematic bases for grouping whereas the HiI/LoC kept to the conceptual and the Lo/Lo seemed restricted to the thematic.

In another test the children were shown drawings of stick figures in various postures. Possible emotional states for each figure were suggested to each child who could then accept or reject the suggestion. The results for the girls showed that while there was no difference between the groups in the degree to which they were willing to accept conventional suggestions the HiI/LoC were particularly loath to accept unconventional ones.

When the children's manifest anxiety was assessed it was found that the anxiety level was lowest for the HiI/LoC, highest for Lo/Lo, and intermediate for the two creative groups. The authors suggested that a moderate level of anxiety facilitates creativity whereas too little or too much is an inhibitor. They see it as a mistake to equate creativity with freedom from anxiety and conclude: 'Creativity need not be all sweetness and light, therefore,

but may well involve a tolerance for and understanding of sadness
and pain. To think otherwise is to fall prey to the rather wide-
spread American stereotype that suffering is always a bad thing
and is to be avoided at all costs.'

In addition to the experimental findings clinical reports were
prepared on various children and were combined into the following
summary:

> High creativity – high intelligence: these children can exercise
> within themselves both control and freedom, both adult-like and
> child-like kinds of behaviour.
>
> High creativity – low intelligence: these children are in angry
> conflict with themselves and with their school environment, and
> are beset by feelings of unworthiness and inadequacy. In a stress-
> free context, however, they can blossom forth cognitively.
>
> Low creativity – high intelligence: these children can be
> described as 'addicted' to school achievement. Academic failure
> would be perceived by them as catastrophic, so that they must
> continually strive for academic excellence in order to avoid the
> possibility of pain.
>
> Low creativity – low intelligence: Basically bewildered, these
> children engage in various defensive manoeuvres ranging from
> useful adaptations such as intensive social activity to regressions
> such as passivity or psychosomatic symptoms.

It would appear that if Getzels and Jackson failed to demonstrate
a distinction Wallach and Kogan did succeed in doing so. Yet in
Scotland a study by Hasan and Butcher (1966) partially replicated
the Getzels and Jackson study with very different results. In this
study 175 Scottish children aged twelve to thirteen and of average
ability were assessed by a battery of creativity tests, intelligence
measures and teachers' ratings of 'desirability of pupil'. The results
showed a correlation of 0.7 to 0.8 between the intelligence and
the creativity tests. It was also found that although the teachers
did express disapproval of the highly creative child with a lower
intelligence this was on account of their low intelligence rather
than their high creativity. The degree of overlap between the
measures of creativity and of intelligence made it virtually impossible to construct four groups as Wallach and Kogan had done.
It does appear that the nature of the creativity measure chosen
is an important determinant of whether creativity will be found

to be separable from intelligence or not. This conclusion is somewhat similar to the one arrived at by Lovell and Shields (1967)
who studied fifty high ability eight- to ten-year-olds (IQs 140+).
Having analysed their scores on a range of tests they found factors
reflecting intellectual ability, the ability to think logically on
Piagetian tasks, plus a series of other dimensions which suggested
that, 'the able pupil is "creative" to different degrees according
to the task that is set him'.

The end of the sixties saw a further development in Intelligence/
Creativity studies when Hudson (1966), using a technique similar
to Getzels and Jackson's with a group of able sixth-form school-
boys, divided them into 'convergers' and 'divergers'. He linked
this division with subject choice, suggesting that convergers would
choose science and divergers arts subjects, as well as with various
personality dimensions. His argument was that although the con-
vergent/divergent distinction was valid it was not correct to equate
divergence with 'creativity'. Hudson however, like Getzels and
Jackson, does not offer convincing evidence that his convergers
and divergers can in fact be separated since the tests which were
used as a basis for dividing them do not fall into two sufficiently
dissimilar sets. However, when Cameron (1967) replicated
Hudson's work with first year Scottish undergraduates she found
some confirmation of the relationship between convergence and
science choice, and divergence and arts choice, in that there was
a relationship between divergence and specialized arts courses,
though not with less specialized courses.

[4]
The creative person

Although the precise nature of the creative process may be difficult to determine, psychologists have been increasingly interested in the characteristics of the creative person and in attempting to identify any environmental influences which may foster creative development. Creative people have been found to be stable and emotionally auto-nomous. However, although relations with their parents were characterized by independence rather than dependence, some researchers report a warm, others a cold home atmosphere. Climate at work, at school, and in the society in general, was found to facilitate creative output, and some training programmes with both children and adults have had a measure of success.

---
1 Creativity and personality

It has often been said that creative people are different from others and can be distinguished on other criteria besides their creativity. Psychologists have attempted to verify this belief in three ways; first by seeing if there is any correlation between certain traits and creativity; second by studying the personalities of a group of generally creative people; and third, which has proved most popular, by studying specific groups of creative people, e.g. scientists or artists.

1.1 Character traits related to creativity

McGuire (1967) writing of the relationship between creativity and emotionality demonstrated that the results of wide-ranging studies of children point to the close correlation between stability and creativity. 'Ineffective' people were characterized by 'Intense self-centred desires and conflicting emotions which stem from a hunger for affection, or loneliness, or feelings of hostility arising out of isolation or rejection by parents and peers'. As children they often exhibited an anti-academic attitude which was assessed by McGuire as being present if 'most often they are named as persons who would *not* ask for help on a school problem (negative academic model)'. They are reputed to 'find school work a disagreeable chore and resent any kind of study (dislikes school)' as well as 'do enough to get by but resent doing anything extra (gets by)'. Such people showed little creative behaviour except in terms of escapist phantasies. A second group he called the 'middle majority' who concentrated on conforming and memorizing rather than thinking deeply or adventurously. The effective person was one who was both able to work and play freely and showed an acceptance of himself and his world.

Effectiveness may be demonstrated by a willingness to take intellectual risks by tackling difficult problems, which for Berlyne (1965) is the characteristic of a creative thinker: 'greater creativity, on the whole, comes from willingness to attack greater or more difficult problems.' This requires courage and Rogers (1954) lists three inner conditions which will lead to such courage. The first is 'openness to experience' which means that the person is able to welcome each experience as it *is* and not misperceive it through imposing a set of rigid categories which he has developed and dare not let go. Openness, for Rogers, means 'lack of rigidity and permeability of boundaries in concepts, beliefs, perceptions and hypotheses'. Second the potentially creative person needs to be able to judge the value of what he does for himself and not only value what others value. And third, he just enjoy toying, or playing with elements and concepts since in such cognitive play the creative juxtaposition will occur.

Both McGuire and Rogers relate creativity to stability and although anxiety may be related to creativity (Wallach and Kogan, 1965) Cattell (1963) warns against confusing anxiety with neurosis. In his studies of scientists (see p. 82) Cattell found no support for linking creativity with neuroticism, indeed he found their emotional stability to be above average. Biographical studies may appear to link artistic creativity with neuroticism but Barron (1967) only found minor signs of this and then only with student writers (see p. 84). When Dellas and Gaier (1970) studied 104 secondary

school children they found that, when IQ was held constant, those
who scored higher on creativity tests were more extraverted and
less neurotic. Similarly Jones (1964) found that the most creative
industrial scientists and technologists were characterized by being
'emotionally stable ... adventurous in outlook, high in degree of
scientific curiosity and low in indication of general anxiety'.

1.2 The creative scientist

Creative scientists have been studied most extensively in an attempt
to understand the composition of their personalities. One of the
earliest studies was Roe's (1952) in which she studied sixty-four
eminent scientists by means of written and projective tests (e.g.
Rorschach 'the "ink blot" test' and Thematic Apperception Test
[TAT]; see p. 235). She found that although all were characterized by a 'driving absorption in their work' there were differences between types of scientists. The social scientists were more
verbally fluent, more independent in attitude towards their parents,
very concerned with human beings and gregarious, whereas the
physical scientists were more likely to feel isolated yet be perfectly
happy in their work.

> ... His work is his life, and he has few recreations, those being
> restricted to fishing, sailing, walking or some other individualis-
> tic activity. The movies bore him. He avoids social affairs and
> political activity, and religion plays no part in his life or think-
> ing. Better than any other interest or activity, scientific research
> seems to meet the inner need of his nature.

Chambers (1964) in trying to differentiate the highly creative
scientists from less creative ones found that the more creative were
more dominant and showed more initiative than the others.
McClelland (1962) was particularly interested in what motivated
the creative scientist to be so dedicated to his work. He first summarized the existing findings as:

1 Men are more likely to be creative scientists than women.
2 Experimental physical scientists come from a background
   of radical protestantism more often than would be expected
   by chance but are not themselves religious.
3 Scientists avoid interpersonal contact.

4 Creative scientists are unusually hardworking to the extent of appearing almost obsessed with their work (yet do *not* show a high need for achievement). [See p. 235.]
5 Scientists avoid and are disturbed by complex human emotions, perhaps particularly interpersonal aggression.
6 Physical scientists like music and dislike art and poetry.
7 Physical scientists are intensely masculine.
8 Physical scientists develop a strong interest in analysis, in the structure of things, early in life.

McClelland suggests a possible reason for this group of characteristics by saying that the young scientist's protestant home may have stressed the importance of curbing impulses, especially the impulse to aggression, and the child dealt with this parental prohibition by retreating from human contacts altogether. Scientists may therefore redirect their aggression into an attempt to understand and dominate nature. This hypothesis led the author to speculate further in order to explain why some scientists became researchers and others did not. He argued that if the child fears aggression he may, according to psychoanalytic theory, attempt to deal with it by 'identifying with the aggressor' or with the most powerful figure in his world namely his father. Terman's data (1954) suggested that research scientists had poor relationships with their fathers and received little understanding or affection from them whereas his non-research group had experienced good relationships with theirs, and this led McClelland to link research orientation with early childhood experience. Cattell and Drevdahl (1955), using Cattell's 16 Personality Factor questionnaire (the 16PF), compared research scientists with both the general population and a group of equally eminent men who were famous for their teaching or administration rather than for research. Both eminent groups were above the population norm in intelligence, dominance and ego strength. The researchers were lower than the administrators on ego strength, and all measures of extraversion but higher in radicalism, self-sufficiency and unsociableness. This avoidance of social contact by scientists was shown (Terman, 1954) to have been present in youth and therefore cannot be attributed to their having become withdrawn after becoming successful adults.

Taylor and Barron (1963) also reviewed previous research and arrived at a list of characteristics which was similar to McClelland's but also had some interesting additions. Productive scientists were found to be characterized by:

1 A high degree of autonomy, self-sufficiency, self-direction.
2 A preference for mental manipulation involving things rather than people: a somewhat distant or detached attitude in interpersonal relations and a preference for intellectually challenging situations rather than socially challenging ones.
3 High ego strength and emotional stability.
4 A liking for method, precision, exactness.
5 A preference for such defence mechanisms as repression and isolation in dealing with affect and instinctual energies.
6 A high degree of personal dominance but a dislike of personally toned controversy.
7 A high degree of control of impulse, amounting almost to over-control: relatively little talkativeness, gregariousness, impulsiveness.
8 A liking for abstract thinking, with considerable tolerance of cognitive ambiguity.
9 Marked independence of judgement, rejection of group pressures towards conformity in thinking.
10 Superior general intelligence.
11 An early, very broad interest in intellectual activities.
12 A drive towards comprehensiveness and elegance in explanation.
13 A special interest in the kind of 'wagering' which involves pitting oneself against uncertain circumstances in which one's own effort can be the deciding factor.

1.3 *Creative non-scientists*

If these are the characteristics of creative scientists to what extent are they similar to those of creative individuals in other fields? Drevdahl and Cattell (1958) obtained a profile based on the 16PF for artists and writers which was strikingly similar to that obtained for scientists. The creative writers, when compared with the general population, were more intelligent, emotionally mature, dominant, adventurous, emotionally sensitive, bohemian, radical, self-sufficient and energetic. These findings were confirmed by

Cross, Cattell and Butcher (1967) who compared art teachers and professional painters with the general population with similar results although the artists score on 'bohemian tendency' (hysterical unconcern) was more than one standard deviation higher than that of the general public. The artists however were found to be more emotionally responsive and anxious than the scientists.

Barron (1967) having studied a group of eminent writers and students on a creative writing course found that the qualities most characteristic of the creative writers were:

1 They appeared to have a high degree of intellectual capacity.
2 Genuinely valued intellectual and cognitive matters.
3 Valued own independence and autonomy.
4 Were verbally fluent.
5 Were aesthetically reactive.

The student writers were much more anxious and moody and appeared to be using their writing as a form of therapy. Barron, like McClelland, was concerned with the writers' motivation and argued that they were motivated by a desire to find ultimate meanings. He also (1955) studied the characteristics of people who had an 'underlying disposition toward originality' when originality was defined as 'the capacity for producing adaptive responses which are unusual'. He found that the originals were characterized by a liking for complexity, independence of thought and 'dominance' by which he meant a desire to dominate not just other people but experience in general. They showed an unwillingness to accept regulation by others, although they were prepared to impose order upon themselves. He concluded:

> The disposition toward originality may thus be seen as a highly organised mode of responding to experience, including other persons, society and oneself. The socially disrated traits which may go along with it include rebelliousness, disorderliness, and exhibitionism, while the socially valued traits which accompany it include independence of judgment, freedom of expression and novelty of construction and insight.

Mackinnon (1960, 1962a and b, 1963) has studied many groups of creative people although he is best known for his study of architects (1962). To collect his sample he asked five experts to nominate the forty most creative architects in the United States;

eighty-six names appeared, sixty-four were invited to take part in the study and forty accepted. Mackinnon then selected two control groups from the 1955 *Directory of Architects*. His findings were many-faceted and only the most significant are reported here. One test (the Myers Briggs Type Indicator 1958) was based on the premise that when people are thinking they are either perceiving (becoming aware of something) or judging (coming to a conclusion about something). It appears that people show a consistent preference for perceiving or judging, the former leading to 'a life that is more open to experience both from within and from without and characterised by flexibility and spontaneity': the latter producing a 'controlled, carefully planned and orderly' life style. The creative architects were significantly more likely to be perceivers than the controls. An even more outstanding finding was that if perception is divided into first 'sense perception or sensation' (a direct form of awareness) and second 'intuitive perception' ('an indirect perception of the deeper meanings and possibilities inherent in things and situations'), *not one* creative architect was a 'sense perceiver' whereas it is estimated that 75 per cent of the general United States population are sense perceivers and only 25 per cent are 'intuitives'.

The creative group accepted higher levels of complexity and disorder in what they perceived than others and were not distressed by this. Independence of thought was highly characteristic of the creative group leading to reasonable, but not outstanding, college achievement. Similarly the creatives' self-image differed from that of the non-creatives in that the first more often described themselves as 'inventive, determined, independent, individualistic, enthusiastic and industrious' in contrast with the others who described themselves as 'responsible, sincere, reliable, dependable, clear thinking, tolerant and understanding'. The creatives also showed more of the feminine side of their nature. Mackinnon comments 'as Jung would phrase it, creative males are not so completely identified with their masculine *persona* roles as to blind themselves to or to deny expression to the more feminine traits of the *anima* [i.e. their feminine part]. In other words they ... have more fully actualised the opposing potentialities of their nature.' The creative person appeared to have an image of himself as creative and to reject repression and suppression as a means of controlling impulses. He also appeared to experience more anxiety than others but had a stronger ego to deal with it. Mackinnon's overall picture of creative architects was one of independent, open-minded men with a strong sense of their own value and the validity of their creative work.

Creative people seem to present a constellation of traits which make them distinct from the general population as Cattell and Butcher (1968) conclude: 'It would almost seem as if the differences between Science, Art and Literature are differences in particular skills and interests only and that the fundamental characteristic of the creative original person is a type of personality.'

---

2 *Environmental influences on the development of the creative person*

2.1 *The family*

> Tom had been raised from an early age by his mother alone. She was an energetic woman who dominated the boy at all times. She told him when he might play, when he must do homework, when he must read 'good' novels, and so on. She insisted that he must play chess with her at a given time each evening, insisted on a certain schedule for piano practice and ran his life completely. She administered severe corporal punishment for trivial offences, and was, overall, domineering, controlling, intrusive and authoritarian. (Cropley, 1967)

Tom, despite distinguishing himself at school and university, made no creative contribution of any kind to his chosen profession.

If creativity is the product of a particular type of personality then it is important to identify the factors responsible for the development of this type of personality. But is the family one such factor? Research results have revealed interesting, yet conflicting, evidence. Roe (1952) describes the average scientist thus: 'He was the first-born child of a middle class family, the son of a professional man. He is likely to have been a sickly child or to have lost a parent at an early age.' Fifty-three per cent of her sample were sons of professional men, not one came from an unskilled labourer's family; none were Catholics, five had Jewish backgrounds and the rest were Protestants. Many more were first borns than could have been expected by chance. Their families did how-ever show some abnormal features, which may be responsible for the independence which characterizes the creative adult. A quarter of the biologists had lost a parent through death or divorce while still young, and a large proportion of social scientists came from homes where the mother was dominant.

When Roe (1951) reported on the responses of her subjects to the TAT (Thematic Apperception Test), she said:

> The attitude they manifest with regard to family relations is rather an unusual one. Its chief aspect is of independence of parents, usually without conflict over it ... a similar independence of other personal relations is generally noticeable. But here, particularly with respect to sexual relations, there is a strong tendency to evade an emotional situation, to give it distance in some way.

In their TAT stories the father figure has a positive image and if rebellion appears it is not accompanied by guilt although more difficulty appears in the mother/son relationships. Terman's (1954) subjects report distance between mother and son rather than conflict or rebellion – and the research scientists also report distant relationships with their fathers. Mackinnon (1962a) on the other hand found that it was often the mother who first fostered her son's artistic potentialities and a minority, who were in no way less creative than the others, were brutally treated by their fathers. Yet, in a subsequent paper (1962b) Mackinnon maintains that 'what appears to have characterised the parents of future creative architects was an extraordinary respect for the child and confidence in his ability to do what was appropriate. They did not hesitate to grant him rather unusual freedom in exploring his universe and in making decisions for himself.'

McClelland (1962) considered child/parent relationships in some detail and concluded that the coldness which characterized the relationship between the eminent scientists and their parents was responsible for their withdrawing from human relationships in general and releasing their aggressive needs in their work. He contrasts them with children from similar Protestant backgrounds who, however, had warm parents and hence were encouraged to enter into social relationships. These children became successful business men.

Weisberg and Springer (1961) in a detailed study related creative behaviour in gifted children to parental behaviour in the home. Three measures of parent/child interaction were particularly closely related to the child's creativity. Creative children were much more likely to have a same sex parent who was expressive (that is spoke openly with the child during the interview) and *non-dominant* (as judged by the extent to which the parent appeared to interfere in the development of the child). Parents who took little notice of their child's periods of regression to more immature modes of behaviour, had children who were more creative than those whose parents either discouraged or encouraged regression. Finally the more autonomy the father had in his job the more creative the child. Other measures were less significant, but still above the chance level; one of these revealed that, although the fathers of creatives had a better relationship with the children than did the mothers, both parents had more intense relationships with their children than did the parents of less creative children. The mothers were less compulsive, and less accepting of the maternal role and the creative children were not forced to conform to parental values. In summary the authors sketched a 'typical' family containing a highly creative child:

> It is not an overly close family unit, with little clinging to each other for support. Conformity to parental values is not stressed in the child, for instance. Nor is it a particularly well-adjusted marriage. The sexual adjustment in the marriage is mediocre, and each parent sees the marriage, and family life, in terms somewhat different than does the other. It is a family in which there is an open and not always calm expression of strong feeling, without that expression being used to bind the child to the values of the parents. Father interacts strongly and positively with the child. Mother interacts with the child quite strongly, but tends often to be ambivalent in her maternal feelings. Father is a man who exercises some authority, both at work and at home. And in this optimal family, when the child regresses, the behaviour is accepted by the parents without discomfort, but parents do not use the child's regression as a crutch by which they can reinforce their own self-esteem. The creative child is often an elder sibling, but is not a particular favourite, in that there is no overvaluation of his or her abilities by the parents.

Getzels and Jackson (1961) compared the family backgroun
their 'high IQ' and 'high creativity' groups and did find
differences although their findings should be viewed with cau
(see p. 73). Both groups of parents were highly educated but the
high IQ group's parents had followed more specialized courses
whereas the high creatives were more likely to be in business and
the wives were more likely to work. The high IQ group's parents
expressed more memories of childhood poverty; they were more
noticing but also more critical of their children and were more
concerned about and dissatisfied with their children's progress at
school. In general the high IQ parents seemed less secure and
more vigilant, the parents of the highly creative children, on the
other hand, were concerned with the child's 'openness to experience, his values, and his interests and enthusiasms'.

That parental behaviour can influence cognitive style is demonstrated by Dawson's (1967) study of two West African tribes.
The Temue who were traditional, mother-dominated and stressed
conformity to adult standards, produced 'field-dependent' children
as measured by Witkin's tests (see p. 69). The Mende who had
considerably less field-dependent children, gave the child responsibility early, used deprivation and not physical punishment, and
were less traditional and mother-dominated.

2.2 The school

The second strongest influence on the child after the family is
the school, and there are two important questions here: firstly,
are some schools more facilitative for creative children than others,
and, secondly, can schools actually foster creativity? The second
question will be dealt with later (p. 96) but the first one has caused
a certain amount of concern among researchers and teachers; however, because of the difficulty of being precise concerning variables
such as 'creativity' and 'classroom climate', the results of the
research should be viewed as tentative.

Mead (1962) poses the problem starkly: 'How can we keep
creativity alive in children – schools and school teachers being what
they are?' She then points out several reasons for the underplaying
of creativity in schools, three of which are important in the British
as well as the American context. First, many teachers may not
in fact wish to teach:

... young women want to be wives and mothers with homes of their own; for them, teaching represents a kind of plateau on which they stand (hopefully only temporarily) between school and marriage. The young men want to be psychologists or educational specialists or administrators; for them teaching represents a tiring activity which slows down their accumulation of credits and degrees and published papers needed for advancement.

(These 'temporary teachers' may, of course, be responsive to the creative production of the children but are unlikely to be sufficiently committed to give such a complex topic the study it deserves.) Second, Mead points out that many career teachers have changed their status by becoming teachers and have adopted the unadventurous, if worthy, standards of the American lower middle class:

> How, then can we expect a young woman who wants to teach – whose aim is to keep the twenty-five or thirty children in her charge well-disciplined, cheerful and passing, who must concentrate on what all of them must accomplish – to welcome a creative child? Isn't everything she stands for antithetical to the values we now urge her to have?

Third, Mead argues that the nation devalues not teachers so much as the *activity of teaching* with the result that teachers will not be able to cherish creativity until the value of their own creative activity, as good as teachers, is recognized.

Mead's speculations were given some support by McElvain, Fretwell and Lewis (1963) who found a significant negative correlation between teachers' creativity scores and ratings of their overall effectiveness by their heads: creativity did not appear to be a desirable characteristic in teachers. Yamamoto (1966) having referred to research which showed creative children to be irritating to teachers, because of their independence, and unpopular with their peers (Getzels and Jackson, 1962; Torrance, 1962a), said bluntly 'we do not know what to do with these crazy kids'. McIntyre, Morrison and Sutherland (1966) reported that when assessing primary school children teachers valued good behaviour, educational attainment and a conforming attitude to school most highly. Roe's (1952) scientists reported being lonely at school and

keeping aloof from classmates. Torrance (1962b) too point
that peer group pressures for conformity and the sc
emphasis on success made it a hostile environment for the ind
dent and adventurous thinker.

However, does the school, or the teacher's attitude, *actually*
have any effect on the creativity level of the pupils? It seems
reasonable to start from the assumption that if creative children
are strong-minded they are unlikely to be affected by their teachers'
attitudes. Yamamoto (1963) found no difference at all in the classroom practice of teachers judged to be high or low on creativity;
and Walker (1967), although he did find differences in classroom
climate between two 'traditional' and two 'creative' schools, also
found that these differences were not reflected in the behaviour
of the pupils on measures of creativity nor did the highly creative
children seem to enjoy school any more at the 'creative' than at
the 'traditional' school. However Torrance (1965) found that at
kindergarten level, teaching with favourable attitudes to creativity
did affect the output of the pupils who had been exposed to a
'creativity training programme'.

The explanation for these findings is not altogether clear but
it is possible that *highly* creative children will remain creative even
in uncongenial atmospheres whereas the *potentially* creative child
requires a sympathetic atmosphere to actualize his potential.
'Latent creativity' is also an important phenomenon that needs
further study: it would appear that children will produce creative
responses when they realize that these are required but inhibit
them if they do not think that they are necessary. Hudson (1966)
reports that when the scientists were asked to respond *as if* they
were arts students their thinking became much more divergent
– as if role playing had released their inhibitions against showing
divergent responses. Similarly Torrance (1965) found that when
children were rewarded for either writing unusual and interesting
stories or writing grammatically correct stories those in the first
condition did write more originally but less grammatically with
the situation being reversed in the second. This indicates that
children will attempt to produce what they think their teachers
want.

Parnes and Brunelle (1967), having reviewed forty training
programmes, concluded that the subjects' creativity levels were
increased by deliberate training programmes. But perhaps the two

best known studies relating teacher behaviour to pupil performance are those of Haddon and Lytton (1968) and Barker Lunn (1970). Haddon and Lytton looked at the effect of formal and informal teaching methods in primary schools on the pupils' level of divergent thinking. They tested 211 children aged eleven to twelve on an adaptation of Torrance's Minnesota Test of Creative Thinking (see p. 67). On all measures the pupils from the informal schools (where child–initiated learning was stressed) showed higher levels of divergent thinking ability. Haddon and Lytton also looked to see if divergent children were less popular with their peers and found that the relationship between IQ (as measured by a Verbal Reasoning Quotient), divergence and popularity was as much a function of the school as the pupils. In other words the pupils valued what the school valued (Table 4.1). In both formal schools VRQ

Table 4.1   *Rank order correlation between VRQ and sociometric status, and between divergent thinking scores and sociometric status*

School		N	VRQ range	VRQ and sociometric status	Divergent thinking and sociometric status
A	Formal	33	135–100	0.137	−0.128
C	Formal	50	126– 70	0.337	0.279
B	Informal	47	135– 85	0.058	0.363
D	Informal	37	135– 61	0.462	0.382

(Haddon and Lytton, 1968)

is more related to popularity than is divergence and in one informal school divergence is more strongly related than is VRQ but in the fourth school both the intelligent and the creative child are popular and the authors comment: 'This school is a particularly delightful one to visit and gives one the impression of informality combined with high standards of work and behaviour. It may be that the ethos of the school ensures esteem for both types of ability ...'

In a parallel study in secondary schools Lytton and Cotton (1969) did not find the same relationship between informal teaching and divergent ability. One hundred and forty-three boys and girls aged fourteen were tested with negative results, perhaps due to the greater complexity of secondary organization whereby in a generally 'informal' school a child may in fact have a 'formal' teacher or learn in a 'formal' department. There was however a higher relationship between VRQ and social class than between divergent ability and class which, the authors suggest, may mean that the environment is less influential in this area of thinking.

Barker Lunn (1970) had a similar hypothesis: namely that informality of teaching method would do more to foster divergent thinking than formal methods stressing academic achievement. She studied 5,500 primary school children giving parallel versions of her test to the children at the end of their third and fourth years. The analysis related difference scores between each time of testing to whether the child was in a streamed or unstreamed school and whether, within the unstreamed school the teacher was progressive. Children with progressive teachers in unstreamed schools showed relative improvement, and lower social class boys showed a significant drop in 'flexibility' scores in streamed schools, but their peers with progressive teachers in unstreamed schools showed an increase. Barker Lunn's work suggests, as does Haddon and Lytton's, that it is not the ethos of the school as a whole that has most effect on pupils but the way in which the teachers they interact with interpret their role and whether their teaching methods are more or less progressive.

2.3 *The working environment*

With respect to adult creativity, the institution or organization within which the adult finds himself seems to be an important factor. Creativity of one kind may be valued in one institution and not in another, nor is it likely that new ideas will always be welcomed by those in positions of power. Gordon (1972) investigated some of the relationships between social milieu, creativity and scientific accomplishment. He studied three groups of scientists – (1) researchers in a defence-oriented research and development firm, (2) chemists and (3) medical sociologists – using Mednick's RAT (see p. 64) as a creativity measure, plus questionnaires, ratings and other measures of productivity and innovation. He found that the RAT did predict creative accomplishment but that the use an organization made of creative ability was related

to the project leader's ability to make grosser or finer discriminations concerning his professional relationships with his colleagues
(in other words whether the director, when assessing his colleagues,
used the whole of a ten-point scale of assessment or whether he
used a narrower band). When all of the director's responses fell
into *one* of three categories 'poor' (five and below) 'moderate' (six
to nine) and 'excellent' (ten) he was called a 'low differentiator';
if his responses fell into more than one category he was judged
a 'high' differentiator. High differentiators led much more 'inno-
vative' projects – their projects were more likely to lead to new
knowledge rather than merely result in an addition to previous
knowledge. The author's explanation for this was that 'project
directors who stress differences (high differentiators) . . . increase
the availability of different types of data enabling themselves and
the members of their group to make remote associations'.

Gordon also hypothesized (1) that the RAT was testing an individual's ability to solve a given problem in an innovatory way
whereas (2) the measures of differentiation reflected an individual's
ability to recognize a problem. If this were so, scores, or combinations of scores, on these measures should predict scientific
productivity in different fields. Accordingly the chemists were
divided into four analytic groups:

1 Integrators: High Differentiators – High RAT.
2 Problem-Solvers: Low Differentiators – High RAT.
3 Problem-Recognizers (focusers): High Differentiators – Low
   RAT.
4 Technicians: Low Differentiators – Low RAT.

It was found that type of productivity was related to analytic style
from which we can conclude that productive research teams require
a judicious combination of people with different types of creative
ability.

Snyder (1969) looked at the effect of institutions of higher education on the development of creativity and suggested that students
in different disciplines may require a different climate: science
students for example, may need more encouragement to take
intellectual risks than engineering students. He therefore investigated the careers of 'creative' students in science-oriented
institutions and found that MIT was losing three times as many
students who, on entering, had shown a liking for seeking 'new

solutions', as they were losing conventional, non risk-taking students. Heist (1967) studied student drop-outs in the United States and found that it was the potentially creative students who were leaving in proportionately greater numbers than the others.

2.4 *The cultural climate*

The culture as a whole may also facilitate or inhibit creative thinking. A culture which tolerates and encourages diversity and the freedom of the individual is likely to be more conducive to creative output than a repressive conformist one. Torrance (1962a) tested children from different cultures and reported that creative development in children varied according to the way the culture responded to the child's curiosity and creative needs. He discussed the Samoan picture in some detail since Samoan children's non-verbal scores were the lowest of all tested. He related these scores to the qualities the culture valued – quietness and conformity – and the values checked by the teacher on the 'ideal pupil questionnaire' – 'remembers well, healthy and always asking questions' (where 'questions' were of the kind 'Is this right?' 'Is this what you want?'). Vernon (1965, 1966) studied English, Hebridean, Canadian, Indian and Eskimo children and reported that while Hebridean children in general scored similarly to the English children, Gaelic speakers, who usually came from isolated rural areas, scored lower. Canadian Indian children had low scores but Eskimo children high ones although economically they were similar. The difference was that the Eskimo culture encouraged adaptability whereas the Indian did not.

Although environmental influences do appear to be relevant it is necessary to avoid the too simple assumption that to change the environment, on the basis of research studies, will increase creativity. As Mackinnon (1962b) warned many years ago:

> We still have no assurance that the conditions in the home, in school, and society, the qualities of interpersonal relations between instructor and student, and the aspects of the teaching-learning process which would appear to have contributed to creative development a generation ago would facilitate rather than inhibit creativity in today's quite different world and far different educational climate.

3 *Fostering creativity*

Given that creative thinking is valuable both for the individual and for society, are there any ways in which the highly creative can be left free to work and the less creative encouraged to develop their powers? Maslow (1962) argued that the first thing to do was to remove the emotional blocks to creativity which occur in the individual. He was concerned, not with productivity but with the 'primary creativeness which comes out of the unconscious' and which can be tapped by the psychologically healthy person who is able to fuse the Primary and Secondary processes and is able to regress at will (see p. 63). Maslow suggested that people could achieve this fusion by psychotherapy or by any technique that enabled the person to face his unconscious and realize that it is not necessarily dangerous. Tumin (1962) had earlier stressed this notion of 'safety' by which he meant 'the condition which prevails when the individual has assurance regarding his basic worth, as measured by the approval and reassurance of others, and thus does not necessarily see his striving for individuality and self-expressiveness as threatening to his status acceptance'. But how in a competitive and status-dominated society can this assurance be given? Within organizations it is often a question of the emotional climate generated by those in control. Gibb (1972) considered how managers could produce a safer and freer climate (Table 4.2). Perhaps the most important single attribute of a manager in creating such a climate, was found to be a high level of trust in himself and in those with whom he worked. Yet an open creative manager will often not fit into a traditional setting so that changes must occur at all levels and the total organization has to learn to be creative. 'T group' (see p. 131) training can facilitate greater awareness amongst colleagues and so do forms of training which alert managers to the fact that rules may be made, not because they are functional, but because making them satisfies the particular manager's needs to control and dominate. Gibb argued that the features in an organization leading to creative output were: 'trust, openness, self-determination and interdependence' and

Table 4.2 *Managing for the release of creativity*

Basic organizational factors	Management behavior and attitudes	Typical effect of management behavior and attitudes
Emotional climate	High trust Low fear	More impulsive, uncensored behaviour Greater risk taking, more error Greater creativity and range of response Trust in own impulse and unconscious life
Communication flow	Free flow of communication Clarity Open strategy and planning	Greater spontaneity in response and feeling Greater expression of foolish, irrelevant, and seemingly meaningless ideas and behavior Greater emotionality More feedback up and down Interaction and 'piggy-backing' of ideas
Goal formation	Allowing self-determination Allowing self-assessment	Reward for risk-taking Sharing and mutual stimulation of ideas Greater diversity and non-conformity More sustained creativity
Control	Interdependent emergent and intrinsic controls residual in life processes	Experimentation with work and structure Open expression of conflict and disagreement Greater innovation Priority of diversity and creativity over conformity

(Gibb, 1972)

stressed that these need to be consciously sought.

A much earlier study (Smith 1959) had reported on favourable and unfavourable conditions for scientific creativity. Subsequent studies (Peltz and Andrews, 1966; Taylor, Smith and Ghiselin, 1963) have largely confirmed Smith's findings and stressed the need for the individual worker's goals to be consonant with the goals of the organization, since considerable stress was caused by a worker feeling pressurized by the immediate needs of the organization, with this pressure being detrimental to his ability to follow his own long term goals. This effect was particularly obvious in hospitals (Gordon, Marquis and Anderson, 1962).

Although most studies concerning the development of creativity stress what the teacher can do for the child, research related to industry would suggest that a productive teacher requires a satisfactory working environment *before* he will be able to improve the environment of his pupils. A similar point is made by Myers and Torrance (1961) who found that there were forces within teachers which opposed innovations. One hundred and fourteen teachers had been asked

to seek systematically and consciously to apply in a reasonable and appropriate way five principles:

1 Treat questions with respect.
2 Treat imaginative ideas with respect.
3 Show your pupils that their ideas have value.
4 Occasionally have pupils do something 'for practice' without the threat of evaluation.
5 Tie in evaluation with causes and consequences.

The authors found that although some teachers were enthusiastic and none opposed the principles, many were completely unable to incorporate them into their teaching. Torrance was well aware of the problems teachers have and the conflicting value systems they are being asked to adhere to and therefore argued (1963b) for a more complex picture of the human mind and personality so that teachers could attempt to develop 'both creative learning and learning by authority ... both moral courage and social adjustment ... both original answers and correct ones ... both discipline and creative behaviour'.

Articles on fostering creativity seem to consist of endless lists of dos and don'ts with precious little evidence of empirical research. One of the better examples of the former is Torrance's (1962) check list for nurturing creativity:

1   Value creative thinking.
2   Help children become more sensitive to environmental stimuli.
3   Encourage manipulation of objects and ideas.
4   Teach how to test each idea systematically.
5   Develop tolerance of new ideas.
6   Beware of forcing a set pattern.
7   Develop a creative classroom atmosphere.
8   Teach the child to value his creative thinking.
9   Teach children skills of avoiding or coping with peer sanctions without sacrificing their creativity.
10 Give information about the creative process.
11 Dispel the sense of awe of masterpieces.
12 Encourage and evaluate self-initiated learning.
13 Create 'thorns in the flesh', making children aware of problems and deficiencies.
14 Create necessities for creative thinking.
15 Provide for active and quiet periods.
16 Make available resources for working out ideas.
17 Encourage the habit of working out the full implications of ideas.
18 Develop skills of constructive criticism.
19 Encourage acquisition of knowledge in a variety of fields.
20 Be adventurous-spirited yourself.

Nevertheless there have been some systematic attempts to foster creativity in the classroom. Crutchfield (1965) and his associates carried out a programme the aim of which was 'to strengthen in the individual child certain cognitive skills which are central to the creative process and to encourage in him certain attitudes and dispositions which favour the use of these skills'. He therefore produced a form of programme aimed to stimulate divergent thinking. The programme consisted of a series of booklets with a continuous story line which the children were able to work through at their own pace. The story concerned two children who were faced with and solved a series of detective problems. Through the fictional characters' problem solving the children were encouraged to develop their own creative problem solving abilities. When the children who had used the programme were compared with matched controls who had not, it was found that they were more efficient in creative problem solving. This superiority extended to other tests not directly requiring problem solving, as for example the 'Dog Improvement Test' (saying how a toy dog could be made more attractive) and the 'Circles Test' (using blank circles as the basis for drawings). But when asked to write a story around five unusual elements the experimental children were no better than the controls.

Olton and Crutchfield (1969) used similar materials but with fifth- and sixth-grade children and extended the design to give the teacher an active role as a discussion leader. Once again the trained group scored higher both at the end of the programme and and after a six-month interval. However Treffinger and Ripple (1965), when they used Torrance's tests and tests of arithmetic problem solving as their post-test, did not find any superiority in the trained group. Rees and Parnes (1970) also used a programmed course for children in academic high schools and found that all children using the programme showed a greater increase in creativity scores than did the control group but that those children who had worked on the programme as a class together with their teacher did better than those who had worked alone. In all of these programmes the best results seem to be obtained when the post-test is similar in kind to the materials used for training and when the class teacher is involved in the training scheme.

Torrance (1962a) stressed the importance of additional support, which goes beyond the class teacher, for creative children. He suggested that school counsellors, social workers or other relevant adults should:

1 Provide a refuge, a safe relationship for highly creative children.
2 Serve as 'sponsors' or 'patrons' for certain highly creative children.
3 Help highly creative children understand and accept their divergence.
4 Listen to the ideas of highly creative children.

5 Recognize creative talent and see that it is given a chance to develop.
6 Help parents and fellow workers understand the problems of highly creative children.

The identification and cherishing of creative talent in children is a difficult and, as yet, little understood procedure. The nurture of adult creativity, whether in teachers or managers, is even more awkward because of the adult's resistance and suspicion. As Tumin (1962) remarked: 'let us not kid ourselves. The way to the creative life for the average man is difficult in the extreme.' However, two approaches which aim at freeing the individual from the blocks which inhibit creativity have been developed: these approaches are 'synectics' and 'brainstorming'.

'Synectics' (Gordon, 1961) means the bringing together of apparently unrelated elements. Gordon and his colleagues believed that people need to understand the psychological processes involved in creative activity before they can improve their own efficiency. Four states in thinking about a problem were isolated and described: first, 'detachment-involvement' in which the person attempts to see the problem in a new light by removing it from its context and at the same time to become motivated to seek its solution; second, 'deferment' which means that the first solution is laid aside; third, 'speculation', allowing the mind to play freely about the problem; and, the fourth stage, 'autonomy of the object' which occurs when ideas related to the solution of the problem appear to take on a life of their own. In a synectics group people are encouraged to learn how to produce each of these states. They are urged to phantasize, to make the familiar strange and the strange familiar by imagining what it would be like to be, for example, a spring or a molecule.

'Brainstorming' (Osborn, 1957) aims to stop the individual judging ideas too soon. Therefore individuals or groups are encouraged, in a non-judgemental atmosphere, to produce as many ideas, on a given topic, as possible. In the first instance it is the quantity and not the quality of the ideas which is important. Evaluation only occurs when all the ideas have been listed. The aim is to 'separate the process of producing ideas from the process of evaluating them'. Parnes (1959, 1960, 1961) studied the effect of brainstorming in detail and concluded that it did increase creative problem solving, enabled the subjects to produce more problem solutions, and more good ideas, and, finally, caused students who had taken courses which included brainstorming to score more highly on Guilford's creativity tests than did students who had not taken such courses. However Taylor, Berry and Block (1958) and Torrance (1961) reported less creative solutions and fewer and weaker ideas from subjects who had used brainstorming.

Further reading

This selection relates to Chapters 3 and 4.

Cattell, R. B. and Butcher, H. J. (1968) *The Prediction of Achievement and Creativity*. New York: Bobs-Merrill.

Mooney, R. L. and Razik, T. A. (eds) (1967) *Explorations in Creativity*. New York: Harper and Row.

Shouksmith, G. (1970) *Intelligence, Creativity and Cognitive Style*. London: Batsford.

Taylor, C. W. (ed.) (1972) *Climate for Creativity*. New York: Pergamon Press.

Taylor, C. W. and Barron, F. (eds) (1963) *Scientific Creativity*. New York: John Wiley.

Section II

Focus:

Social aspects
of the classroom

[5]
Social interaction
and social perception

To understand the classroom as a context for learning requires, as we have seen, such cognitive concepts as intelligence and ability, thinking, problem solving, cognitive style, teacher expectation and creativity. We now turn to the classroom as a social system and this requires a different set of concepts. Here we are not concerned with an individual's capacity to respond to environmental stimuli of a cognitive kind but with his response to other human beings who live alongside him and either facilitate or inhibit his learning.

When humans gather together in groups of two or more they interact with each other. Their mode of interaction is not random and through it each individual attempts to structure, and hence make meaningful, the situation in which he finds himself. In the classroom both pupils and teachers are attempting to structure the experience they are having and, although there will be a certain amount of communality in their perceptions, it must be remembered that, as individuals, their perceptions may differ significantly leading to unintentional misunderstandings. The study of the regularities in interaction, and of an individual's meaning making attempts, is the concern of both psychologists and sociologists in that this topic marks the interface of the two disciplines. Social interaction needs to be both described and explained – descriptive studies are valuable in drawing attention to the mechanics of social behaviour – thus illuminating what is normally taken for granted – since systematic study is necessary for a person to become self-conscious concerning his behaviour. Nevertheless description is not enough as we have also to explain the function of the behaviour which characterizes the human species in order to develop a theory with predictive power.

Social interaction implies sequencing and reciprocity, i.e. A's action produces a reaction in B which, in turn, modifies A's subsequent action. Therefore each unit of behaviour has to be seen in its context as part of an ongoing process and be judged accordingly. When an individual is in a social situation his behaviour differs from when he is alone since he takes into account the fact that he is either actually or potentially, the object of another's regard. Why it should be felt that 'private' behaviour is behaviour that cannot be revealed fully to another, but only selectively exhibited, is an intriguing question which cannot be pursued here. Whatever the reason, a person in a social situation does behave in a way he considers to be more adequate than his private behaviour and by observing the behaviour of others he attempts to make enough sense of the situation to judge what would constitute appropriate behaviour on his part.

1 *Methods of research*

If a psychologist is interested in studying social interaction he has to do it in such a way that his results are capable of being reproduced by others replicating the experiment. It is not enough for his observations to be no more than descriptions of how individual people behaved in a particular situation, rather he is concerned with general laws of behaviour which enable predictions to be made as to how people, who share the characteristics of the experimental subjects, would behave if a situation similar to the experimental one occurred.

1.1 *Laboratory studies*

Experimental social psychologists would argue that if their experiments are to be replicable then the variables must be limited, the methodology explicit, and the situation circumscribed. This has given rise to laboratory studies of social interaction in which subjects' responses to certain limited situations are described. Asch's (1956) conformity study is a classic of this kind. He was interested in the effect of group influence on individual judgement and therefore set up a situation in which there was a group of seven to nine students of whom all but one were aiding the experimenter. The students gathered in a room, arranging themselves in a row with the naive subjects (the one not aiding the experimenter) at one end, and were told that the task was to do with 'the discrimination of length of lines'. They were then shown two cards one with a single line on it, and one with lines of varying length, and asked which of the three lines was equivalent in length to the single line. The students working in collaboration with the experimenter all gave a unanimously incorrect answer so that the naive subject was left with a conflict between what he himself thought and what the group said. What happened? With 123 naive subjects giving twelve judgements each, 37 per cent of the judgements were incorrect, that is 37 per cent of their judgements conformed to the group, whereas a group of control subjects, who worked alone, gave accurate judgements.

One alternative to using 'collaborators' or 'stooges' is the technique of the simulated group (Blacke and Brehm, 1954). In this type of experiment the subject is placed in a booth and is given to understand that adjoining booths are occupied by other subjects; they are, in fact, empty. Before he gives his response he is told that he will hear or see the responses of the others on a display board. The experimenter then varies the responses to suit his purposes and measures the extent to which the one experimental subject conforms to what he believes to be the responses of other members of the 'group'. The disadvantage of laboratory methods is that if the situation is made too simple it becomes unlike a real life situation in which the participants are receiving, processing and responding to more diverse information, and this may mean that laboratory studies show us how people respond in laboratories but not in real life. In an attempt to make laboratory studies more realistic subjects are told that the experiment is to do with 'y' when the experimenter is actually concerned with 'x', e.g. behaviour in the waiting room. An example of this is Schachter's (1959) study of the relationship between anxiety and affiliation. In his study subjects were led to believe that the experiment they were about to take part in would involve the receiving of painful, but not damaging, electric shocks, and that there would be a waiting period of about ten minutes before the start of the experimental session. They were then divided into two groups; the first group were told that they could wait together with others due to take part in the same experiment or wait alone, and the second group were told that they could wait with others who were waiting to see their professor or alone. In the first group six out of ten chose to wait with the others, in the second group all preferred to wait alone. From this Schachter concluded that anxiety causes a wish to affiliate but only with those who face a similar threat.

Another alternative is to equip laboratories with two way mirrors thus enabling psychologists to observe people interacting in groups without the subjects being affected by the presence of the observer. This method is particularly appropriate for observing a group such as a therapy or task group over a series of sessions in order to follow changes in the internal dynamic of the group and the development of interpersonal conflict or co-operation.

1.2 *Re-analysis of 'real life' data*

An alternative to the laboratory method is to analyse real life data in terms of the variables in which the experimenter is interested. Schachter (1959) had found a relationship between birth order, anxiety, and affiliative need in that anxious later-borns did not choose to be with others whereas anxious first-borns did. This led him to hypothesize that, when troubled, later-borns would solve their problems by drinking, i.e. a non-social activity, and first-borns by psychotherapy. When he looked at the results of Bakan's (1949) studies of alcoholism, he saw that later-borns were over-represented among chronic alcoholics and early-borns under-represented. He then analysed Wiener Stieper's data on 'the psychometric prediction of the duration and outcome of outpatient psychotherapy' and found that the hypothesized relationship held.

1.3 *Systematic and participant observation*

If results which are both applicable to the real world and replicable are required, psychologists can make use of systematic observation in a naturalistic setting. Many of the studies of class-room behaviour come into this category, for example Kounin's (1970) study of classroom management and those relating to teacher style (see p. 173). Even greater realism can be achieved by infiltration or participant observation whereby the psychologist becomes a member of the group he wishes to study and attempts to observe it from the inside. Patrick (1973), for example, met, as a participant, a Glasgow gang twelve times in 1966–7 and as a result of this was able to gain an understanding of the boys' behaviour and value system in terms of the importance of territory, status and being noticed. As a result of his work he concluded that

> the Glasgow juvenile gang, then, in my opinion has little internal cohesion of its own; it exists to oppose others and to provide coveted status for its members and especially its leaders ... it wasn't the strongest or the fittest, the tallest or the brightest boys who became leaders or lieutenants of gangs, but the most psychologically disturbed, those with lowest impulse control.

In order to assess the value of such participant observation studies it is necessary to have them in sufficient quantity to determine whether the findings do indeed describe behaviour which is lawlike, and hence generalizable, or whether they are applicable only to the specific situation described.

1.4 *Self-reports*

Perhaps the most obvious way of finding out the salient features in any piece of social interaction is to ask the participants what their opinions and motives were. Research which has used this method (for example the work of R. D. Laing) has drawn attention to the disparity between different participants' perceptions of the nature of the situation. In Laing and Esterton's study (1964) of, so called, schizophrenic girls he recorded interviews with both the patients and the members of their immediate family and obtained contrasting reports (Table 5.1).

Laing sees the causes of the person's illness in this mismatch of perceptions but it may well be that this is characteristic of many social situations which could not be described as pathological.

1.5 *The field interview*

A popular variant of the above is the field interview in which people are either interviewed and asked a systematic series of questions or are asked to complete a questionnaire. This method is open to some of the same objections as laboratory studies in that people

Table 5.1 *Parent v. child views*

Daughter's view	View of mother and father
Blackness came over her when she was eight.	It did not. Her memory is at fault. She was imagining this. This showed a mental lapse.
She started to masturbate when she was fifteen.	She did not.
She was worried over her examinations.	She never worried over examinations because she always passed them, and so she had no need to worry. She was too clever and worked too hard. Besides she could not have worried because they would have known.
She masturbates now.	She does not.
Her mother and father tried to stop her reading.	Nonsense: *and* she had to be torn away from her books. She was reading too much.
She was not sure whether they could read her mind.	They thought they knew her thoughts better than she did.

(Abridged from Laing and Esterson, 1964)

may, when answering a question, say that they would behave in a certain way when, in fact, they would not do so in a real situation.

1.6 *The effect of the research method*

Whatever research method is used the same serious problem arises and this is that the psychological experiment is itself a social situation: a factor which has to be taken into account when assessing the findings. The effect of the experimenter cannot be ignored nor the experimental equipment. Orne and Scheibe (1964) showed that when the briefing for a sensory deprivation experiment differed so that, in the first condition, it was made to seem to have an element of risk by taking the subject's medical history, making him sign a form relieving 'the Massachusetts mental health service from legal responsibility for the consequences of the experiment', and providing a button in the room, marked 'emergency alarm', as against a second condition without these measures, it was found that subjects who were tested in the first condition showed significantly more deprivation symptoms (e.g. perceptual aberrations, intellectual dullness, anxiety, spatial disorientation, and restlessness) than those in the second, although in fact the amount of deprivation was identical. From this they concluded that, 'subject's behaviour can be differentially manipulated by altering the implicit and explicit cues in the experimental situation, and further that subjects may react to social cues, or demand characteristics, in such a way, as to confound experimental results'.

Rosenthal and Rosnow (1969) have considered this question at some length and argue that there are two kinds of experimenter effect; the first concerns his influence on his own observations and the second his influence on the responses of his subjects. It would seem that experimenters do make unintentional recording errors which are biased in the direction of their hypothesis but that these are usually insignificant in the final analysis. With respect to the second dimension of interactional effects the results are more serious. For example Rosenthal (1966, 1967) showed that male experimenters were more friendly towards their subjects than female experimenters and that female subjects were more 'protectively' treated than male subjects which led him to suggest that when an experiment shows a sex difference this could be due to the different ways in which the experimenter treated the male and female subjects. Personal characteristics of the experimenter such as race, anxiety and warmth can also have differential effects on the subjects' responses. In addition the behaviour of the subjects can affect the experimenter and his response to them in turn influence other subjects. In an earlier experiment (1965) Rosenthal, Greenfield and Carota set up a situation in which one group of experimenters had their hypothesis confirmed by their first subjects, who were stooges, and another group of experimenters had their hypothesis disconfirmed by their first subjects who were also stooges. These two groups of experimenters obtained significantly different results with respect to the experimental task and personality measures with their subsequent subjects who were not stooges.

2 *Elements of social interaction*

In order to understand any social situation Sherif and Sherif (1969)
list four sets of factors which need to be taken into account. First,
those which relate to the people taking part, for example similarities
or differences in sex, age, class, or occupation, and the extent to
which the participants are known to each other. Second, factors
relating to the nature of the interaction, that is whether it is a
work, social, or problem solving situation. Third, the quality of
the place where interaction takes place, whether luxurious, run
down, or prestigious since participants will vary their behaviour
depending on the location of the activity; the location itself sets
up expectations concerning the type of action deemed to be appropriate and too much deviation on the part of some will dis-
orientate others. Finally account must be taken of the relation of
an individual to the above sets of factors in terms of his social
standing, sex, role in the activity, and degree of familiarity with
the location. In any situation participants themselves need to be
sensitive to these significant dimensions.

When adults interact there are at least two types of information
to be processed: the verbal, and the non-verbal.

2.1 *Verbal elements*

Speech is a central component in any social situation and although
participants do attend to the overt content of the communication
they are also influenced by *how* a statement is made, as well as
what is said, and also by the choice of words used to convey the
message.

The explicit verbal content of social interaction is the aspect
to which the participants pay most attention as it appears to be
the most direct aspect of communication. Spoken language, has
its own ritualistic elements and for social interaction to proceed
smoothly these rituals must be correctly performed; for example,
a telephone conversation requires that the answerer speaks first
(Schegloff, 1968) and there are specific rituals for greeting depending on the length of time since the last encounter and the degree
of intimacy between the parties (Goffman, 1971).

Direct communication. It is direct communication (*what* is said) that appears to have the most cognitive content. Runkel (1965) points out that 'the meaning of any spoken phrase depends on the expectations within which it is embedded' which leads him to define the communication process as 'an interaction between cognitive fields', and to hypothesize that 'the similarity of structure between two cognitive fields increases the efficacy of communication between them'. To test this hypothesis he checked students' and instructors' responses to certain key statements which were related to the course but were not directly linked to the course content. Having found a group of students who were 'colinear', that is shared a similar cognitive outlook, with their instructors, and a group who were not, he looked at the scores obtained by these two groups of students on 'quizzes', given during the course on course content and found that 'colinearity' with the instructor did result in higher scores on quizzes. These scores were not related to differences between the students as measured by the American Council on Education's test of scholastic aptitude. The interesting aspect of this study is that the original statements were not related to course content and therefore his results suggest that a student who shares a similar cognitive field to his instructor will gain more from communication with him than a student who does not, even if the content of the communication is of equal relevance to both students.

Sociolinguistics. Sociolinguistics, unlike psycholinguistics which concentrates on the development of language within an individual, has been defined by Ervin-Tripp (1964) as 'the study of verbal behaviour in terms of the relations between the setting, the participants, the topic, the functions of interaction, the form and values held by the participants about each of these'. (1) By setting is meant both the time and the place of the interaction and the expected behaviour in such places, (for example a lecture as opposed to a picnic). (2) Participants are distinguished by their social role and status (see p. 135) and their role within the communication so that those with the highest status are seen both to speak more frequently and to receive more communication from lower status participants. (3) The topic is the overt content, and (4) the function of an interaction refers to the effects that the speaker intends it to have on the listener (e.g. he can make requests, offer information, or express emotions or attitudes). Most sociolinguistic research is concerned with the interaction of two or more of the above variables of setting, participants, topic and function, and smooth social interaction is dependent on the appropriate use of language bearing in mind these discrete components of any act of communication.

Voice.   The work of Lambert (1967) and Giles (1971) suggests that accent and intonation do affect a person's judgement of another's personality and that a regional accent may arouse prejudice. In a recent experiment (Giles, 1976) two groups of seventeen-year-old school children were asked by the experimenter to write an essay on psychology. When speaking to the first group the experimenter spoke standard English, but when speaking to the second group he used a Birmingham accent. A second experimenter then asked the students to write a pen-portrait of the first experimenter and to rate him on such traits as intelligence, likeability, honesty and popularity. The first group were found to write longer essays and pen-portraits, and rated the experimenter as more intelligent than did the second group. Giles concluded that a standard English accent makes a more favourable impression than does a regional accent. Soskin (1953) claimed that vocal communication gives two types of information; the one, 'semantic', is the familiar words and phrases, and the other, 'affective', is the individual non-verbal aspects of vocal production. Laver (1963) divided the 'affective' into three distinct types of information – the biological, the psychological and the social. Biologically the voice can indicate the sex and age of the speaker and also his physiological state, e.g. sexual arousal. Psychologically, there does seem to be some support for associating a harsh voice with dominance and a soft one with submission. Socially a voice can convey class as Hoggart (1957) noticed:

> There is the cracked but warm-hearted voice, slightly spitting through the all too regular false teeth, of some women in their forties ... There is a husky voice which I have often heard ... among working-class girls of the rougher sort; it is known among the more 'respectable' working-class as a 'common' voice.

Voice can also relate to occupation so that for example clergymen, teachers, and disc jockeys develop a characteristic form of delivery.

2.2 *Non-verbal elements in social interaction*

There is often a discrepancy between what A says and what B hears. A large proportion of this discrepancy is due to *non-verbal* aspects of interaction which may be entirely unconscious accompaniments of the verbal message, but which fill out the verbal message for the listener in a way which may or may not be in accordance with the speaker's intention. Non-verbal behaviour covers such factors as proximity, bodily orientation, the communication of status differences and liking, gesture, facial expression, the expression of emotion, eye contact and direction of gaze. These factors have the function of setting the emotional climate for the interaction and facilitating its process by, literally, signalling whether the communication will continue or is shortly to be terminated.

Abercrombie (1956) makes a useful distinction between non-verbal elements which can be independent of the verbal elements of a conversation and those which must be dependent on them, e.g. hand gestures.

Body motion.   The study of body motion, as distinct from verbal behaviour, is known as 'kinesics' and Birdwhistell (1961) defines this study as 'the science of body behavioural communication'. Body motion can be studied as a patterned system which must be learned by every individual if he is to participate fully as a member of his society. When a person speaks to another, the face is the most revealing source of non-verbal cues, the hands and the feet the least. This is apparent by the convention that we can refer to a person's non-verbal facial cues by saying, 'why do you frown?' or 'you look puzzled' but we cannot say 'your hands are tense or your legs express fear', nevertheless hands and legs do reveal unexpressed emotions. In a study by Ekman and Friesen (1969) people were shown parts of the body as filmed during interaction and it was found that the viewers made different assessments of the subject depending on the part of the body that they had seen, for example, those who saw the head only believed the subject to be 'healthy and co-operative' while those who only saw the body perceived her as 'cocquettish, excited, seductive' and much younger than those who viewed the face.

Both Birdwhistell (1968) and Kendon (1964) give a method for analysing facial changes in terms of eyebrow, eye, mouth and head position, and these facial changes usually signal the emotional state of the person, for example happy, sad or aroused. Perhaps the most revealing part of the face is the eyes, and eye movements have been shown to be significant determinants of both the process and nature of an interaction. Kendon (1967) has shown how eye movements during speech are formalized and signal when a person wishes to speak, to continue speaking, or to stop. There is initial eye contact before speaking after which the speaker looks away, then an intermittent gaze during speech with the listener looking more than the speaker so that his eyes are, as it were, ready to be 'caught' when the speaker looks to get feedback, and, finally, the speaker looks up to signal that he is about to terminate his utterance. Eye contact also signals emotional state in that there is more eye contact when the pair like each other, a stare can suggest aggression or domination, rapid eye blinks anxiety and widened pupils attraction or arousal. However, people are taught to control their facial expression and it may be that other parts of the body are more revealing. Ekman and Friesen (1969) showed that 'hand toss' is judged to represent uncertainty or defensiveness and 'hand shrug rotation' frustration or exasperated anger. Krout (1954) claimed that there are some regularities in hand movements so that fear is expressed by putting a hand to the nose, aggression by fist gestures, and affection by holding two fingers, or holding the index finger between two fingers.

Body posture and orientation.   A more gross dimension is that of posture and bodily orientation during interaction, which can express status differences, emotion, or degree of liking. People do not usually sit directly opposite one another but at an angle. However, Mehrabian (1968) suggests that there are sex-difference cues in orientation which have to be taken into account. Generally speaking, 'greater relaxation, a forward lean of trunk towards one's addressee, and a smaller distance to the addressee communicated a more positive attitude to the addressee than a backward lean of posture and a larger distance'. Mehrabian also observed that:

> for male communicators (in the order of their importance) more eye contact, smaller distance, and a relative absence of an arms akimbo position are part of an attempt to communicate a positive

attitude. For females, the corresponding cues (also in order of importance) are a relative absence of the arms akimbo position, smaller distance and arm openness. Also, a male communicator can convey his lower, as opposed to higher, status relative to his addressee using the following cues (in order of their importance): head tilt close to horizontal rather than head hanging, a relative absence of the crossing of one leg or foot in the front of the other, more eye contact, a relative absence of arms akimbo position, less leg relaxation, less hand relaxation, and more direct shoulder orientation. For female communicators the corresponding list (also in order of importance) is less hand relaxation, head tilt closes to horizontal rather than head hanging, more eye contact, greater arm openness and more direct shoulder orientation.

He found (1969) that for men shoulder orientation was more direct with a high status addressee, but that less direct body orientation was used when an addressee was very much liked. Women used extremely indirect orientation with disliked addressees, moderately indirect with liked ones, and least indirect with neutral ones. Relaxation also showed sex differences in that men were found to be tense with disliked men but relaxed with disliked women. Women communicated dislike with a greater degree of relaxation as exemplified by 'sideways lean' when seated.

Proximity. There are clear conventions, which differ between cultures, concerning the distance that people choose for comfortable interaction: for conversation five feet is usual, intimacy decreases distance and status differences are signalled by greater distance as well as in greater relaxation by the higher status participant. In a study of the behaviour of Arabs and Americans, Watson and Graves (1966) showed that Arabs do sit more directly opposite each other than Americans, they also sit closer, are more likely to touch each other, have more eye contact and speak more loudly. (An interesting extension of this study would be to see how Arabs and Americans would modify their proxemic behaviour when interacting with each other.) Heshka and Nelson (1972) found that women who were strangers sat further apart than men who were strangers, that pairs of young people sat closer than did others, and Lott and Sommer (1967) that people chose seats

further away from another person when that person was described
as either of high or low status. When studying disturbed children
Fisher (1967) observed that disturbed children place models of
adults further apart than did adjusted children. In an experiment
with his students Garfinkel (1964) asked each of those collaborating
with him to choose a friend and, whilst talking, to put his face
close to his friend's. The result was acute embarrassment, especially
between men, and the attribution of a sexual intention. Even when
the purpose of the experiment was explained to the 'naive' students
they remained embarrassed and wanted to know why they had
been selected as the ones to be approached. Overcrowding can
cause behavioural changes and Hutt and Vaizey's (1966) finding
that children became more aggressive as the playground became
more crowded may have implications for arriving at an acceptable
density in school classrooms, whether traditional or open plan.

Non-verbal behaviour has some of the characteristics of a dance
in that interaction will be smooth if the participants pay attention
to the implicit rules and rhythm. This question of compatibility
is especially important for teachers since it would be unlikely that
a class would contain a homogeneous sample and therefore the
teacher has to be the one to be aware of the problems inherent
in an attempt to interact with others who may have a social
performance incompatible with his own. A hypothesis that would
be worth testing is that incompatibility in non-verbal social
behaviour between teacher and pupil could be as significant a
variable with respect to failure in communication, as incompatible
linguistic codes.

3 *Social perception*

A significant determinant of any interpersonal act is the nature
of the impression the participants form of each other, either initially
or during the course of interaction. The analysis of social perception
has shown that people do form impressions and attribute qualities
to each other and that this perceptual process can be biased in
various ways; it can also affect the subsequent encounter so that
first impressions become, in Merton's (1957) phrase, 'self-fulfilling
prophecies'. Perry and Boyd (1972) distinguish person perception
from impression formation and define the former as a means of

organizing the social world and the latter as the evaluation of it; however, it is not always possible to keep the two processes distinct.

Person perception combines processes used for the perception of objects and for concept formation in that it is used to predict future behaviour, is based on previous experience and is essentially inferential. The perceiver creates a form of imaginative reconstruction out of the other's overt behaviour. Thus the other's behaviour is ordered to give it stability and consistency, perhaps to the detriment of accuracy, in the perceiver's attempt to create a meaningful whole, as if he were motivated by a 'will to meaning'. The subsequent interaction is guided by the participants' impressions of each other.

3.1 *Impression formation*

Although the naive realist would maintain that there is direct perceptual access to another, a little reflection will show that impressions are constructed out of the behaviour of the person perceived, the context of the perceptual act, and the expectations and sensibilities of the perceiver. In his classic study Asch (1946) claimed to show that forming an impression of personality was an organized process. He gave his subjects two identical lists of traits describing a person, with the one difference that the first list contained the word 'warm', whereas in the second list this was replaced by the word 'cold'; the words common to both lists were, 'intelligent, skillful, industrious, determined, practical, cautious'. He then asked his subjects to describe the people characterized by these traits. The results showed that the substitution of one word totally altered the subjects' response so that the person described as cold was consistently seen in more negative terms despite the other positive attributes. In further studies some traits such as 'honest, strong, serious and reliable' were not affected by being linked with 'warm' or 'cold'.

It could be argued that people do not use lists of traits as a basis for perceiving others and therefore this study is somewhat unrealistic.

Two more naturalistic studies were those of Weinstein and Crowdus (1968) and Kelley (1950). The former put each of their subjects with another person in a waiting room. The other then left and a third person entered who gave the subject positive or negative information concerning the first person. The subjects were later asked to evaluate both the people they had met in the waiting room. They found that men were more affected by negative and women by positive information. Kelley (1950) showed that if students were given identical descriptions of a visiting lecturer, before they met him, in which one description contained the word 'warm' and the other the word 'cold', those students who had received the 'cold' description actually spoke less in the discussion following the lecture. Izzett and Leginski (1972) showed that if a person gives positive information about himself this results in a less favourable impression than if the information had come from a third party, but that the reverse is true for negative information, so that if one person gives another negative information concerning himself the other will have a more favourable impression of him than if he had been told the negative information by a third person.

Dornbush *et al.* (1965) questioned children aged between nine and eleven years concerning their perceptions of their peers. They found that the categories used were related to the *perceiver* not the *perceived*, i.e. if A called B 'clever' this meant that A was likely to use the category 'clever' or 'dumb' when describing C, D, or E; it did not mean that B was likely to be perceived as 'clever' by other children. In other words B may *be* clever, but he will only be described as such by a child using that category and his cleverness will not stimulate the categorization in a child who has not been applying that category to others. The authors concluded that, 'the most powerful influence on interpersonal description is the manner in which the perceiver structures his interpersonal world'. Morrison and Hallworth (1966) analysed the peer ratings made by girls in a Scottish secondary school and found that, generally three dimensions were used; first 'social extraversion', based on judgements of sociability, cheerfulness, generosity and co-operation; second 'pleasant classmate' which stressed courtesy, loyalty and co-operation with teachers; and, third 'non-academic leader', i.e. ability at games and leadership. The age of the father and the sex of the child were found to modify perception and Tonkey (1972) warns that perception of people is influenced by role perception and therefore the situational context also needs to be taken into account.

However, person perception, unlike object perception, is a two-way process. The object of perception is a human being similar to the perceiver and the perceiver realizes that he is, in turn the object of the other's perception. This reciprocity has two main results; the perceiver both attributes 'mental' qualities, e.g. intentions, abilities and attitudes to the person perceived, and is himself affected by experiencing himself as perceived.

3.2 *Attribution of intention, responsibility and ability*

As children mature they develop notions of causality and come to accept that whatever happens is caused. It is not surprising, therefore, that both children and adults attribute intentionality, and hence responsibility, to others. Heider (1958) suggests that the attribution of responsibility has four stages: in the first, a person is held responsible for all effects that can be seen as being related to him in some way even if he is not the agent, e.g. the owner of a car is seen as responsible for an accident even if he is not driving; at the second stage he is responsible if he is the agent, say the driver of the car, even if, in fact, he could not have avoided the accident; at the third stage people are seen as responsible if they could have anticipated the incident, and in the fourth they are responsible if they intended the effect. The final stage has the added refinement of taking into account environmental factors which may have affected the agent and hence become mitigating circumstances. Walster (1966) showed that adults will attribute differential amounts of responsibility to the agent depending on the outcome, so that a man whose car accidentally ran away was judged more responsible when a child or man was injured than when there was either no harm done or merely damage to the car.

Work on the attribution of ability is especially relevant for education, and research suggests that the initial attribution may be biased so that subsequent changes in performance will be attributed to the child's own diligence or the teacher's skill depending on the context rather than on an objective assessment of performance. Jones *et al.* (1968) let subjects watch 'pupils' solving problems. All the pupils solved fifteen out of thirty problems but their patterns of success were different. Pupil A solved them correctly in a random order, B had ascending success, that is most failures at the start of the sequence, and pupil C had descending success, i.e. most failures at the end of the sequence. Pupil C was consistently judged to be more intelligent and was judged, incorrectly, to have solved more problems correctly than the others. When the subjects who had been watching were themselves asked to solve problems, those who had an ascending pattern were more confident in their own ability. The study points to a potential mismatch of perception: if Pupil A has an ascending success rate he will feel confident but the teacher however will attribute less ability to him than to pupil C who exhibits a descending success rate. First impressions here seem significant to the extent of distortion.

Johnson, Feigenbaum and Weiby (1964) performed a particularly ingenious study which illustrates both the initial attribution of ability and the teacher's subsequent responses to changes in a pupil's performance. In this study eighty subjects taught arithmetic concepts to fictitious 'students'. The response of the 'students' was in fact controlled by the experimenter. In the first test student A performed high and student B low. The subjects attributed the cause of the students' performance to internal factors in the students and not to their teaching. Positive characteristics were attributed to A and negative to B. The experimenter then told all the subjects that indeed A's real characteristics were positive and told half the subjects that B's characteristics were also positive, i.e. that he had a high IQ, a good past record, and that his father was a professional man. The other half were told that B had negative characteristics, i.e. a low IQ, bad past record and father was a non-professional. The teaching situation was then repeated followed by a second test in which A performed high and B either high or low. There were thus four possible conditions with reference to B: B had positive characteristics and high performance on the second test, positive characteristics and low performance, negative characteristics and high performance, negative characteristics and low performance. At the end of the second test A was again rated higher despite improvements in B's performance. The results showed that when B improved the subjects tended to see themselves as responsible but B as responsible when he did not improve. There was thus a tendency to balance perception by attributing negative qualities for negative behaviour and vice versa.

Psychology, unlike physics, is not usually noted for clear-cut results, but in this area the findings are beginning to take a firmer shape. Beez (1970) showed that when children taking part in a head start programme were randomly assigned to a 'high' ability or a 'low' ability group and teachers were given fake psychological data concerning the pupils' ability level, this assessment affected both the teacher's behaviour and the pupil's performance. One of the teachers' tasks was to get the children to recognize symbols, like road signs, presented on separate cards. The results showed that not only did teachers attempt to teach more to the high ability group – 87 per cent of the 'high' ability teachers taught eight or more symbols but only by 13 per cent of those expecting low performance did so – but also that the 'high' ability group actually learnt more signs: their mean was 5.9 whereas for the 'low' ability group it was 3.1, that is 77 per cent of the 'high' ability group learnt five or more signs but only 13 per cent of the 'low' did so. Findings of this magnitude, which point to the importance of expectation as opposed to 'actual' IQ or ability, have serious implications for teachers and pupils in the schools today.

Teachers can also attribute ability as the result of manipulation by the students. Singer (1964) explored the relationships between students' grade point averages and their score on a test designed to measure their manipulative ability, or Machiavellianism, (Mach. V). He found a correlation for men between Machiavellianism and grade point average but not for women. For women the correlation between GPA and physical attractiveness was significant for first-borns. Singer hypothesized that the first-born attractive girls were given the benefit of the doubt when grades were being awarded because the professors could associate their names and faces. When he tested this it became apparent that first-born girls did tend to sit in the front of the class, speak to the lecturer after the class and visit him in his room more often than later-born girls. He concludes: 'The results imply that the poor college professor is a rather put upon creature, hoodwinked by the male students (later born) and enticed by the female students (first born) as he goes about his academic and personal responsibilities.' However, when the faculty were tested they scored higher on Machiavellianism than the students so Singer ends with the hope that, 'the academicians are fighting strategem with strategem'.

3.3 *Teacher expectation*

Rosenthal and Rosnow (1969) reviewed several studies to do with experimenter/teacher expectation which seem to indicate that, 'considering the studies of human learning and ability as a set, it appears that the effects of experimenter expectancy may well operate as unintended determinants of subjects' performance'. One of the studies reviewed showed that when the experimenter administering a Wechsler Intelligence Scale for Children (WISC) expected the child to be 'above average', the child scored, on average, 7.5 points above the child who was expected to be 'below average', although, in fact, both children were of average intelligence. In the school situation, the study by Rosenthal and Jacobson (1968) is well known. In this, pupils whom their teachers had been led to expect to 'bloom' during the year did show an increase of four points in IQ, although they had originally been chosen at random. An interesting aspect of this study is the attitude of teachers towards the children. The children expected to improve were rated more positively by teachers in terms of their adjustment, affection and future success than those children who were not expected to improve but, in fact, did so. This second group were given negative evaluation and were perceived as displaying undesirable behaviour. The authors comment: 'If a child is to show intellectual gain it seems to be better for his real or perceived intellectual vitality and for his real or perceived mental health if his teacher has been expecting him to grow intellectually.' Having reviewed several studies Rosenthal (1966) concludes that seven out of ten experimenter/teachers do affect the performance of their subjects with the bias towards their own expectation.

The alarming work of Rosenhan (1973) demonstrates the effect of expectation. In his study eight normal people pretended to have psychiatric symptoms, that is they claimed to hear voices saying 'empty', 'hollow' and 'thud', and were admitted to mental hospitals. Once inside they behaved perfectly normally but, having been classified as ill, their normal behaviour was perceived as abnormal to the extent that doctors ignored their reasonable questions and, when one 'patient' spent his time writing up his experiences this was recorded as 'patient engages in writing behaviour'. One 'patient' was kept in hospital for fifty-two days and the average stay was nineteen days. These results are understandable if, as

Bruner, Shapiro and Tagiuri (1958) maintain, impression formation is like concept formation in that it is, necessarily, based on incomplete information and has to be built up in a way that seems coherent to the perceiver. As Walter Lippmann remarked: 'For the most part we do not see and then define, we define first and then see.'

3.4 *Consistency bias*

It can thus be demonstrated that the attribution of ability and 'mental' qualities can be influenced by the perceiver's bias. Bias is also created by the tendency to associate one attribute with another, so that people who are warm are also expected to be friendly, and by the desire for consistency, these two perceptual processes lead the perceiver to create stability of perception across groups and within individuals. This type of structuring can lead to stereotyping whereby whole national groups or social classes are defined by a limited number of traits and each member of the group is deemed to have these characteristics. His behaviour is then 'prejudged' in the light of his national or class membership, irrespective of his actual behaviour.

In order to maintain perceptual stability the person has to deal with contradictory information concerning others. Hastorf, Schneider and Polefka (1970) made a threefold classification of ways of minimizing inconsistency; first a relational tendency by which the inconsistent trait is reinterpreted or new traits added to make the whole more consistent, second the odd trait can be discounted or ignored, or third, by linear combination, whereby final impression is the result of combining all the traits. Whether traits are equally weighted has generated a considerable amount of research and there does seem to be support for the view that people seek balance or congruity although Triandis and Fishbein (1963) showed that prejudiced subjects follow the congruity principle less than unprejudiced when a trait towards which they are prejudiced is present.

There are, however, considerable individual differences in people's willingness to accept contradictory information so that cognitively simple judges use one-dimensional categories and ignore inconvenient traits, whereas more complex judges are prepared to live with ambiguity. It has been suggested that authoritarians are less willing to tolerate ambiguity. In his study of the authoritarian personality, Adorno *et al.* (1950) pointed out that high authoritarians were characterized by the simplicity of their perceptions, in particular their refusal to attribute negative qualities to their parents.

Seeking for consistency affects both the perceiver's view of others and his view of himself, i.e. his self-concept and his 'being-for-others'. Combs and Snygg (1959) summarize the position by saying:

... we have seen that (1) man, like the universe of which he is a part, characteristically seeks the maintenance of organisation; (2) that the organisation man seeks to maintain is the organisation of which he is aware, namely, his phenomenal self; and (3) that, because man lives in a changing world and is aware of the future as well as of the present, maintenance of the self requires not simple maintenance of the status quo, but an active seeking for personal adequacy.

3.5 *Role of the person perceived*

The person perceived is both aware that he has, or wishes to have, certain qualities, and that his beliefs about himself can be confirmed or disconfirmed by another's perceptions. Heider (1958) considered this question in some detail and maintained that

The experience of being scrutinized pulls p very strongly into the interpersonal process going on between p and o. Because o's judgment of him is often vital to p in a uniquely personal way, he seeks to inform himself of this evaluation. If he believes that o's reception is favourable, p's reaction may become strengthened and more organised; but if he is insecure about o's reaction, or believes it is negative, p's action may go on with a conflicting and interfering content present in p's life space.

He disagrees with Sartre's (1956) more negative view that, 'Either the other looks at me and alienates my liberty, or I assimilate and seize the liberty of the other', saying that to be the object of another's perception is not to literally become an object in the thing sense.

3.6 *Self-image and self-esteem*

A person's self-image and self-esteem is an important determinant of social interaction and social psychologists have been concerned with its effect on behaviour and the extent to which it is composed of the reactions of others. Coopersmith (1967) sees the development of self-esteem as the result of acceptance by parents who 'are concerned and attentive towards their children ... [who] ... structure the worlds of their children along lines they believe to be proper and appropriate and ... [who] ... permit relatively greater freedom within the structures they have established'. He concludes that 'children with high self-esteem are more likely to identify, as well as more likely to have a favourable model with which to identify'.

Different levels of self-esteem have discrete behavioural concomitants, with those high in self-esteem being socially poised, low in anxiety, and likely to obtain positions of influence; those with medium self-esteem are similar but have the 'strongest value orientation and are most likely to become dependent upon others', while those with low self-esteem are anxious, withdrawn and passive. When Coopersmith looked at the relationship between self-esteem and academic performance he found that 'The correlation between subjective self-esteem and intelligence is .25 and that between self-esteem and academic achievement is .30'. Thus both correlations were statistically significant, but also showed that while ability and academic performance were significantly associated with self-esteem, they were not wholly responsible for developing it.

Videbeck (1960) studied the extent to which a person's assessment of his own capabilities is affected by others' comments on his ability. Having got students from introductory speech classes to rate themselves on items beginning, 'if you were required to ... how adequately could you...', he then submitted them to a test after which half were given negative and half positive feedback. The results confirmed the hypothesis that self-ratings would change in the direction of the feedback. However, there are probable individual differences in reaction, for as Kennedy and Vega (1965) showed, both white and black students responded to blame with lowered performance when the examiner was white, but black students showed improved performance when the examiner was black.

If smooth and accurate social interaction requires A to perceive B in a way which takes account of B's perception of himself and B's actual abilities and intentions, then skill in social perception is important for teachers and all those who have to work with people. There has been some, rather unrelated, work on the characteristics of a good judge (see Cook, 1971, for a review), which suggests that intelligence can be related to this ability and that perceptual skill is not a unitary trait; judges are more accurate depending on the class of the person they are judging so that usually similarity between perceiver and perceived is correlated with accuracy.

Can people learn to be more sensitive and accurate in their perceptions of others? Jecker, Maccoby and Breitrose (1965) do give some evidence that teachers can be trained to judge their pupils' comprehension more accurately during a lesson by recognizing and interpreting certain significant non-verbal cues. Perhaps greater clarity concerning initial assumptions and the processes of perception would also be helpful. Nilsen (1954), speaking of assumptions which are barriers to communication, includes several assumptions which are equally applicable to perception. He says: 'One assumption appears to be basic in this area, namely, that in a given situation the communicator assumes he knows enough about that situation.' This knowledge leads him to assume that others see things as he does, that people are consistent over different contexts, and that 'the communication process in a given situation has little or no relation to other events in the same situation'.

Further reading

Argyle, M. (1969) *Social Interaction*. London: Methuen.
Argyle, M. (ed.) (1973) *Social Encounters*. Harmondsworth, Middlesex: Penguin.
Cook, M. (1971) *Interpersonal Perception*. Harmondsworth, Middlesex: Penguin.

Danziger, K. (1975) *Interpersonal Communication*. London: Pergamon Press.

Ekman, P. (1972) *Emotion in the Human Face*. London: Pergamon Press.

Goffman, E. (1971) *Relations in Public*. Harmondsworth, Middlesex: Penguin.

Hargreaves, D. H. (1972) *Interpersonal Relations and Education*. London: Routledge and Kegan Paul.

Hastorf, A. N., Schneider, D. J. and Polefka, J. (1970) *Person Perception*. Reading, Mass.: Addison-Wesley.

Laver, J. and Hutcheson, S. (eds) (1972) *Communication in Face to Face Interaction*. Harmondsworth, Middlesex: Penguin.

Morrison, A. and McIntyre, D. (eds) (1972) *Social Psychology of Teaching*. Harmondsworth, Middlesex: Penguin.

Livesley, W. J. and Bromley, D. B. (1973) *Person Perception in Childhood and Adolescence*. London: John Wiley.

Wheldall, K. (1975) *Social Behaviour*. London: Methuen.

Yee, A. H. (ed.) (1971) *Social Interaction in Educational Settings*. Englewood Cliffs, New Jersey: Prentice-Hall.

[6]
Groups and social influence

In the last chapter social interaction was considered as a general phenomenon, but of particular interest to the teacher is the aspect of group behaviour. A group is an interactive system, and is thus distinct from a collection of people in a railway carriage or a queue, none of whom may respond to the presence of the others. Interaction requires that each of the members of a group should be attentive and responsive to the behaviour of the others. A class of thirty children may be treated by the teacher as one group but, in fact, this larger group can often be seen to be composed of smaller groups which overlap each other. Although psychologists have paid most attention to the behaviour of small groups of two to twelve people this is not to say that the characteristics of small groups may not also be evinced by larger groups. The study of small groups, although concentrating on the group/climate/intention dimension, also needs to take into account individual personality and needs, together with such concepts as role, status, and norm. In response to these variables the group develops a characteristic structure and process in order to maintain its existence and carry out its task, i.e. perform, to the satisfaction of its members.

---

1 *Groups*

1.1 *Types of group*

There are four main types of group each of which may be further subdivided; firstly, social groups which come together because they share a common social purpose for example family, sporting, recreational and special interest groups; secondly, groups which

cohere because of the interpersonal attraction of the members as
in friendship groups; thirdly, task groups which meet because they
have a specific problem to solve; and finally, therapy or personal
growth groups. Many groups represent a combination of these
pure types, such as those which begin as task groups and develop
into friendship groups, or groups which have elements of both
social and interpersonal attraction.

Group work can be used as a means of training people to be
more sensitive in their interpersonal encounters. The best known
of these methods is the T (Training) group in which people meet,
usually in a residential setting to take a course lasting for periods
of a few days, a week, or two weeks, in order to explore how they
respond to others and how others perceive their response. Smith
(1969) outlined four areas of behaviour relevant to T group training:
the first, 'public behaviour' is overt and needs no further analysis;
the second, 'blind behaviour' is behaviour which is apparent to
others but not to the person himself – T group training can make
a person aware of blind behaviour so that he can use this new
knowledge in future dealings with people; the third, 'hidden
behaviour' is behaviour of which the person is aware but conceals
from others, he can learn in a T group how much of this could
be revealed; and the fourth, 'unconscious behaviour' is not
perceived by either the person or the group and the T group does
not concern itself with this. Therapy groups are intended for people
with various forms of psychiatric disturbance who are enabled,
by meeting as a group with a trained leader, to work through their
problems together.

1.2 *Group characteristics* (norms, roles, status)

Individuals behave differently in company from when alone and
a significant determinant of an individual's public behaviour is
the type of group in which he finds himself. Perhaps the most
obvious characteristic of a group is that it forms norms. The concept
'norm' has many different interpretations but a simple way to con-
ceptualize it is to think of it as similar to a force field, that is
it marks out an area of acceptable and unacceptable behaviour
and indicates to participants what is consonant or dissonant with
the belief system of the group. There is thus some measure of
flexibility. Those members who are most acceptable to the group

are usually those who approximate most closely to the norm, be it a norm of work, value, level of performance, or appearance; but some deviation, within limits, is allowed. If a member deviates too far the others will attempt to bring him into line, but if he persists in deviating he will, ultimately, either have to modify the group norm or leave the group. Individuals who tend to adhere to the norms will, over time, build up credit so that they may then deviate until their credit is exhausted. Hollander (1958, 1960) called this 'idosyncratic credit' and showed that, in a problem solving situation, the person who had agreed on procedures in the early stages was more able to innovate later than one who had disagreed while procedures were being developed.

The process of inducing people to adhere to group norms is known as conformity (see p. 148), however a prior question is how and why group norms come into existence during the initial phase of group formation. Argyle (1969) suggested that, 'shared patterns of behaviour are adopted by group members because this enables them to attain group goals and satisfy interpersonal needs'. Thibaut (1968) looked into the finding that normative methods of control were preferable to control by a single individual when individual control could be equally successful as a means of attaining group goals. The results of his experiments supported the theory that in a situation in which A could exploit B, and B might be attracted by other relationships, so that each is a threat to the other (if B withdraws A loses his power, and hence B threatens A, yet A is in the position of power and thus threatens B) the two may agree on a set of norms which limits the power of A and removes B's power to withdraw so that they can work together with their mutual threat removed. In this study Thibaut quoted a comment by Wells to the effect that a third disinterested party might be necessary, in this case the experimenter, to facilitate the acceptance of normative rules.

But Wells further hypothesized that informal norms would develop without the presence of a third party when there was mutuality of interest. It is possible that norms originate from some external standard, be it the values of the culture or the work expectation of the teacher, from which the individual members of the group decide how far it is acceptable to deviate, thus setting up a range of behaviour around the originally externally set standard. For example a group of children may work to a norm of doing slightly less work than the teacher asks, and will thus produce more work for a teacher who asks for more. Others, who accept the norm set by the teacher, may be overworked if the teacher is expecting a short fall and therefore setting more work than he expects in fact to be done. It is possible that the question of norms is at the back of the phenomena outlined by Jackson (1964) that children, despite their original ability, do become 'A' 'B' and 'C' stream children once they have been in a stream for a sufficient length of time, and this factor needs to be taken into account, along with the effects of teacher expectation, in assessing a child's performance (see p. 273).

The term *role* refers to an 'expected pattern of reciprocal behaviour' and within a group different members will play different roles. A person alone cannot have a role, they only arise when people are in relationship with one another. The term role can be used widely, for example in relation to the woman's role or the role of a husband or wife, but in the small group context it refers more specifically to the behaviour which characterizes a particular individual in that group. He may be the one who initiates new activities, who facilitates the activities of others, who is an expert in the task, or who acts as a critic or a clown. A problem with roles is that once a person has been cast or has cast himself in a certain role, it may be difficult for him to change, as the equilibrium of the group is based on a certain pattern of role relationships, and for one to change might upset the equilibrium thus causing others to put pressure on him to maintain the *status quo*. A person's role in a group can lead to stress and anxiety if that person is asked to play two incompatible roles, for example a woman who is expected to be both feminine, in a submissive male-ego-building sense, and critical in response to the demands of a particular task. If, then, a role is the result both of a person's own predispositions, and others' expectations of him, how exactly does this process of social influence work? Kahn (1964) offers an illuminating model of role relations (Fig. 6.1).

It would seem that in any organization or group certain positions have to be filled and the occupants of those positions have to behave in a way which is consonant with the expectations of others. Goffman (1956) dealt with roles at some length when he presented his dramaturgical model which stressed the 'on stage' 'off stage' aspects of social behaviour and argued that, 'roles represent

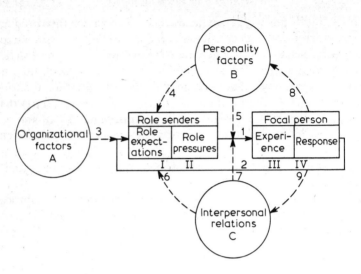

Fig. 6.1 *A theoretical model of factors involved in adjustments to role conflict and ambiguity*

1. Circle A: Organization as a whole, its size and product etc. The relation of the person to the organization, his rank etc.

2. Arrow 3: Represents a causal relationship between organizational variables and the role expectations and pressures, which are held about and exerted towards a particular position.

3. Circle B: Personality factors.
   Arrow 4: Some traits which can evoke or facilitate certain responses from role senders.
   Arrow 5: Role pressures *on* the person.

4. Circle C: Interpersonal relations.
   Arrow 6: Pressures exerted by role senders in response to interpersonal relations between them and X.
   Arrow 7: Different interpretations of pressures depending on personal relations between focal person and role senders.

5. Arrow 2: The way the focal person complies will affect future behaviour of role senders.
   Arrow 9: Response of focal person leading to long-term changes in relations between focals and senders.
   Arrow 8: Changes in personality organization due to reaction to role experience.

(Kahn, 1964)

reciprocal obligations. X is expected by Y to behave in a certain way and in return Y has to treat X with the respect due to his position.'

Closely related to the concept of role is that of *status* which refers to the power dimension in a group. It is purely a function of group membership in that it only occurs when people evaluate each other. This results in a social hierarchy with those at the top having more power than those lower down. A person is said to have high status if he is successful in initiating action or inter-action within a group. The member with high status is the one whose ideas, over time, are those which are acted upon by the group, not necessarily the individual who speaks most or who offers most ideas. However Bavelas, Hastorf, Gross and Kite (1965) in a series of neat experiments showed that if they experimentally manipulated the amount a member spoke he was judged by the other members to be making a better contribution and his socio-metric status (see p. 143) rose with the increase in speech.

The matter however may be more complex, as Willard and Strodbeck (1972) suggest that it is speed of response which makes other members see the quick responder who 'jumps in' as com-petent and as a potential leader. A person may also have status purely because he occupies a certain position, for example the throne, but it may also be gained by a member having a specific expertise which is of value to the group (thus status can change as the group task changes), or by a member showing adherence to group norms and being clearly and effectively involved in group activities. This led Homans (1961) to see status as recognition by the group in return for rewards gained for the group. Problems can arise in this kind of situation when a person is expected to have status by virtue of his position as, for example a manager or a professor, and turns out not to have the necessary expertise. If the situation cannot be resolved to the satisfaction of the group the result will be the group's own gradual disintegration.

1.3 *Group structure*

Group structure is perhaps best conceptualized diagrammatically as drawn by Davis (1969) (Fig. 6.2). In (a) there is a clear chain of command leading to a hierarchical structure; in (b) one person is dominant and the members each relate to him but do not differ in status with respect to each other; in (c) the situation is similar with A being central rather than dominant, in (d) and (e) the structure is more democratic with (e) representing more interaction in that each member relates to every other one; (f) and (g) represent two-way interaction between some members with (g) appearing to be a more closely knit group.

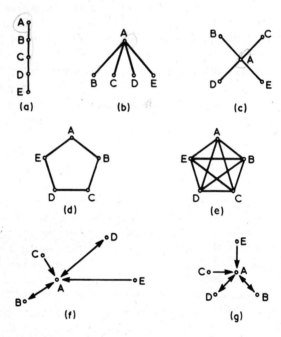

Fig. 6.2 *Group structure*
(Davis, 1969)

1.4 *The development of a group*

Given that an individual behaves in a certain way within a group, how does a group, as a group, develop? Tuckman (1965) suggested that there is a parallel between the development of group structure and the execution of the task activity (Table 6.1).

Table 6.1 *Relationship between group structure and task activity*

Group structure (i.e. the pattern of interpersonal relations)	Task activity
1 Testing and dependence	1 Orientation to the task; i.e. an attempt to identify its parameters
2 Intragroup conflict	2 Emotional response to task demands, some resistance
3 Development of group cohesion; harmony of maximum importance	3 Open exchange of relevant interpretations
4 Functional role relatedness; group becomes a problem solving instrument	4 Emergence of solutions

(Tuckman, 1965)

[handwritten annotation: NOT MUNDANE! V. Important]

Such mundane considerations as physical location may also *[handwritten: Bring in Nicholson]* affect the nature of group interaction and the role any particular individual plays within a group. Festinger, Schachter and Back (1950) were able to show that in apartment buildings geographical location was a significant determinant of sociometric choice. The lay-out of each of the buildings was the same (Fig. 6.3) and each flat was occupied by a young married couple studying at MIT. Each couple was asked to name its three closest friends. The

[handwritten annotation: change in ratios over time]

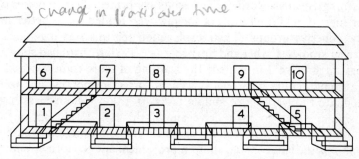

Fig. 6.3 *Schematic diagram of Westgate West Building* (Festinger, Schachter and Back, 1950)

findings were that in general couples named those living nearest to them. However, couples in central flats were named more often by other couples on the same floor, whereas couples in end flats were more likely to be named by and to name people on the upper floor. Since the data was collected from several buildings, choices must be related to the geographical position of the rooms and not to the personal characteristics of the occupants.

1.5 *Group effectiveness*

Being a member of a group can enable a person to arrive at a better solution to a problem than he would have achieved alone, and also to learn more effectively. The superiority of group problem solving might be thought to be merely the result of a group representing the pooled expertise of the individual members. However it is likely that there are other dynamic factors at work particularly in terms of affect.

In a study of group cohesiveness and individual learning Lott and Lott (1966) hypothesized that individuals would perform better on learning tasks when they were in a more cohesive group (that is with better liked others), than when they were in a less cohesive group. Having used sociometric tests (see p. **000**) to assess degrees of liking, primary school children, from the fourth and fifth grades were divided into groups of three or four of the same sex. The groups were of four kinds: (1) high intelligence with high cohesiveness; (2) high intelligence with low cohesiveness; (3) low intelligence with high cohesiveness; and (4) low intelligence with low cohesiveness. The children were then given the task of learning Spanish words. The results confirmed their hypothesis for high IQ children but not for low who tended to do better in low cohesive groups. Their explanation for this was ingenious. Earlier studies (Farber and Spence, 1953; Taylor, 1956) had shown that 'high drive' can impede the learning of more complex tasks, by strengthening incorrect as well as correct responses, but will facilitate the learning of simple tasks. If group cohesiveness has a similar effect to high drive and if the task would appear a complex one for the low IQ children but a simple one for the high IQs the latter should show improvement and the former none. Nevertheless the authors did not report individual measures and it is possible that the pooling hypothesis (that the group represents the result of the members' expertise) is at least as powerful as that of cohesiveness.

Leadership. The effectiveness of a group is dependent on several variables such as the personal abilities of the members, the environmental context, the nature of the task and the quality of the leadership. The leadership variable is a significant one and has generated a good deal of research, firstly into the characteristics of leaders, secondly into group climate and thirdly into leader/follower transaction. A famous study of the second kind by Lippitt and White (1943) appeared to show that when children were exposed to leadership of various styles – in this case authoritarian, democratic and laissez-faire – their behaviour varied accordingly and this study favoured the democratic. However, the matter is, perhaps, more complex, as exemplified in a later study by Weschler, Kahone and Tannenbaum (1961). In this examination of laboratory groups, group A was led in a restrictive way by a 'brilliant young scientist' and group B in a permissive way by an older 'fatherly' type of man. The members of each group were then asked to rate, amongst other things, their morale and productivity on a five-point scale. Both groups were then rated on morale and productivity by seven senior members of the laboratory administration. The rating showed that Group A was more productive, in the view of their superiors, than the low-morale members thought, and that group B, with higher morale, was assessed by their superiors as less productive. This suggests that different styles of leadership are more or less effective in relation to different types of outcome.

To think of the teacher as a leader draws attention to two discrete aspects of his role; firstly, as a leader of children in a classroom, and secondly as a leader of adults when he is in the role of head of department or head of a school. Turner and Lombard (1969) listed three things which they believe a leader ought to be able to do:

1 He has to understand and manage the translation of an expanding body of knowledge into practical concrete behavior.
2 He has to be able to listen to himself, and see this as both more important and more difficult than listening to others.
3 He has to develop and express in his behavior a central

concern for every individual's potential as a human being; he has to value individual growth and development for himself and others not as a means to an end but as his own major purpose in life.

They stressed that what this requires is:

The administrator's ability to increase his awareness and understanding of how he feels about events in which he is involved and other people with whom he interacts. Sometimes in the midst of my involvement, and at other times when I reflect on what has taken place, I have to ask myself this question and listen with skill to my answer: How is what I am aware of experiencing outside of myself being affected by what I may not be aware of experiencing inside.

Fiedler (1967) has suggested a contingency model of leadership which states that 'the group's performance will be contingent upon the appropriate matching of leadership style and the degree of favorableness of the group situation for the leader'. To arrive at this he divided task groups into three kinds in terms of the members work relations: first, 'interacting' in which successful task performance requires that the members work together and are thus interdependent; second, 'coacting' where although the task is a joint one, the members can work on it independently; and, third, 'counteracting' in which the members wish to reach a common goal but to do this requires that they take part in a bargaining process in order to resolve the different points of view within the group to the satisfaction of the members. Obviously the effective leader will need to be utilizing different skills depending on the type of group. In the first case he is concerned with co-ordinating the members' work so that it runs smoothly, in the second with the individual performance and attainment, and in the third with acting as moderator so that the conflict is productive in terms of the final outcome (Fig. 6.4).

It is necessary to distinguish leadership activities which are directed towards attaining the group goal and those which are concerned with maintaining the group in existence as a group. The first of these is the responsibility of the task leader, the second of the socio-emotional leader. The task leader will be respected but his very competence can be seen as threatening to the self-

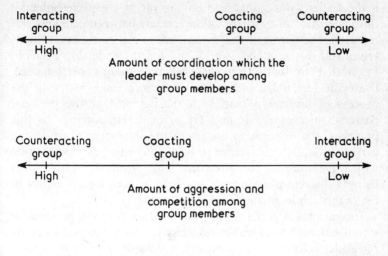

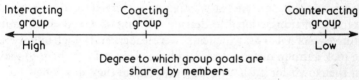

Fig. 6.4 *Schematic comparison of interacting, coacting and counteracting groups in three dimensions*
(Fiedler, 1967)

esteem of the other members. The socio-emotional leader restores the others' self-esteem and maintains group coherence. However if the group is well organized and accepts the task leader he will be less threatening and hence there will be less need for a socio-emotional leader. Burke (1967) showed that when there was low interest in the task the socio-emotional leader had to increase his activity as the task leader proposed more solutions, but when there was high task interest this was not necessary.

In a useful review of the question of leadership Hollander and Julian (1969) outlined four aspects of the study of leadership which they believed needed to be pursued. First, leadership should be seen as a question of influence within a specific group pursuing a particular task; second, it develops over time and is successful

→ 4 task leaders → make others task work

if the leader gains status by fulfilling the role expected of him; third, a leader must initiate action, mediate between members and represent the norms of the group both to the participants themselves and to the outside world; and fourth, leadership needs to be related to the effectiveness of the group's performance. Generally Hollander and Julian were more concerned with the process of leadership than with the outcome or the personal characteristics of the leader. Of particular importance to this process is the response of the group and the extent to which the participants allow the leader to lead – he must, as it were, rule with the consent of the governed. Thus leadership rather than being a discrete phenomenon needs to be seen as one aspect of the highly labile interaction system known as a group.

Increasingly it is the transactional, rather than the personal or situational, aspects of leadership which are being stressed whereby the leader is legitimized by providing rewards and in return gains status and esteem. An early study by Merei (1949) is a good example of transactional leadership. Having observed children in a nursery school to see which ones were leaders and which followers, he took a group of followers out of the class and left them to play on their own for an hour a day. Over time they developed their own pattern of interaction in terms of the games they played and 'ownership' of various toys. He then introduced one of the leaders into the group. When the leader attempted to exercise his authority he failed. That is, once the social pattern was set a new leader could not achieve dominance without the agreement of the followers.

Participant characteristics. However, group effectiveness is also determined by the characteristics of the participants and the situation. Participant characteristics are of crucial importance when, for educational reasons, there has been deliberate interference with the composition of the group. Children naturally form friendship groups but it is becoming increasingly popular for teachers to divide children into groups with the deliberate intention of mixing different levels of ability. Dahllöf (1971) reviewed studies in Stockholm (Svensson, 1962), Växjö (Carlsson, 1963) and Utah (Borg, 1965) and showed that there was a consistent, if non-significant trend for pupils in positively selected classes to have higher attainment than those in comprehensive (i.e. non-selected) classes but that there was no difference between those in comprehensive and negatively selected classes. However subsequent work showed that, if teaching remained traditional, the same level of attainment in comprehensive classes as in positively selected ones required more time, and the taking of more time on elementary work could prejudice the quality of more advanced work. Thus the characteristic of participants will affect the nature of the group's performance and requires an institution to have clear aims – i.e. with what group outcomes it is most concerned – as well as requiring flexibility of approach from the teacher.

1.6 *The analysis of groups*

If a teacher wishes to know more about the nature of the group with which he has to deal there are two established ways of doing this. Firstly he can use the sociometric technique originally devised by Moreno (1934) which describes the social structure of a group in terms of its friendship patterns or task pairs; it is essentially a way of measuring the static structure of a group at a particular moment. The teacher asks each child in the class to choose one or more children with whom he would like, or, in some instances, dislike, to play, do a project, or go to camp – the precise form of the question is determined by the nature of the information required. Having noted the choices they can be represented by a sociogram which will enable the teacher to see how the children in a class, cluster, whether any child receives no choices and is therefore a neglectee, or an isolate who neither gives nor receives choices; the teacher can also distinguish those children who receive a significant number of choices from more than one group and are known as 'stars'. With a larger group, usually over thirty, a sociomatrix is used which can show both the amount and direction of interaction. The analysis of sociometric data is more complex than its collection, since if the teacher is concerned with the sociometric status of a child he is not only interested in how often he was chosen, but also in whom he was chosen by, and how often rejected and by whom. Summing up the number of choices a child receives can give a guide to his sociometric rating or popularity. Alternatively checking the number of significant others chosen by the child can indicate his level of security since it is hypothesized that secure children will need less significant others and will

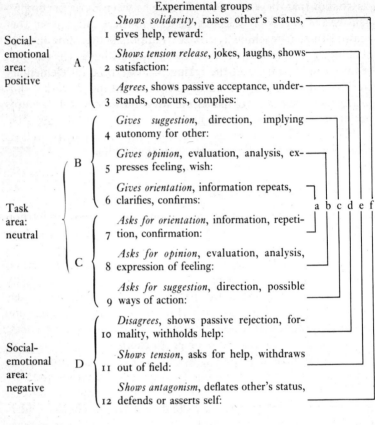

Fig. 6.5 *Interaction analysis schedule.*
(Bales, 1951)

Experimental groups

Social-emotional area: positive — A
1 *Shows solidarity*, raises other's status, gives help, reward:
2 *Shows tension release*, jokes, laughs, shows satisfaction:
3 *Agrees*, shows passive acceptance, understands, concurs, complies:

Task area: neutral — B
4 *Gives suggestion*, direction, implying autonomy for other:
5 *Gives opinion*, evaluation, analysis, expresses feeling, wish:
6 *Gives orientation*, information repeats, clarifies, confirms:

C
7 *Asks for orientation*, information, repetition, confirmation:
8 *Asks for opinion*, evaluation, analysis, expression of feeling:
9 *Asks for suggestion*, direction, possible ways of action:

Social-emotional area: negative — D
10 *Disagrees*, shows passive rejection, formality, withholds help:
11 *Shows tension*, asks for help, withdraws out of field:
12 *Shows antagonism*, deflates other's status, defends or asserts self:

a b c d e f

Key:

a Problems of communication
b Problems of evaluation
c Problems of control
d Problems of decision
e Problems of tension reduction
f Problems of reintegration

A Positive reactions
B Attempted answers
C Questions
D Negative reactions

therefore make less choices. Thus sociograms can be valuable aids to the teacher in helping him to understand the informal network of the class and therefore to attempt to improve the environment of the neglected or isolated child.

As a way of studying the dynamic process of the group an observer can record all instances of interaction in the group, its nature and the participants. Perhaps the most famous of these schedules is that of Bales (1951) (Fig. 6.5). His theoretical division of group process into areas with similar problems arising in each, enabled him to arrive at a coherent scheme for observation. To apply the schedule the observer has a check list on which he marks the category number of each statement, who made it, and to whom. This data is then used to arrive at a profile of the group in terms of the percentage of statements made in each category; a matrix shows the originator of the statements, whether they were addressed to the group as a whole, or to a particular person and, finally, a sequential analysis shows proportional changes in the incidence of statements in the major groups of categories. Despite the elegance of Bales' scheme it is not easy to administer and requires considerable practice on the part of the observer. As Sprott (1958) pointed out, in Bales' groups

> The air is not, as in most committees, loud with the sound of the grinding of axes. In real life situations all these factors complicate the situation. Information is distorted by self interest; immediate inferences; people have to be cajoled, delicately handled and so forth because of their sensitivity or pride of rank or because of their power.

This approach has now developed into the study of classroom interaction (see p. 162).

1.7 *Groups and teaching*

If a teacher understands group behaviour, how does this knowledge help his teaching? Getzels and Thelen (1960) have a useful model of the classroom as a social system showing the various dimensions which need to be taken into account (Fig. 6.6). Studies of the relationship between group behaviour and learning, however, seem to be more related to higher education and slanted to the psycho-analytic approach to groups (Richardson, 1967) which although

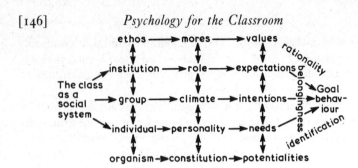

Fig. 6.6 *The classroom as a social system*
(Getzels and Thelen, 1960)

illuminating requires a closer relationship between the teacher/
leader and the group than the average school teacher can have
with classes of thirty children whom he may see only once or twice
in the week. Nevertheless the work of Abercrombie (1970) may
be of relevance even to those who are not involved in higher
education. Group learning is seen as differing from class teaching
in that when a teacher addresses a class as a whole, whether
formally in a lecture or by more informal exposition, the tendency
is to see each student as an individual learning in isolation from
others so that students learn alongside others but not with others.
In a tutorial the emphasis again is on an individual student but
there is a two-way interaction between the tutor and student
whereas in the seminar the aim is to exploit the interaction
between student and student as well as between tutor and student,
in order to increase their grasp of the subject matter. An extension
of this is syndicate work in which the group works alone, or with
the occasional presence of the teacher, and aims to produce a report
at the end.

When forming groups teachers may decide to make them complementary, either academically so that all levels of ability are
represented, or sociometrically as a way of increasing contacts for
isolates or neglectees. Or they may decide to group them on the
basis of common academic or sociometric attributes. Having
formed groups the teacher needs to consider seating arrangements,
whether communication should be patterned or free and whether
the leader should be designated or left to emerge. When faced
with a problem, either in the classroom or in the staffroom, a
knowledge of group variables such as role, status, norm, participant

characteristics and context together with the effect of social influence factors, should help the teacher to follow the problem solving sequence outlined by Schmuck, Chesler and Lippitt (1966). They suggest that a problem must first be identified, its causes diagnosed either by a questionnaire or verbal questions, and a plan developed for dealing with it which will take into account both the teacher's and the pupil's potentialities for contributing to the solution. These initial phases should then be followed by direct action through adapting teaching and interpersonal strategies in the light of the former analysis and the theoretical insights. A period of feedback and evaluation may then follow.

Perhaps the major finding for the school teacher is that groups do have a dynamic of their own and that it is necessary for him to understand the dynamic of a particular group in order to adapt his teaching to be consonant with it. As with leadership, 'good' teaching is not, in many senses, a generalized trait: what makes it good is whether it is effective in a particular context and this will be determined by the nature of the interaction generated by a particular group.

2 Social influence in groups

Being a member of a group does appear to alter an individual's behaviour so that it is more consonant with that of the group as a whole. This change is the result of social influence and is of particular relevance to education, as children are, developmentally, susceptible to pressure and, indeed, much of education is concerned with attempting to make norms comprehensible and thereby encourage adherence to them. Henry (1966) is persuasive when he points out that in American schoolrooms children are learning more than one thing:

A classroom can be compared to a communications system, for certainly there is a flow of messages between teacher (transmitter) and pupils (receivers) and among the pupils; ... But there is also another interesting characteristic of communications systems that is applicable to classrooms, and that is their inherent tendency to generate *noise*. *Noise*, in communications theory, applies to all those random fluctuations of the system which cannot be controlled ... In a classroom lesson on arithmetic, for example, such *noise* would range all the way from the competitiveness of the students, the quality of the teacher's voice ... to the shuffling of the children's feet. The striking thing about the child is that along with his arithmetic – his 'messages about arithmetic' – he learns all the noise in the system also ... The most significant cultural learnings – primarily the cultural drives – are communicated as noise.

In the past social influence has been largely equated with the study of conformity, and, indeed, this is an important aspect, but this emphasis should not overshadow the significance of non-conformity and of influential minorities.

2.1 *Types of conformity*

In order to understand the phenomenon of conformity several distinctions must be made at the outset. Hollander and Willis (1967) distinguished between descriptive and inferential levels of analysis. The earliest studies, for example Asch (1956) (see p. 106) were mainly descriptive claiming to show that when one person is exposed to the social influence of a larger group his responses are likely to be modified in order to be more consonant with those of the larger group. Thus conformity was seen as a change of 'opinion, attitude, or performance with respect to some outside norm'. The conformer changed his behaviour in the direction of the norms of the group as he perceived them. As a further refinement Beloff (1958) pointed out that there are at least two forms of social conformity, namely acquiescence and conventionality. By acquiescence she meant movement in response to group opinion within a specific situation, and by conventionality a more general adherence to the 'tenets, attitudes and mores of a subject's culture or subculture'. Conventionality is therefore the result of many instances of acquiescence. This distinction led her to hypothesize that those subjects who were acquiescent were likely to be conventional and vice versa. To test this she used two measures of conventionality, based on the aesthetic and political preferences of the experimental subjects' reference group, and correlated these with the subjects' degree of acquiescence in the experimental situation. She found that for men there was a relationship between political conformity and acquiescence and for women between aesthetic preference and conventionality.

A famous series of studies of value as descriptions of social influence processes are those of Milgram (1963, 1964, 1965a, 1965b, 1974) who showed the extent of both group and individual social influence in what were, originally, studies of destructive obedience. He made a distinction between 'action' and 'signal' conformity; in the former the yielder has to *act* in accordance with his conformist response whereas, in the latter, he merely 'signals', that is *says*, that he agrees.

In the first experiments (1963) the subjects were blue-collar workers who responded to newspaper advertisements requesting help in an experiment. When they arrived at Yale they were met by a serious white-coated experimenter and were told that they were to take part in an experiment to study the effect of punishment on learning. They then chose who were to be the 'teachers' and who the 'learners' (in fact the election was rigged so that the experimental subjects were always the teachers). The 'learner' then went into an adjoining room and the subjects were shown the experimental apparatus, which consisted of a display board showing switches which were to deliver an increasing level of electric shock to the learner. They were told that the shocks would be extremely painful but they would not inflict permanent damage and were instructed to question the learner and shock him for every mistake he made up to the maximum level of 450 volts. The experiment then began and if the subjects appeared uncertain whether they should continue they were told, 'the experiment requires it' or 'it is absolutely essential that you continue'. During this process the learner, although in fact not being shocked, feigned signs of distress to the extent of pounding on the wall at 300 volts, after which there was 'no more response'. Afterwards the subjects were told that they had not shocked the learner. Here, then, were a group of Americans being asked to inflict extreme pain on companions merely because a high status experimenter in a prestigious institution had requested them to do so and paid their expenses. The important question was at what stage in the experiment would they refuse to continue. The results (Table 6.2) show that the majority (65 per cent) continued to the end.

Milgram (1964) then varied this to see the effect of group

Table 6.2 *Distribution of break-off points*

Verbal designation and voltage indication	Number of subjects for whom this was maximum shock
Slight shock	
15	0
30	0
45	0
60	0
Moderate shock	
75	0
90	0
105	0
120	0
Strong shock	
135	0
150	0
165	0
180	0
Very strong shock	
195	0
210	0
225	0
240	0
Intense shock	
255	0
270	0
285	0
300	5
Extreme intensity shock	
315	4
330	2
345	1
360	1
Danger: severe shock	
375	1
390	0
405	0
420	0
XXX	
435	0
450	26

(Milgram, 1963)

pressure. In this experiment the subjects were alone initially and were told that they could choose the level of shock, that is they did not have to keep increasing it. These same subjects then repeated the experiment as members of a group of four in which, unknown to them, the other members were stooges. If the learner were to make a mistake all four members of the group could suggest a shock level and the lowest would be taken, and the experimental subjects were told that they were to speak last and administer the shock. The three stooges suggested ever-increasing levels of shock. The results (Fig. 6.7) show that the subjects gave higher levels of shock in the group situation but did not go as high as the stooges suggested. In another experiment (1965a) Milgram looked

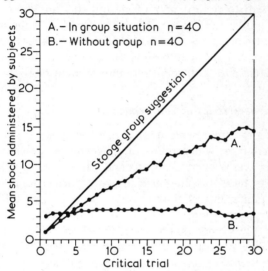

Fig. 6.7 *Mean shock levels in experimental and control conditions over thirty critical trials*
(Milgram, 1964)

at the effects of a disobedient group. In this situation at the tenth error the first stooge said that he would not go on despite the experimenters protests and at the fourteenth the second stooge refused. In this condition the naive subjects were much more likely to stop before the end so that the group seems to have counteracted the influence of the experimenter.

Milgram's distinction between action and signal conformity is an extension of Kelman's (1958) between 'public' versus 'private' change. Kelman suggested that there are three discrete responses to attempted social influence namely compliance, identification, and internalization. In compliance, A conforms to B because B can reward or punish him, and therefore A's change is dependent on B's power and the change will only be exhibited when B is in a position to affect A. Compliance tells us nothing about A's private opinions, merely his public behaviour – that is he signals conformity, but may only act on it if B is present. With identi-fication, A conforms because he feels he has something in common with B and his relationship with B is important. Thus, as long as the relationship lasts, A will conform to B irrespective of whether B is present to reward or punish, and this implies a private as well as a public adherence to B's norm. Internalization means that A finds that he agrees with B and therefore changes his mind in response to B's arguments, thus the change becomes part of A's value system and is thus entirely independent of B.

2.2 *Characteristics of conformers*

In all of the experiments quoted there were some subjects who did not conform which raises the question of the characteristics of conformers. Wiener, Carpenter and Carpenter (1956) found that conformity measures did correlate with other types of behaviour such as punctuality. Beloff (1958) reported a sex difference in that high ascendency (as measured by the AS Reaction Study Inventory) in women and low ascendency in men correlated with acquiescence whereas high neuroticism in men (as measured by the Maudsley Personality Inventory) and low neuroticism in women correlated with acquiescence. In addition Beloff found that authoritarianism seemed to be related to conformity. This led her to conclude that acquiescent women are more stable, and acqui-escent men more submissive and neurotic. This is an interesting result and her interpretation is that if many acts of acquiescence lead to someone who is submissive, one could expect conventional women to be true to type and thus be acquiescent. On the other hand the conventional picture of a man does not stress submission so that a conventional man who is acquiescent in a group is, by definition not conforming to the wider norm of male behaviour: he will thus feel a measure of conflict and this could explain the higher neuroticism scores of the acquiescent men. Men are therefore faced with two inconsistent positions: either they conform to the wider norm and do not acquiesce in a group, or they acquiesce to the group norm and thus violate the wider norm. Women, on the other hand, can acquiesce in a group and, by their acquiescence, adhere to the wider norm; their behaviour is thus consistent. It would be interesting to replicate this study using women who are adhering to a different norm of female behaviour, for example members of a women's liberation group, to see if their responses would be similar to those of the men.

In a very early study Newcomb (1943) showed that conformity and independence are not, necessarily, unitary concepts. The same response of conformity may have different interpretations depending on the context. He looked at Bennington, a small women's college, at which students were mainly from conservative homes and came with a conservative set of values, whereas the faculty were radical. What then was the effect of the faculty's radicalism on the attitude of the students over the three-year period of their stay? Newcomb divided those who had been radicalized and those who had not, into several subsets.

1 *Non conformers* – i.e. they remained conservative.
   (a) Those who were not aware of the radical norm and who had therefore not changed. They clung together and reinforced each other's attitudes.
   (b) Those who were aware of the college radical norm and rejected it.
   (c) Those who were aware but were keener on their parents values and therefore did not change.
2 *Conformers* – i.e. those who changed in a radical direction.
   (a) Those who were not aware that they had changed, they had just drifted with the tide.
   (b) Those who were aware of the change and agreed with the faculty attitude.
   (c) Those who were aware and actively trying to change others.

There has been a considerable amount of work on the relationship between birth order and conformity (Becker and Carroll, 1962; Becker, Lerner and Carroll, 1964, 1966). These experimenters argued (1966) that if a distinction is made between normative and informational material (Deutsch and Gerard, 1955) first-borns, who are prone to look to others for approval and support (see p. 108), would conform in a normative situation – that is where approval was invoked, whereas later-borns, who use others as a reservoir of information, would conform more when the others offered information. To oversimplify, first-borns look to others to see if they are lovable, later-borns to see if they are correct. Therefore in a study (1964), using the classic Asch situation (see p. 106) that had twenty-four first-born subjects, and twenty-four later-borns, with eighteen of the sample being Puerto Ricans. The hypotheses were:

1 First-borns will yield more frequently than will later-borns.
2 Puerto Rican children will yield more frequently than will native American children.
3 First-born Puerto Ricans will yield more frequently than will later-born Puerto Ricans or first-born native Americans, who, in turn, will yield more frequently than will later-born native American children.

Their hypotheses were confirmed but it was shown that first-born Puerto Ricans did not yield more than later-born Puerto Ricans which may suggest that the birth order effect is specific to certain cultures. They then varied the conditions (1966) and found that if the group was to be rewarded by tickets to a match for a correct solution the first-borns yielded most, but in a memory condition, when the Asch (1956) lines were removed and the subjects had to remember the originals, the later-borns yielded most, that is they deferred to peers when information was involved. This study shows that different people will conform depending on the situation and the *kind* of dependence on others required.

The circumstances and structure of a situation can also affect conformity as Milgram (1965b) demonstrated in a further variation on his original study in which he increased the saliency of the learner. Here he had four conditions: first, remote feedback as in the first experimental condition; second, verbal contact with the learners saying 'experimenter, get me out of here'; third, the learners and the teachers in the same room; and fourth, a touch condition in which the teachers had to press the leaners hands onto the electrodes to administer the shock. The results indicated that increased saliency caused the subjects to abandon the experiment earlier. Thirty-five per cent of the subjects defied the experimenter in the original condition, 37.5 per cent in voice feedback, 60 per cent in proximity, and 70 per cent in touch proximity. In the 'Bridgeport' experiment (1965b) the experimental design was the same as the Yale condition but the experiment took place in a rundown office block by a group ostensibly called 'Bridgeport research associates' and the subjects were told that this was a private firm doing research for industry. The result was a lower level of obedience but still 48 per cent of the subjects continued to the end.

Salmon (1969) studied sixty primary school boys aged ten to eleven to see the extent to which they conformed to peer or to adult pressure. She found that conforming to one or the other was associated with the degree to which the child accepted peer or adult values. She had administered a sociometric test two years previously and found that the children who enjoyed high social status at that time were more likely to conform to peers at the time of her present experiment whereas those who currently had high status showed no such effect.

2.3 *Non-conformity*

Jahoda (1959) having surveyed the conformity literature wondered how non-conformity was possible and remarked that nevertheless, 'the task of psychology ... is to understand human behaviour and not merely the behaviour of majorities however large or significant'. She presented a scheme for classifying types of conformity (Table 6.3) in terms of the person's initial investment in the issue, whether they changed position and whether their private opinion differed from their public one. Although we may thus distinguish many levels of conformity, independence is capable of even more variations. A distinction is sometimes made between 'anti-conformers', in other words those who always go against the majority and are thus as dependent on majority opinion as those who conform, and 'independents' who sometimes yield and sometimes maintain their original position. Moscovici and Faucheux (1972) argued that if the larger group was lacking in consensus another member was less likely to conform, thus drawing attention to the importance of behavioural style in inducing conformity. They maintained that social influence is exemplified by two processes in addition to

Table 6.3 *Types of conformity and independence*

Initial investment in issue	Yes				No			
Adoption of advocated position	No		Yes		No		Yes	
Private opinion differs from public opinion	No	Yes	No	Yes	No	Yes	No	Yes
Designation of process	a	b	c	d	e	f	g	h

(Jahoda, 1959)

conformity namely 'normalization' and 'innovation'. Normalization is a bargaining process by means of which individuals reach
consensus; to arrive at the final statement each adapts his original
position slightly until a general agreement is obtained and outright
conflict avoided. Innovation, or successful social influence by
minorities, is less researched than conformity but Moscovici and
Faucheux argued that innovation requires a conflict situation so
that group norms are eroded and the stage is set for the creation
of a new norm. This insight allowed them to make the following
distinction: '[innovation] revolves around the creation of conflicts,
just as normalization revolves around the avoidance, and conformity around the control or resolution of conflicts.'

2.4 *The function of social influence*

Since people in groups do influence one another, *why* do people
respond to social influence? There are several theoretical approaches to answering this question. If a person is concerned with
making sense of the world in which he lives it seems likely that
he will attempt to order its elements in a way which reduces
ambiguity and results in a balanced picture. Starting from the idea
of balance, Festinger (1957) produced the idea of dissonance by
distinguishing between propositions which are 'consonant' with
one another – that is they follow logically or psychologically (a
generous man will give money freely); those which are 'dissonant'
or mutually exclusive (a generous man who turns out to be a miser);

and propositions with an irrelevant relationship (a generous man who has red hair). Having made this distinction, he argued that people dislike dissonance and will change their attitudes or opinions in order to reduce it. The strength of his theoretical formulation was that it led to some non-obvious experimental predictions which were subsequently upheld. Festinger and Carlsmith (1959) required their experimental subjects to spend an hour on a boring task and then gave them either $1 or $20 to tell another subject, who was awaiting his turn, that they had an exciting time. At the end of the experimental session a control group (who had worked on the full task but had not had to lie about it), the $1 liars and the $20 liars were asked to say how much they had in fact enjoyed the task. The $1 group expressed most liking for the task which, in dissonance terms, means that since $1 could not justify the lie, they had to pretend to themselves that the task really was interesting whereas those being paid $20 could believe that the task was dull but that the high payment justified the lie. Obviously this result can be interpreted differently but nevertheless the reduction of dissonance as a motivating force in social interaction needs to be taken seriously.

Other theorists (Thibaut and Kelley, 1959; Nord, 1969) posit a simpler, capitalist exchange model which says that people are influenced by others because of the psychological rewards this brings them. Social behaviour thus becomes a market place, or stock exchange, wherein people are motivated to maximize their rewards and minimize their losses through compliance or domination by means of negotiation and bargaining. This model seems intuitively acceptable but raises the more awkward question as to what is rewarding about the rewards; why do people value a social approval, or, for that matter, why do they act to reduce dissonance? A speculative answer to this would be along the lines that man is a social animal and hence strategies of social behaviour are an essential part of his species' being. To say that men exist in groups is not therefore to tell us something additional about man but rather to draw attention to one element in the definition of the concept 'man'.

Further reading

Abercrombie, M. L. J. (1970) *Aims and Techniques of Group Teaching.* Pamphlet No. 2. London: Society for Research into Higher Education.
Davis, J. H. (1969) *Group Performance.* Reading, Mass.: Addison-Wesley.
Fiedler, F. E. (1967) *A Theory of Leadership Effectiveness.* New York: McGraw-Hill.
Gahagan, J. (1975) *Interpersonal and Group Behaviour.* London: Methuen.
Milgram, S. (1974) *Obedience to Authority.* London: Tavistock.
Smith, P. B. (1973) *Groups within Organisations.* London: Harper and Row.

[7]
Classroom behaviour

If psychology is the study of human behaviour then the analysis of classroom behaviour falls within its province, despite the fact that a considerable amount of this work is not done by psychologists nor is it normally reported in the more widely known psychological journals. The analysis of classroom behaviour by any one of the methods described in this chapter, is one way of teasing out the complex interactive variables that together form 'a class'. It also underlines the fact that a classroom is a social system which cannot be understood if this dimension is inadequately considered.

Initially, interest in classroom behaviour arose out of attempts to characterize 'effective' teaching and, as in leadership research (see p. 139), there were attempts to link teacher characteristics with pupil achievement. Although there were some positive findings, as Gages' (1965) five components of effective teaching – warmth, cognitive organization, orderliness, indirectness and problem solving ability – and Gross and Herriott's (1965) linking of higher morale, increased professional performance by teachers and high pupil achievement with heads who exhibited 'executive professional leadership'. In general these studies proved to be unwieldy and unreliable: 'these studies have yielded disappointing results: correlations that are non significant, inconsistent from one study to the next, and usually lacking in psychological and educational meaning' (Gage, 1963).

A similar approach was to relate teacher personality to pupil behaviour and perhaps the largest study, which has a certain relevance, was the Teacher Characteristic Study carried out under Ryans' direction (1960) which covered more than 6,000 teachers. He found that it was possible to extract certain contrasting characteristics which could then be used for diagnostic purposes (Table 7.1).

Table 7.1 *Teacher characteristics*

Warm, understanding, friendly *v.* aloof, egocentric, restrictive classroom behaviour.

Responsible, business-like, systematic *v.* evading, unplanned, slipshod classroom behaviour.

Stimulating, imaginative *v.* dull, routine classroom behaviour.

Favourable *v.* unfavourable opinions of pupils.

Favourable *v.* unfavourable opinions of democratic classroom procedures.

Favourable *v.* unfavourable opinions of administrative and other school personnel.

Learning centred (traditional) *v.* child centred (permissive) educational viewpoints.

Superior verbal understanding (comprehension) *v.* poor verbal understanding.

Emotional stability (adjustment) *v.* instability.

(Ryans, 1960)

As in leadership research, studies of characteristics were accompanied by, and gave way to, situational studies which stressed 'the teacher in the classroom'. This approach gave rise to two related methods of research, firstly studies of 'classroom climate' and, secondly, the systematic observation of teacher/pupil or pupil/pupil interaction in which the techniques of interaction analysis were also often used to assess classroom climate.

were arguing that teacher/pupil relations were interdependent and that pupils' emotional and teachers' professional needs had to be met in order to generate a positive atmosphere. During the 1960s, studies of classroom climate became more sophisticated and complex with Schmuck (1966) relating teacher behaviour to climate. He found that teachers with a positive emotional climate spoke to more pupils, made specific statements of praise to pupils who had been co-operative but made general statements when they wished to control unruly behaviour, unlike teachers with negative climates who concentrated on fewer pupils, took little notice of slower pupils, and both rewarded less and punished individuals more for misbehaviour. During this decade environmental variables were included, for example Biddle and Adams (1967) discussed four contributory variables, namely teacher behaviour, pupil behaviour, social environment and physical environment, and Gump (1964) went so far as to argue that teachers were most effective when they manipulated the environment rather than when they acted as a stimulus.

However, once the classroom became an area of research its very complexity caused the categories of analysis to multiply as in Cornell, Lindvall and Saupe's (1952) 'classroom observation code digest' in which the dimensions used were:

1 *Differentiation* ... the extent to which provision is made for individual differences among students.
2 *Social organization* ... the type of group structure and the pattern of interaction among individuals.
3 *Initiative* ... the extent to which pupils are permitted to control the learning situation.
4 *Content* ... the source and organization of the content of learning.
5 *Variety* ... the extent to which a variety of activities or techniques are used.
6 *Competency* ... differences in the technical performances of teachers.
7 *Classroom climate* ... social emotional climate.

It therefore soon became apparent that there was a need to make a more systematic choice of variables to be coded.

In the late fifties Medley and Mitzel (1958, 1959) developed OScAR (Observation Schedule And Record) which '... was

designed to permit recording of as many possible significant
aspects of what goes on in a classroom as possible, regardless of
their relationship to any dimension or scale' (Gage, 1963). This
was considerably more sophisticated than earlier attempts and led
on to the serious study of interaction analysis which flourished
in the sixties.

A more recent and important study in the classroom climate
tradition was that of Kounin (1970) which combined both field
study and observation but was primarily concerned with the techniques of classroom management. Kounin defined 'successful'
classrooms as 'those having a high prevalence of work involvement
and a low measure of misbehaviour in learning settings'. Through
videotapes, interviews and questionnaires, he correlated certain
forms of teacher behaviour with their amount of 'success' in the
classroom. There were five major behavioural categories: first,
'withitness' and 'overlapping' which referred to the teacher's ability
to know what was going on, 'having eyes in the back of her head',
and being able to attend to two things at the same time ('withitness' was found to be the most significant and was an important
factor in teacher success); second, 'smoothness' and 'momentum'
which covered the teacher's ability to keep the pace going during
recitations and in transitions from one activity to another; third,
'group alerting' and 'accountability' which distinguished the
teacher who could catch and maintain the attention of the group
rather than concentrate solely on an individual child to the exclusion
of the others (this measure indicated that keeping children involved
and alert was more important than following up their work); fourth,
'valence' and 'challenge arousal'; and fifth, 'seatwork variety' and
'challenge' which together underlined the importance of variety,
especially for younger children.

1.2 Interaction analysis

Interaction analysis is a systematic means of analysing classroom
behaviour in terms of predetermined categories. The most usual
method is for an observer to either sit in a classroom or to work
from audio or visual recordings. He has a schedule, or system
(see Table 7.2), which assigns category numbers to 'bits' of
behaviour. He can then either write down a category number each

time the behaviour, speaker or topic changes; or he can use time sampling so that, for example, every three seconds, he writes down whichever category is appropriate for the behaviour taking place at that particular moment. Whole lessons or parts of lessons can be coded, and the specific method – whether change or timed units – is stipulated in the schedule.

Table 7.2 *Categories for the Flanders system of interaction analysis*

Indirect influence	1* Accepts feeling: accepts and clarifies the feeling tone of the students in a non-threatening manner. Feelings may be positive or negative. Predicting or recalling feelings are included.
	2* Praises or encourages: praises or encourages student action or behaviour. Jokes that release tension, not at the expense of another individual, nodding head or saying, 'um hm?' or 'go on' are included.
	3* Accepts or uses ideas of student: clarifying, building, or developing ideas suggested by a student. As a teacher brings more of his own ideas into play, shift to category five.
	4* Asks questions: asking a question about content or procedure with the intent that a student answer.

Teacher talk

Direct influence	5* Lecturing: giving facts or opinions about content or procedure; expressing his own ideas, asking rhetorical questions.
	6* Giving directions: directions, commands, or orders to which a student is expected to comply.
	7* Criticizing or justifying authority: statements intended to change student behaviour from non-acceptable to acceptable pattern; bawling someone out; stating why the teacher is doing what he is doing; extreme self-reference.

8* Student talk–response: a student makes a predictable response to teacher. Teacher initiates the contact or solicits student statement and sets limits to what the student says.

Student   9* Student talk–initiation: talk by students which
talk   they initiate. Unpredictable statements in response to teacher. Shift from 8 to 9 as student introduces own ideas.

10* Silence or confusion: pauses, short periods of silence and periods of confusion in which communication cannot be understood by the observer.

---

* There is NO scale implied by these numbers. Each number is classificatory, it designates a particular kind of communication event. To write these numbers down during observation is to enumerate, not to judge a position on a scale.

(from Flanders, 1970a)

In *Mirrors for Behaviour II* (a most useful compendium of systems), Simon and Boyer (1970) characterize observation systems as a 'meter language' which they say should be, 'descriptive rather than evaluative, deal with what can be categorized or measured and must deal with *bits* of action or behaviour not global concepts'. They group the categories covered by the systems into seven main classes:

1 Affective – the emotional content of communication.
2 Cognitive – the intellectual content of communication.
3 Psychomotor – non verbal behaviours, posture, body position, facial expression and gestures.
4 Activity – what is being done that relates a person to someone or something else (e.g. reading or hitting).
5 Content – what is being talked about.
6 Sociological structure – the sociology of the interactive setting, including who is talking to whom and in what roles.
7 Physical environment – description of the physical space in which the observation is taking place, including materials and equipment being used.

Perhaps the easiest way of gaining an overview of this vast and expanding field is to consider selected systems in more detail with examples of some categories (for full details of these and other systems consult Simon and Boyer, 1970).

Flanders' category system. Probably the best known of all systems is that of Flanders (Table 7.2) which relates to classroom climate and is particularly concerned with the balance between 'initiation' and 'response'. By 'initiation' Flanders (1970a) means, 'to make the first move, to lead, to begin, to introduce an idea or concept for the first time, to express one's own will', and by response 'to take action after an initiation, to counter, to amplify or react to ideas which have already been expressed, to conform or even to comply to the will expressed by others'. He has now produced an expanded system (Flanders, 1970b) in order to get a finer analysis. A further elaboration is that of Amidon and Hunter (1970) which uses affective and cognitive categories in order to tease out more complex response behaviours.

Coding teacher behaviour. There are, as is to be expected, many schedules relating specifically to teacher behaviour. Hughes was concerned with the teacher's ability to create a climate for learning by analysing various functions of teacher behaviour, for example controlling, aiding, developing and clarifying content and responding to pupil's needs. A most inclusive system is the 'taxonomy of teacher behaviour' of Openshaw and Cyphert (Table 7.3). Based on other category systems it is designed to provide the data for comparative studies of teacher behaviour. In contrast Ribble and Schultz's system focuses on a single problem namely 'the congruence between the teacher's choice of objectives to be implemented and the behaviour chosen to implement those objectives'.

Table 7.3 *Categories for a taxonomy of teacher behaviour*
(M. K. Openshaw and F. R. Cyphert)

A given encounter is categorized in each of the four dimensions. Each encounter may have shifts within the *Sign dimensions*. Furthermore, a given behaviour may be classified in more than one category of the *Function dimension*. Any change in the *Source* and *Direction* dimensions indicates a new encounter.

Table 7.3 *Categories for a taxonomy of teacher behaviour—cont.*

The instrument is presented in brief form below:

I.	Source dimension	Indicates the origin of an encounter.
	A. Originate	The source of the behaviour is undiscernible within the classroom setting.
	B. Respond	The source of the behaviour is some discernible aspect of the classroom setting.
II.	Direction dimension	Indicates the target to which the behaviour is directed.
	A. Individual	Behaviour focused on one person.
	B. Group	Behaviour focused on more than one person but less than the total class.
	C. Class	Behaviour focused on the whole class.
	D. Object	Behaviour focused on inanimate element in physical environment.
III.	Sign dimension	Indicates the mode of communication of an encounter.
	A. Speak	Behaviour characterized by spontaneous speech.
	B. Read	Behaviour characterized by oral reading of (printed) written matter.
	C. Gesture	Behaviour characterized by purposive body movement.
	D. Perform	Behaviour characterized by demonstration, non-verbal illustration, singing, etc.
	E. Write	Behaviour characterized by chalkboard presentation, writing on a chart, or overhead projector foil, etc., but excluding drawing.
	F. Silence	Behaviour characterized by an absence of other signs.
	G. Laugh	Behaviour characterized by inarticulate sound of mirth or derision.
IV.	Function dimension	Indicates the purpose of the behaviour within an encounter.
	A. Structure	Set the context and focus of subsequent subject matter and/or process.
	1 Initiate	Introduce and launch an activity, task, or area for study.
	2 Order	Arrange elements of subject matter and/or process in a systematic manner.
	3 Assign	Designate required activity.

B. Develop   Elaborate and extend within an established structure.
  1 Inform   State facts, ideas, concepts, etc.
  2 Explain   Show relationship between ideas, objects, principles, etc.
  3 Check   Request information concerning understanding.
  4 Elicit   Solicit a verbal response that states facts, ideas, concepts, etc.
  5 Test   Conduct a written quiz or examination – dictate questions, supply answers, without explanation.
  6 Reinforce   Confirm or sustain an idea, approach, or method through reiteration.
  7 Summarize   Restate principal points in brief form.
  8 Stimulate   Foster student involvement and participation.

C. Administer   Execute tasks of classroom routine and procedure.
  1 Manipulate   Arrange elements of the classroom environments, personal and physical. (Cause others to do something.)
  2 Manage material   Provide or co-ordinate use of media, supplies, or materials.
  3 Routine   Request information regarding compliance with individual, class or school expectations (regulation).
  4 Proctor   Monitor classroom during group activity, testing, student teacher performance, etc.

D. Regulate   Establish and maintain interpersonal relations.
  1 Set standard Impose or guide development of standards of behaviour.
  2 Support   Express confidence, commendation, or empathy.
  3 Restrict   Reprimand, threaten, punish, etc.
  4 Assist   Provide personal help; does for.
  5 Inquire   Ascertain student involvement.
  6 Monitor-Self Recognize and interpret teacher's behaviour. (Check own understanding.)

E. Evaluate   Ascertain the relevance or correctness of subject matter and/or process.

1 Appraise	Verify by appeal to external evidence or authority.
2 Opine	Judge on the basis of personal values and beliefs.
3 Stereotype	React without stated reference to criteria or person.

Further refinements

1. The addition of the *Direction dimension* was found to be necessary when the system was checked against the paradigm theorized to contain the essential elements of teacher classroom behaviour. There is a need for still further testing of this dimension.
2. The *Stimulate* sub-category could be more critically defined so that some of those behaviours without observable relationship to the extension of the content or process of the lesson formerly coded under *Develop – Stimulate* could more logically find a place under the *Regulate* category.

(from Simon and Boyer, 1970)

Schedules related to cognitive aspects of the classroom. Some schedules pay attention to cognitive aspects of classroom behaviour and arise from a particular theoretical orientation towards cognitive development for example that of Aschner–Gallagher which draws on Guilford's theories of intellect (see p. 11). This particular schedule has five major categories: (1) cognitive memory, (2) convergent thinking, (3) evaluative thinking, (4) divergent thinking, (5) routine thinking. In a short, but revealing, system Gallagher (1970) uses three-number codes to reflect his division between content and skills, levels of conceptualization and types of teaching. A particularly interesting system is that of Denny, Rusch and Ives on the relationship between the teacher's behaviour and the pupils' creative thinking.

The analysis of non-verbal behaviour. Predictably the majority of systems rely on verbal behaviour but there are a minority which attempt to code non-verbal behaviour. Lindvall, Yeager, Wang and Wood focus on pupil activity and Spaulding's two complementary schedules are unique in being designed to be used with pupils as young as two years. Hall has developed a system for describing proxemic behaviour which is detailed and inclusive and is 'to describe behaviours which make up cultural patterns about which most people are not aware but which profoundly affect interactions' (see p. 117).

Analysis of specific subject areas. Some systems relate to specific areas of teaching such as science and mathematics. One of these (Wragg, Table 7.4) is British and is an attempt to apply the Flanders system in the context of a foreign language lesson, to compare teacher/pupil interaction when English is being spoken with the interaction when the foreign language is being spoken.

Table 7.4 *Categories for the Wragg system* (E. C. Wragg)

	In native language	In foreign language	
	1	11	Accepts feeling: accepts and clarifies the feeling tone of the students in a non-threatening manner. Feelings may be positive or negative. Predicting and re-calling feelings are included.
Indirect influence	2	12	Praises or encourages: praises or en-courages student action or behaviour. Jokes that release tension, not at the expense of another individual, nodding head or saying 'uh huh?' or 'go on' or their equivalent in the foreign language are included.
	3	13	Accepts or uses ideas of student: clarify-ing, building, or developing ideas or suggestions by a student. As teacher brings more of his own ideas into play, shift to category five or fifteen.
	4	14	Asks questions: asking a question about content or procedure with the intent that a student answer.
Teacher talk	5	15	Lectures: giving facts or opinions about content or procedure; expressing his own idea; asking rhetorical questions.

Table 7.4 *Categories for the Wragg system—cont.*

	In native language	In foreign language	
Direct influence	6	16	Gives directions: directions, commands, or orders with which a student is expected to comply.
	7	17	Criticizes or justifies authority: statements, intended to change student behaviour from non-acceptable to acceptable pattern; bawling someone out; stating why the teacher is doing what he is doing, extreme self-reference.
	8	18	Student talk-response: talk by students in response to teacher. Teacher initiates the contact or solicits student statement.
Student talk	9	19	Student talk-initiation: talk by students, which they initiate. If 'calling on' student is only to indicate who may talk next, observer must decide whether student wanted to talk. If he did, use this category.
	10	20	Silence or confusion: pauses, short periods of silence, and periods of confusion in which communication cannot be understood by the observer. For silence following talk in the foreign language use category 20.

(from Simon and Boyer, 1970)

A slightly different approach is that of Herbert (1967) who presented a system for analysing *lessons*, not teacher/pupil interaction, starting from the idea of a lesson having six components (Fig. 7.1) which together make up a lesson. The 'structure' of the lesson is thus 'the pattern of changes that have been effected in the components through the course of a lesson'. Herbert's system charts each component change, thus revealing the structure of the lesson, with the sole aim of making the teacher aware of what he is doing. His modesty concerning the utility of such instruments is applicable to virtually all classroom research, 'It will not necessarily make them better teachers. The relationship between the criticism and the practice of any art, craft, or science is always problematical.'

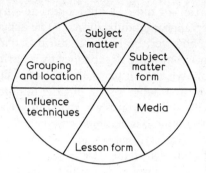

Fig. 7.1 *Components of the lesson*
(Herbert, 1967)

Limitations of interaction analysis. Interaction-analysis systems are impressive instruments but teachers may wonder how effective they are in practice. Many are used on initial training courses as a means of alerting student teachers to the multi-dimensional nature of classroom activity; but they are likely to be of even more use to the established teacher who wishes to improve his performance, as they do claim to provide an objective way of assessing what he is, in practice, doing compared with what he thinks he is doing. They are, of course, a reliable tool for educational researchers provided they are used for testing hypotheses and not applied indiscriminately. However, there are some limitations of their usefulness in that they can be difficult to administer accurately and thus require the operators to be well trained. The amount of data generated may also prove difficult to analyse without easy access to a computer. It is for these reasons that the relatively simple Flanders system has proved so popular.

Although these systems give information on what is happening in the classroom and when, they ignore the question 'why' thus making it impossible to analyse the different intentions behind behaviour which may appear superficially similar. They thereby fail to take into account how that behaviour is perceived and interpreted by the participants. The context of the behaviour is

largely unexamined so that, for instance, in a formal school where
the major teaching strategy is teacher exposition, a teacher who
uses even a small amount of indirect questioning may be perceived by the pupils as permissive, whereas in a 'free range' school
the *same* proportion of indirect questioning to direct exposition
would make her appear unduly formal. The schedules of both
teachers would, however, be identical and differential effects on
pupil performance could only be explained by referring to the effect
of that particular style in that particular school. Thus the systems
can give data on the teacher's style but the interpretation of the
significance of this style requires a wider study relating to school
ethos and teacher/pupil expectations.

Perhaps their greatest disadvantage is that the categories are
pre-determined and even if they are based on a well-established
theoretical position, or intuitively credible, the suspicion remains
that the teacher or researcher by concentrating on those aspects
of the situation identified by the schedule may overlook other
aspects which are as relevant, if not more so, to the object of his
inquiry. Nevertheless, the complexity of human interaction neces-
sitates some selection and these systems, which provide a rationale
for selection, do have an obvious value.

Before using any system the teacher/researcher would be wise
to examine the assumptions underlying the schedule, for example
the nature of its theoretical background as in the Aschner–
Gallagher schedule based on Guilford, or Solomon's based on
Piaget and Bruner, which focuses on the teacher's ability to work
with levels of 'imagery' in the classroom. Other schedules assume
a certain teaching style (cf. Flanders), or are intended for pupils
of a certain age. Very few, if any, seem to take account of the
possibility of the host of trivial interruptions that beset the average
classroom and would interfere with time sampling. If the observer
is not clear on these points he may try to apply a system in a
totally unsuitable situation with the result that the coding will be
neither valid nor reliable.

The fact that the majority of systems are American should not
deter the British teacher, as one British schedule (Barnes) produced
similar profiles in Britain and America, suggesting that the role
of teacher is perceived and played in a similar manner in both
countries. But it is to be hoped that more British schedules will
be developed.

1.3 *Contextual studies*

An alternative means of observing behaviour in the classroom is to use an unstructured, open-ended field observation approach which attempts to gain information on a wide range of phenomena. As early as 1951 Wright, Barker, Nall and Schoggen were arguing that 'an adequate psychological ecology of the classroom must describe the psychological habitats that *are* brought about in the setting and the particular behaviours which these habitats engender'. This they felt indicated the need for observers who would keep a full, anecdotal, record leading a 'naturalistic', unstructured, description of the pupils' behaviour. Sometimes called the 'anthropological approach', this orientation has its roots in both the participant/observer studies of sociologists or anthropologists and the descriptive sketches of the fictional or semi-autobiographical writers.

This type of research usually takes place over a lengthy period with the observer aiming to integrate himself with the class. His methods range from direct observation, through questionnaires, to lengthy, informal interviews with both pupils and teachers. It is surprising that classroom research for at least a decade has failed to make use of such an obvious source of information as the participants themselves. When attempting to understand classroom behaviour no one seems to have thought of asking pupils and teachers what they thought they were doing and listening carefully to their answers.

Delamont (1976) made an extended study of this kind, in a girls' private school and was able to show how valuable this approach is as a complement to interaction analysis. Having looked at the Flanders schedules of eighteen teachers she considered four in detail. These four she called Latin A, Latin B, Physics A and Biology A. Latin A and Latin B were similar to each other in their proportion of acceptance of ideas and in their low proportion of pupil-initiated speech, but differed considerably in the proportion of questioning to lecturing in their speech. Physics A and Biology A were both unlike the other scientists by having a lower proportion of questioning and lecturing than their colleagues, and a higher proportion of pupil-initiated speech. They also accepted and used a higher proportion of pupil contributions.

For her analysis she picked out four themes: (1) the physical ng created by each of the teachers; (2) their personal appearance; (3) the pupils' opinions of each teacher; and (4) evidence from dialogue recorded during their lessons. The results showed that Latin A had a permanent classroom, with almost bare walls into which the pupils entered in silence. She dressed in classic tweeds, and taught by formal methods from a fixed position in front of the class. The extracts from her lessons showed that she was clearly in control, asked the girls, in turn, to translate one sentence and demanded answers. The pupils only spoke when they corrected one another's mistakes. Their opinion of her was unanimous – 'frightening', 'cross', 'strict', 'efficient', 'makes us work' and 'a really good teacher'.

In contrast Latin B did not have a permanent classroom and often arrived together with the pupils at the room allocated to her for that period. Her clothing was fashionable, she carried knitting around in a shopping basket and had a large engagement ring on her finger. Her teaching methods were informal and she often sat in a relaxed manner perched on a pupil's desk. She asked the girls to speak, encouraging them to give their own interpretations. The pupils had a much wider range of opinions on her than on Latin A. There was agreement that she was 'easily led astray' but otherwise some found her 'good' others 'bad' some 'efficient' others 'inefficient'.

The science teachers, although having similar Flanders profiles, when looked at in more detail, turned out to have very different classrooms. Biology A had a new laboratory full of exhibits which expressed life and movement. She, like Physics A, was married with children which was unusual in this school, but her style of dress was similar to her colleagues'. The other science staff kept their lessons moving swiftly, using worksheets and timetables, and with brisk talk and rapid movements drilled the pupils. Biology A, in contrast, gave the impression of having plenty of time. She moved slowly, never drilled the girls and was always prepared to discuss other aspects of biology as they arose. The lesson extracts showed that she emphasized deduction. The pupils realized that this teacher's style was unlike her colleagues but felt that her methods were effective and that they remembered more even though she appeared to 'teach' them less.

Physics A had an old and somewhat stuffy laboratory and chose to keep her electrical equipment in chocolate boxes. She was more casually and more brightly dressed than the others but her lessons 'appeared rushed and disorganized', making the girls unsure what they were meant to be doing. Frequently the practical work ran overtime leaving the girls no chance for discussion and causing them to rush to get the room cleared up. Her lesson extracts showed that her approach was more disjointed although she was clearly attempting a 'guided discovery' approach. The pupils agreed that she was 'muddling' and felt that her methods were ineffective. Their assessment of her was 'a nice clever person who was *unable* to teach'.

A study such as this points up the intensely personal nature of classrooms and the need for research which can take account of these important dimensions in a systematic manner.

1.4 *Transactional studies*

These various approaches to the study of classroom behaviour have led to an increased emphasis, which again parallels leadership research, to the transactional nature of the situation. The 'good' teacher may well be the rare 'will o' the wisp', but 'good' teaching in a particular context is clearly related to certain types of teaching strategy being more or less effective for certain types of pupil. Washburne and Heil (1960) carried out a neat transactional study by dividing teachers into three categories – 'spontaneous', 'orderly' and 'fearful' – and then further subdivided each category into two groups – 'superior', 'inferior' – depending on the warmth of their relationships with pupils. Pupils were then classified as 'strivers', 'docile conformers' and 'opposers'. All possible combinations were then examined for their effect on pupil achievement and the results showed that a scale of 'effectiveness' could be produced.

The three most effective styles were, in descending order:

1 Superior orderly (warm, dominant, orderly).
2 Superior spontaneous (warm, expressive, lively, independent, encouraged pupils to express their own ideas).
3 Superior fearful (warm, conscientious almost obsessive and fearful).

The poorest style was the inferior spontaneous.

In terms of pupil characteristics it was shown that 'strivers' did well regardless of teacher characteristics, 'docile conformers' were most successful with 'superior spontaneous teachers' and 'opposers' were unsuccessful with all teachers but were best when they had 'superior orderly' teachers. Results like this have supported Thelen's (1967) argument that pupils and teachers should be matched, calling the belief that teachers should be equally effective with all pupils a 'profound hypocrisy'. He hypothesized that if teachers were asked to identify pupils with whom they thought they had been successful, and if they all identified the same students, it could be concluded that 'teachability' was a unitary trait but if they chose different students then matching pupils to teachers might seem a potentially useful strategy. The findings were that teachers *did* differ in the students they chose, and therefore a study was carried out which compared classes composed of children perceived as 'teachable' by their teacher with a control class selected at random from available children. Although this design was chosen it was possible that pupils would not choose the teachers who chose them and therefore the match of pupil choice with teacher choice would not be exact. However, to control both factors appeared to raise considerable practical problems and teacher choice became the basis of selection.

'Teachability' classes were composed by asking the teachers to name the pupils they found 'teachable'. These pupils were then given a wide range of tests. Their particular patterns of responses were then compared with the responses of the pupils who were to take part in the experiment. Where the responses of the 'experimental' pupil matched those of the 'chosen' pupil, he or she was allocated to the teacher who had originally chosen the pupil. To oversimplify, if teacher X had chosen children who scored high on items A, B and C, and teacher Y children who had scored low on those items, then when the test had been administered to the larger population, pupils with high A, B, C scores were assigned to teacher X and those with low A, B, C scores to teacher Y. The teachers then taught a 'teachable' class and a 'control' class for a year. The results showed that although the 'teachable' classes were 'more work-oriented, less inattentive, less distractable', and had 'more work solidarity, more enthusiasm in the teacher's approval of work, less rigidity, more flexibility in teaching and greater permissiveness with respect to disruptive behaviour', the correlation with achievement was zero with five classes showing superior gains and eight inferior gains. Thelen concludes that, 'Teachability grouping facilitates the accomplishment of some or most of the teacher's purpose, and in most cases, makes him more effective with whatever methods of teaching he has developed. Such facilitation, however, has educative outcomes only to the extent that the teacher's purposes are educative.'

Using case studies of five of the teachers in the experiment Thelen was able to show that

> one teacher appeared to want more vigorous, personally involving interaction with his students, another wanted a class that could penetrate deeper into the principles of algebra; another wanted a pleasant, friendly, non work oriented class that would make him feel more adequate, another wanted a class in which he could combine 'counseling' with teaching.

Provided the teacher's and children's wants were similar a supportive classroom climate would result, but one wonders if parents, who wish their children to achieve, would be particularly heartened by these results. There seems to be an assumption that a supportive atmosphere is to be welcomed as a means to the end of pupil learning but Thelen's work suggests that the means can become an end in itself to the mutual satisfaction of both pupil and teacher with the price being the divorce of 'schooling' from 'education'.

2 *Teacher/pupil interaction*

To speak of 'transactional' studies draws attention to the importance of teacher/pupil perception and pupil/pupil perception and interaction. Thelen (1967) has contrasted the way teachers categorize pupils into broad categories, 'good' (teacher-facilitative), 'bad' (teacher-hindering or obstructing), 'indifferent but nontoxic' (hardly noticed) and 'sick' (anxiety arousing); but with the complexity revealed by a factor analytic study of pupils, 'We had to discard the notion that there would be a few, neat, and all-inclusive categories of students'. Teachers did, however, as his main study showed, differ in the qualities they picked out as indicating that a pupil was teachable. McIntyre, Morrison and Sutherland (1966) made some illuminating observations when they inquired into which pupils teachers thought were worth 'taking trouble over'. In this study they demonstrated the complex nature of teachers' assessment of pupils. Teachers in middle-class schools were most interested in and concerned for boys perceived as 'pleasant', that is, those who conformed to classroom behavioural norms; whereas in suburban working-class schools it was the 'clever boy' and in urban working-class schools the 'hard working and attentive' boy. The 'ideal girl', on the other hand, was less differentiated, she was either a 'good pupil' in terms of quietness and good behaviour or valued as sociable and a leader. Older teachers, in general, were more interested in the pupils' attainments and work attitudes and younger teachers in their behaviour in class.

Nash (1976) considered this question from the pupils' viewpoint and, using a modification of Kelly's (1955) (see p. 210) technique for eliciting constructs, was able to abstract six bi-polar constructs of pupils' overriding expectations concerning teacher behaviour. These were:

1 Keeps order – unable to keep order.
2 Teaches you – doesn't teach you.
3 Explains – doesn't explain.
4 Interesting – boring.
5 Fair – unfair.
6 Friendly – unfriendly.

He argued that the children had a well-developed sense of what was acceptable teacher behaviour and what was not, and well-intentioned teachers who deviated too far from the norm were not liked. As an illustration of this he described the response of two teachers, with differing approaches, to the attempts of their pupils to 'try them out' by shouting out 'clever' remarks etc. Mrs. C. always realized and quietly met the challenge thereby showing that she perceived the situation in the same way as the children, whereas Mrs. A. tended to initially ignore challenging remarks. She reported that her aim was to get the pupils 'to internalize a value system'. What happened in practice was that when the first challenge was ignored subsequent challenges became more and more overt until the class became out of hand and she had to restore order by more authoritarian means than those used by Mrs. C. Nash maintains that trouble arose because she refused to define the situation in the way the class defined it and hence used a style that did not meet the pupils' expectations. Walker and Adelman (1976) stress the importance of understanding the significance classroom jokes and informal talk have for the participants, since they maintain that both teachers and pupils develop distinct identities during the course of a year, or even years, of working together and hence their speech becomes a kind of 'cryptic shorthand'. In informal classrooms identities are less easily developed, since there is less of an audience at any one time, but, once developed, they are 'personal' rather than 'social' identities. These identities give classroom interaction a 'long-term meaning' which would be incomprehensible to an observer on a brief visit.

Stubbs (1976) considered the function of teacher talk in some detail and found that teachers were mainly concerned with controlling the class by 'continually explaining, correcting, evaluating, editing and summarising'. Much time was spent merely in keeping in touch with their pupils. The author draws out eight functions of classroom language (Table 7.5) and shows that certain characteristics of teacher talk are very specific to the teaching situation. For example the remark 'what do you mean by X' is frequently used by teachers but not by pupils, who would be more likely to rephrase it as 'I don't understand that'; nor would it be used by teachers in speech with other adults since, Stubbs comments, it would lead to '"what do you mean", "what do I mean?",' sequences, or to the teacher being perceived as a teacher and therefore rejected.

Table 7.5 *Types of classroom language*

1 Attraction or showing attention.
2 Controlling the amount of speech ('anything else you can say about it?' 'Who's that shouting and screaming?').
3 Checking or confirming understanding.
4 Summarizing.
5 Defining.
6 Editing ('I take it you're not exaggerating?' 'That's getting nearer it').
7 Correcting.
8 Specifying topic.
9 Keeping children on the topic.

(Stubbs, 1976)

Bellack and her co-workers (1966) also researched the question of language in the classroom in some detail and concluded that present practice (that which *is* rather than what *ought* to be) can be described in terms of 'the rules of the classroom game of teaching'. In general 'the classroom game involves one person called a teacher and one or more persons called pupils. The object of the game in the classrooms observed is to carry on the discourse about subject matter, and the ostensible payoff of the game is measured in terms of the amount of learning displayed by the pupils after a given period of play.' They found five general rules – first, that they were four basic moves, all pedagogical, initiatory moves which consisted of structuring and asking for responses, and the reflexive moves of responding and reacting; second, the teacher participated most in the game; third, the teacher structured the content and the discussion and usually, but not always, initiated the discussion of irrelevant issues; fourth, all players preferred the 'empirical mode of thought (fact-stating and explaining)' to the 'analytical mode (defining terms and interpreting statements)' and the use of 'evaluative statements (opinioning and justifying)'; fifth, there was no single winner:

> Rather there are relative degrees of winning and losing, and the teacher's winnings are a function of the pupil's performances. This is a peculiar, but important, characteristic of the game. While the teacher undeniably has the greater power and freedom in the course of play, he is ultimately dependent on his pupils for the degree of success he achieves in playing the game.

Within these general rules Bellack identified specific rules for both teachers and pupils when soliciting or responding, and structuring; for example

> 'The teacher's primary role is that of solicitor', or 'The pupil's primary role is that of respondent'. The pupil most often solicits the teacher rather than a fellow pupil and when announcing the activity for a sub-game, the teacher generally states that the class will 'talk about' or 'take up' a specified topic; rarely is he more specific in indicating the type of oral activity. From experience the pupil understands that the class will engage in a verbal exchange consisting primarily of soliciting by the teacher and responding by the pupils.

3 Pupil/pupil interaction

Pupil/pupil interaction is much less researched than teacher/pupil interaction. Flanders and Havumaki (1960) showed that teacher behaviour can influence pupil behaviour since pupils who were praised by the teacher were found to receive more sociometric choices from other pupils. In their experiment teachers consistently praised pupils sitting in odd numbered seats in the experimental group and praised at random in the control group. Subsequently pupils who had sat in the odd numbered seats in the experimental group received significantly more choices than their peers.

A pupil's morale and behaviour is affected by his view of himself and his relationship with his peers. Individual morale is a function of the degree of similarity between the individual's view of himself as he is and as he would wish himself to be. Schmuck (1963) showed that classrooms with widely spread liking choices (diffuse liking structure) had a more positive climate than those with narrowly focused liking structures and that pupils who had a low status were more aware of this in the narrowly focused structure. Pupils who accurately perceived their low status were academic underachievers and had more negative attitudes towards themselves and their schools than did those who accurately perceived their high status. Pupils who actually had low status but perceived themselves as having higher status achieved more and had more positive self-images than did their more perceptively accurate peers.

What determines whether a child will be popular? Kohn (1966) found a high correlation between a child's initiating acts towards others and their acts towards him and his positive acts towards others and theirs towards him. But the most active children were more negatively treated. This suggests that 'the child creates his own environment'.

There are however some personal characteristics which account for children being perceived as acceptable by their peers. Morrison and Hallworth (1966) studied adolescent girls and found that, when assessing peers, three main dimensions were used: first 'social extraversion', which was related to 'sociability, cheerfulness, generosity and co-operation with other pupils' and which the authors hypothesize, is linked with sociometric status; second, 'the pleasant classmate' who is dependable and courteous towards others; and third, the 'non-academic leader' related to interests, games ability and leadership. These dimensions do not entirely overlap with those used by teachers suggesting that a child's status may differ when he is with peers and when with adults.

Sugarman (1968) explored the way in which children in school formed informal peer groups and the norms and values operating in these groups. His subjects were 540 fourth-form boys in four London secondary schools. He was able to categorize four types of groups (Table 7.6). Boys from homes with a lower 'intellectual

Table 7.6 *Categorization of four types of peer group*

Peer group	Achievement	Conduct	Number of peer groups	Number of pupils
Type I	Good	Good	24	99
Type II	Good	Bad	17	73
Type III	Bad	Good	9	61
Type IV	Bad	Bad	12	63

(Sugarman, 1968)

quality' who belonged to group I were found to score more highly in general in adjustment to school than did the boys from homes of 'higher intellectual quality'. However there was no evidence that boys in *any* of the groups would favour one of their peers who merely excelled in academic work. However, in all four groups popularity was associated with achievement and this, surprisingly, was particularly marked in groups III and IV. Poor conduct, although having some relation with leadership in group I and III, was negatively related to popularity in all four groups. Finally those children who had a well defined peer group were the most likely to be overachievers.

Further reading

Amidon, E. J. and Hough, J. B. (eds) (1967) *Interaction Analysis: Theory, Research and Application.* Reading, Mass.: Addison-Wesley.

Bellack, A., Kliebard, A., Hyman, H. M., Smith, R. T. and Frank, L. Jr (1966) *The Language of the Classroom.* New York: Teachers College Press.

Flanders, N. A. (1970) *Analysing Teaching Behaviour.* Reading, Mass.: Addison-Wesley.

Gage, N. L. (ed.) (1963) *Handbook of Research on Teaching.* Chicago: Rand McNally.

Herbert, J. (1967) *A System for Analysing Lessons.* New York: Teachers College Press.

Kounin, J. S. (1970) *Discipline and Group Management in Classrooms.* New York: Holt, Rinehart and Winston.

Siegel, L. (ed.) (1967) *Instruction: Some Contemporary Viewpoints.* San Francisco: Chandler.

Simon, A. and Boyer, E. G. (eds) (1970) *Mirrors for Behaviour* (2 Vols.). Philadelphia: Classroom Interaction Newsletter in co-operation with Research for Better Schools.

Stubbs, M. and Delmont, S. (1976) *Explorations in Classroom Observation.* Chichester, Sussex: John Wiley.

Thelen, H. A. (1967) *Classroom Grouping for Teachability.* New York: John Wiley.

Travers, R. M. W. (ed.) (1973) *Second Handbook of Research on Teaching.* Chicago: Rand McNally.

Section III

Focus:

The individual
in the classroom

[8]
Individual
development

*In previous chapters the phenomenon of social interaction has been
described and certain aspects of it reviewed, but one component has
been missing and that is 'the individual' who interacts with the social
milieu. A concern with social interaction needs to be complemented
by the study of the individual's own interaction, i.e. the internal
dialogue between the 'I' and the 'me'.*

*During their school years children are learning to interact with
adults and peers, to internalize the norms of their own culture, or
subculture, and to appreciate both the formal structure of law and
government and the informal structure of socially valued or pro-
hibited behaviour. In a pluralist society in which children are bombarded with conflicting values from parents, peers, school and the mass
media, it is clear that the development of an autonomous adult personality is likely to prove difficult so that adherence to a particular
norm, or conformity to a certain subculture becomes an attractive alternative to autonomy. Furthermore, the classroom in order to be understood, needs to be viewed as a place in which each individual is
attempting to make sense of the situation in which he finds himself,
and the meanings thus made need to be thought of as differing from
individual to individual, according to each one's perception of the situation.*

1 Infancy and early childhood

Many attempts to explain behaviour place considerable emphasis
on the early years mainly because it is thought that it is during
this period that a person develops his characteristic orientation

towards the world. Once developed this orientation is not seen by the individual as a construct but rather as an accurate representation of what the world, and in particular the social world, is. The social perceptions developed in infancy are thought to become the foundation of the adult's response to others, and although an adult can change a specific response, to attempt to restructure his whole mode of response is, psychologically if not literally, to ask him to be born again.

1.1   *The infant's main task: differentiation*

The infant's major task is one of differentiation; that is he must develop a way of ordering the stimuli to which he is exposed according to some principle of selection. Differentiation and selection require systematic categorization and it is the construction of a categorical framework subsequently applied to the diffuse environmental stimuli, which constitutes the major task of learning in the early years. How is this achieved? It can be argued, as Lenneberg (1967) maintained with respect to language development, that the infant is born with some kind of filtering device by means of which he is able to begin the task of categorization:

> There are certain cerebral functions which mediate between sensory input and motor output which we shall call generically *cognitive function* ... cognition is regarded as the behavioural manifestation of physiological processes. Form and function are not arbitrarily superimposed upon the embryo from the outside but gradually develop through a process of differentiation. The basic plan is based on information contained in the developing tissues.

It has been held however that at birth the infant is a *tabula rasa* which takes whatever impressions are available. Watson (1928) formulated this clearly: 'The human being at birth is a very lowly piece of unformed protoplasm, ready to be shaped by any family in whose care it is first placed.' However this view seems only to be applicable with respect to the adult behaviour that the child will exhibit, that is whether he becomes a tinker, tailor, soldier or sailor, it does not appear to rule out the possibility that the child has inborn modes of functioning which enable him to make contact in the first place with the family that will shape him. Indeed if the child is going to be affected by significant others a necessary precondition for this would seem to be the infant's ability to recognize these others as significant. In human terms the baby is unformed but if he were put in an eagle's nest he would not fly, nor could he be shaped at all if he could not distinguish some salient stimuli to respond to.

These complex processes of differentiation and categorization are thought to develop out of the neonate's repertoire of reflex behaviours originally related to survival. Bowlby (1953) argued that the first instinct is to cling rather than to suck and Harlow and Zimmermann's (1959) work supports this. They showed that when infant macaque monkeys were exposed to surrogate mothers, one of which was made of wire mesh and the other of soft material, if they were frightened they would cling to the cloth rather than the wire mother. In a further study the infant monkeys were divided into two groups one of which had a wire mother, which contained a feeding bottle, while the other group had a non-feeding cloth mother and were fed by hand. Both groups developed an attachment to their mother surrogate, but when frightened the infants with the cloth mother would cling, relax, and then observe the strange object whereas those with the wire mother would rush to the mother initially, but would then clutch themselves or rub against the side of the cubicle. However one might expect a frightened animal to cling in the hope of being removed from the dangerous situation whereas a hungry animal could be expected to seek the mother who feeds. Infants do, however, show a sucking pattern which Wolff (1967) has shown to be rhythmical and to occur in sleep so that it can not be only related to motor feedback or to the presence of the breast. Similarly crying and eye movements have been shown to be organized in time sequences (Pretchl and Lenard, 1967) once again suggesting that infant response is initially ordered rather than merely a random response to external stimuli. Nevertheless for behaviour to develop to any extent some form of environmental trigger would seem to be required.

1.2 The role of the mother

Such 'natural' instinctive behaviour does not of itself, however, shed much light on the development of 'social' or 'cultural' patterns of response. Social patterns require social mediation which has

led many theorists to concentrate on the significance of the mother
or mother substitute, that is to underline the rather obvious point
that adult interpersonal behaviour is likely to be affected by an
early experience of interaction with another person. Underlying
most of these theories is a paradigm which sees the infant as motivated to seek gratification; if this search is frustrated he is thought
to develop anxiety and much subsequent behaviour can then be
interpreted as a means of reducing such anxiety. The significance
of the mother, or mother substitute, as a social mediator is emphasized in the work of John Bowlby (1953, 1969, 1973). He hypothesized that 'the child's tie to his mother is a product of the activity
of a number of behavioural systems that have proximity to the
mother as a predictable outcome', and argued that the original
function of such behaviour was protection from predators. For
the last twenty years he has been stressing the ill effects that accrue
if a child is separated from its mother once the attachment bond
has been formed, or if the initial bond is prevented from being
developed. He argues that separation will lead to protest, despair
and detachment and sees infant separation as *a* key to adult anxiety,
thus echoing but modifying Freud's view (1926) that 'missing
someone who is loved and longed for is the key to an understanding
of anxiety'.

The 'maternal deprivation' hypothesis has been widely, but
perhaps rather uncritically, accepted. Rutter (1972) suggests that
the adverse consequences which appear to follow separation from
the mother are less likely to be a result of the loss of the mother
as such. They may be caused by a 'disruption of the bonding
process' in general. In some circumstances separation does not
appear to affect bonding and hence bonding and attachment should
not be thought of as synonymous. The most significant bond
formed by a child need not be to its mother nor even to a female,
although since mothers traditionally interact more with their young
children than do others, this is likely to be the case. Similarly the
person with whom the child forms the main bond need not be
the most important person in his life. Rutter concludes that:

> The concept of 'maternal deprivation' has undoubtedly been
> useful in focusing attention on the sometimes grave con-
> sequences of deficient or disturbed care in early life. However,
> it is now evident that the experiences included under the term

'maternal deprivation' are too heterogeneous and the effects too varied for it to continue to have any usefulness.

Yarrow and his colleagues (1974) compared a group of adopted children's behaviour at age ten with their infant experiences and looked at the effect of separation on later development. They found that several infant environmental variables were significantly related to later IQs for boys but not for girls (Table 8.1). The level and appropriateness of the stimulation offered by the mothers

Table 8.1 *Correlations between dimensions of maternal care in infancy and intellectual development at ten years*

Environmental variables	WISC Total IQ		
	Group	Boys	Girls
Physical contact	0.38**	0.68**	0.12
Acceptance	0.33*	0.55**	0.11
Positive emotional expression	0.27*	0.50**	0.03
Emotional involvement	0.35**	0.46*	0.24
Communication	0.29*	0.47*	0.11
Individualization	0.33*	0.48*	0.20
Appropriateness of stimulation	0.32*	0.48*	0.16
Achievement stimulation	0.22	0.43*	0.08

** Significant at 0.01 level.
* Significant at 0.05 level.

(Yarrow, 1974)

seemed particularly important for their son's later development. With respect to social behaviour at age ten once again the correlations were only significant for the boys:

... social effectiveness, a measure of the degree to which the child can relate with ease and contribute constructively to a social situation, and depth of relating, his capacity to relate on a meaningful level, with closeness and discrimination, to his parents, his siblings and his peers, – are related significantly for boys to several dimensions of early maternal behaviour, namely communication, individualisation, positive emotional expression, and appropriateness of stimulation. (Tables 8.2, 8.3, 8.4)

Table 8.2 *Correlations between dimensions of maternal care in infancy and depth of relating at ten years*

	Depth of relating		
	Group	Boys	Girls
Communication	0.34*	0.42*	0.27
Appropriateness of stimulation	0.30*	0.43*	0.19
Individualization	0.32*	0.37	0.28
Positive emotional expression	0.21	0.42*	0.00

* Significant at 0.05 level.

(Yarrow, 1974)

Table 8.3 *Correlations between dimensions of maternal care in infancy and social effectiveness at ten years*

	Social effectiveness		
	Group	Boys	Girls
Communication	0.41**	0.50*	0.29
Appropriateness of stimulation	0.27*	0.43*	0.00
Individualization	0.35**	0.41*	0.29
Positive emotional expression	0.23	0.45*	0.00

** Significant at 0.01 level.
* Significant at 0.05 level.

(Yarrow, 1974)

Table 8.4 *Correlations between dimensions of maternal care in infancy and social dominance at ten years*

	Group	Boys	Girls
Positive emotional expression	0.22	0.42*	0.03
Social stimulation	0.30*	0.45*	0.20
Achievement stimulation	0.28*	0.41*	0.20
Sensitivity	0.33*	0.43*	0.26

* Significant at 0.05 level.

(Yarrow, 1974)

However, for both sexes, children who were separated from their foster mothers after six months, when presumably a relationship had been formed, were, at age ten, less able to form different levels of relationship with people than were the children who had either experienced no separation or whose separation had occurred before six months of age. In their conclusion they state that

> One cannot draw the nice simple conclusion that the early environment is decisive for later development. But one can say that the affective relationship with the mother in infancy and maternal stimulation are variables that must be entered into the predictive equation along with a multitude of other constitutional givens, a variety of other experiences throughout childhood.

1.3 *Forming primary relationships*

Rather than considering the significance of early relationships Schaffer (1971) concentrated on, 'The manner in which the infant forms the primary relationship and on the mechanisms that bring about selective social behaviour'. He argued that infants were more interested in certain types of stimuli than others and that human beings were more salient than inanimate objects; thus the first category that the infant develops is that of 'human being'. He then learns to differentiate between familiar humans and strangers. This can be said to have occurred when the child exhibits fear of strangers and recognition of the mother or members of the family. Having made this initial classification the infant positively seeks out the known and becomes attached to his mother. He is then able to explore his environment secure in the 'knowledge' that he has a base to return to.

Throughout this period the relationship has a transactional quality in that the child can affect the adult by crying or smiling and the adult can affect the child both by his response to the child's initiative and by stimulating the child. The transactional nature of such social behaviour as 'babbling' was shown by Rheingold, Gerwitz and Ross (1959) who conducted an experiment with twenty-one three-month-old infants. In this study the experimenter, on the first two days, leant over the cot with an expressionless face and counted the number of times the infant vocalized. For the next two days if the infant vocalized when the experimenter was leaning over the cot he, or she, would cluck, smile and pat the infant's stomach; on the final two days the experimenter acted as in the first two days. The results showed that there was a dramatic increase in vocalization on the days when the experimenter responded and as strong a decrease when he did not.

1.4 *Early learning by imitation*

Schaffer (1971) traced the early development of social recognition, that is the differentiation of significant from strange adults. Once this is accomplished the child is able to learn by imitating the known models. Learning by imitation can take several forms, at its simplest it is just copying but if the child perceives the model as having desirable qualities which he would like to have he may wish to be like the model and hence copy his behaviour – thus becoming 'identified' with the model even to the extent of responding to the model's successes and failures as if they were his own. On the other hand he may copy the model through fear of disapproval if he fails to do so. This can lead to a form of identification – 'identification with the aggressor' (A. Freud, 1937) whereby the child appears to behave in a way which models the behaviour of a feared adult. It is thought that this may reduce anxiety but this explanation is not entirely convincing and it may be simply that, in the absence of other models, the child copies the only one present.

There are several competing theories of imitation learning: Miller and Dollard (1941) argued that the imitative acts are initially accidental but are repeated if they are followed by praise or reward, whereas Mowrer (1950) saw the reward as internal and arising out of the satisfaction derived from behaving like the loved person. Bandura, Ross and Ross (1963) tested three theories by seeing which model the child would imitate given a choice. The first theory, 'status envy' says the child will copy the model who *possesses* the goods or qualities which he desires. The second is Mowrer's theory of 'secondary reinforcement' which says the child is intrinsically rewarded by behaving like a model whom he has grown to value, and the third, or 'social power' theory, says that it is the model who has the power to *give* the rewards who will be copied.

To test these theories the authors composed groups of three consisting of two adults, one male and one female, and one pre-

school child. There were two variants, in the first one an adult
(A_1) had control of the toys and gave them to the other adult (B+)
while the child watched; in the second, one adult (A_2) again had
control of the toys but this time he gave them to the child while
the other adult (B−) was ignored. Then both the adults in the
groups, watched by the child, performed tasks in an idiosyncratic
way and the question was, which adult (i.e. A_1, A_2, B+ or B−)
would the child imitate when he was performing the same tasks?
(A control group merely watched the adults perform the tasks
before doing so themselves.) 'Status envy' theory says the child
would copy the adult (B+) who had been given the toys that he
wanted; 'secondary reinforcement' that he would copy the adult
who gave the toys to him (A_2): and 'social power' the adult (A_1,
A_2) who had the control of the distribution of the toys, irrespective
of whether the toys were given to him or to the other adult.

The control group showed no preference for one adult over
another, therefore any preference shown by the experimental group
must be attributable to the role played by the model in the experimental condition. The results showed a highly significant preference for the model who controlled the distribution of the toys,
although aspects of the behaviour of both models was imitated.
Although it could be argued that this could be a form of 'status
envy' in that the model who had control could have been perceived
as *having* the toys in a more absolute sense than the model who
was dependent on his generosity, there were some interesting side
effects, as for example the finding that if the child subject was
a boy, the controller of the toys female and the ignored adult male,
the child was more likely to imitate the ignored male. In a follow
up interview the authors report: 'A number of these children were
firmly convinced that only a male can possess resources and, therefore, the female dispensing the rewards was only an intermediary
for the male model.' The boys were also more likely to imitate
men whereas the girls were ambivalent.

1.5 *The pyschoanalytic approach to infant learning* (Freud,
    Klein, Sullivan)

A powerful group of theorists (e.g. Freud, Klein and Sullivan)
are concerned not with the *mechanism* of learning so much as with
what is learned since they begin from a concern with the infant's

wishes or desires. It is obvious that no infant can immediately satisfy all its instinctive desires and hence social development becomes the development over time of a form of equilibrium between what is wanted and what can be obtained. It is the nature of the balancing mechanism which becomes the person's characteristic form of response and it is this regularity of response which is known as personality. The work of Freud is much too extensive and complex to be covered here, but he does adumbrate a neat model for a balance mechanism in that he sees behaviour as being explicable in terms of the relative strength of three modes of response. These modes of response however should not be thought of as three separate entities in a state of perpetual warfare, like superpowers controlling a nuclear arsenal, rather they are complementary processes which together can create a stable state. He calls these the Id, the Ego and the Super Ego.

Freud sees the neonate as a seething mass of undifferentiated desires. The Id – this seething mass – can only wish since by its very nature it cannot conceive of a reality which is not itself and hence cannot seek its satisfaction in an external world. It is the Ego which takes account of the external world and attempts to modify the desires of the Id so that they can be met in the real world. The Ego would thus seem to be dependent on the infant's early differentiation of itself from others. If the Ego is concerned with what *can* be done the Super Ego is concerned with what *ought* to be done since it is the result of the child's taking in, and making part of himself, the moral standards of his environment. In a very different sense this too represents a filtering process since, presumably, the Id can wish for anything, and the Ego then has to filter out what *cannot* be done and the Super Ego what *ought not* to be done. If the relevance of this for understanding the behaviour of children in the classroom is rather unclear, an aspect of Freud's theory of anxiety and its repression (1926) may exemplify the real power of what may appear to be no more than an attractive metaphor.

He argued that the infant may experience a situation in which his wishes are frustrated and hence develop anxiety: the significant point is that this experience may predate the full development of the Ego, which would enable the infant to dissolve the anxiety in a realistic manner; instead the immature Ego seeks safety in flight and represses the wishes of the Id which it cannot cope with.

The Ego has thus, through failing to respond to the Id,

> ... narrowed its sphere of influence. The repressed instinctual impulse is now isolated, left to itself, inaccessible, but also uninfluencable. It goes its own way. Even later as a rule, when the Ego has grown stronger, it still cannot lift the repression; its synthesis is impaired, a part of the Id remains forbidden ground to the Ego.

When a situation, similar to the one in which the original frustration occurred, recurs in adult life anxiety is aroused but is not recognized by the Ego and hence the Ego cannot deal with it.

Nevertheless it is there and affects the individual's behaviour. It is as if the architectural Ego has built a house on what it believes to be solid rock only to find that it is shaken by tremors from an underground volcano, the existence of which it is not only unaware but *incapable of hypothesizing*. This notion of behaviour motivated by unconscious wishes, which cannot be recognized or controlled, leads to an explanation of behaviour not in terms of the nature of the case but in terms of what a person dreams the case to be.

Klein (1960) although accepting a similar balance mechanism to Freud's, views its development differently as a result of her work with children, and lays more stress on the first year of life. Her view is that the Ego exists from birth and that the infant unconsciously experiences his inevitable frustrations as though they were 'inflicted by hostile forces'. In response the infant both makes the external events part of himself (introjection) and reshapes his perception of the external world in accordance with his own feelings (projection). That is, if he is hated he believes he is hateful (introjection), and if he hates he believes he is hated (projection). This interplay of projection and introjection is thought to continue throughout life. If a good dependable mother is introjected the developing Ego will be strengthened; however, since even the most loving mother must frustrate the child, the infant feels anger and hate towards the object it also loves. This feeling of anger causes guilt and, Klein argues, the Super Ego develops out of this feeling of guilt during the fifth or sixth month of infancy. The infant has thus to balance these conflicting emotions with the additional problem that he is both developing and applying the balance mechanism at the same time.

Adult behaviour is seen as a reflection of the inner world developed in infancy. Thus, some adults have an optimistic belief in other people whereas others who are 'too much dominated by suspicion and self pity, turn even minor disappointments into disasters'. Furthermore, successful identification with parents and other adults by the infant will result in an adult who can enjoy the pleasures and achievements of others vicariously, but the infant who did not find sufficient satisfaction for his impulses will become the greedy or envious adult who is never satisfied with the success he achieves and resents the success of others. Since nothing can totally satisfy the unlimited wishes of the Id such an adult is doomed to dissatisfaction and will attribute the cause of this to the assumed malevolence of others rather than to his own unresolved infantile wishes. Klein concludes:

> If we look at our adult world from the viewpoint of its roots in infancy, we gain an insight into the way our mind, our habits, and our views have been built up from the earliest infantile phantasies and emotions to the most complex and sophisticated adult manifestations. There is one more conclusion to be drawn, which is that nothing that ever existed in the unconscious completely loses its influence on the personality.

Sullivan (1955a, 1955b) had a different, but related, view of development. He regarded personality as essentially a product of interpersonal relations, so that mental disorder is really interpersonal disorder. Personality therefore is the result of experience, and thus we should not say that experiences are something we have but rather that we are totally shaped by them. The infant is seen as having the potentiality to be human but this can only be actualized through interaction with adults and peers. This potential human has certain needs, for physical comfort, tenderness, the stimulation of the oral, anal, visual and auditory zones, the need to grow and develop its capabilities, and generally the need for security and satisfaction. As a result of the way in which these needs are met, and the 'reflected appraisals' of others (i.e. the infant's understanding of others' perception of him), the child will develop a sense of the 'good me' the 'bad me' and the 'not me' – the latter being those aspects of the child's behaviour which have caused such conflict with significant others that he is unable to subsume them even as part of the 'bad me', and they become not just things that should not be done but things that are not being done.

The original contribution of Sullivan is his view that needs are only comprehensible in the context of a real or phantasized inter-personal situation leading to his theory of 'reciprocal emotion'. During childhood and adolescence the individual, through intense socialization, is building up a repertoire of expectations and re-sponses, and, most important of all, a self-concept through his perception of others' perception of him. A healthy self-concept will enable the adult both to interact smoothly with others and to develop himself further.

2 The middle years and adolescence

If we view the early years as a time of developing a balance mechanism and characteristic orientation to the world, the middle years can be seen as a period in which the child uses his developing powers to extend his range, to inhibit behaviour which incurs the disapproval of parents and peers, and to construct a model of the social world. However it must be remembered that these processes are in fact concurrent, with perhaps no more than a greater emphasis on one or the other at any one time.

2.1 Moral development

Henry (1966) views the inhibition of undesirable responses as learning to want what the culture requires, and this process has been studied in detail by writers of various theoretical persuasions, usually under the umbrella term 'moral development'. This can, for convenience, be separated from social development but should be seen as intimately connected with cognition, social and emotional development. A socially desirable response has three prerequisites: the child must know what is required, he must want to do it, and he must actually do it. The first of these, that is the question of moral judgement, has been most extensively studied by Piaget (1932) and his followers, notably Kohlberg (1963), who described a de-velopmental sequence in the child's understanding of what is right and what is wrong. Both used a technique of telling stories which contained moral dilemmas and asked the child what the agent in the story should have done. Piaget distinguished between 'heteronomous' morality, when the child accepts that what adults say is wrong is, in fact, wrong (in this period rules are sacrosanct so that they cannot be changed to suit the participants in a game), and 'autonomous morality' when rules are binding by mutual agreement and wrong doing is judged in terms of the child's internalized higher order principles rather than by adult fiat. Kohlberg extended Piaget's work and proposed three levels of development, first the 'premoral', second, 'conventional role conformity' and third, 'self accepted moral principles'. The following extract from Kohlberg (1963) shows each level including sub-stages, giving six stages in all.

1. Pre-conventional level

At this level the child is responsive to cultural rules and labels of good and bad, right or wrong, but interprets these labels in terms of either the physical or the hedonistic consequences of action (punishment, reward, exchange of favours) or in terms of the physical power of those who enunciate the rules and labels. The level is divided into the following two stages:

Stage 1: The punishment and obedience orientation. The physical consequences of action determine its goodness or badness regardless of the human meaning or value of these consequences. Avoidance of punishment and unquestioning deference to power are valued in their own right, not in terms of respect for an underlying moral order supported by punishment and authority (the latter being Stage 4).

Stage 2: The instrumental relativist orientation. Right action consists of that which instrumentally satisfies one's own needs and occasionally the needs of others. Human relations are viewed in terms like those of the market place. Elements of fairness, of reciprocity, and equal sharing are present, but they are always interpreted in a physical pragmatic way. Reciprocity is a matter of 'you scratch my back and I'll scratch yours,' not of loyalty, gratitude, or justice.

2. Conventional level

At this level, maintaining the expectations of the individual's family, group, or nation is perceived as valuable in its own right, regardless of immediate and obvious consequences. The attitude is not only one of *conformity* to personal expectations and social order, but of loyalty to it, of actively *maintaining*, supporting, and justifying the order and of identifying with the persons or group involved in it. At this level, there are the following two stages:

Stage 3: The interpersonal concordance or 'good boy – nice girl' orientation. Good behaviour is that which pleases or helps others and is approved by them. There is much conformity to stereotypical images of what is majority or 'natural' behaviour. Behaviour is frequently judged by intention – 'he means well' becomes important for the first time. One earns approval by being 'nice'.

Stage 4: The 'law and order' orientation. There is orientation towards authority, fixed rules and the maintenance of the social order. Right behaviour consists of doing one's duty, showing respect for authority and maintaining the given social order for its own sake.

3. Post-conventional, autonomous, or principled level
At this level, there is a clear effort to define moral values and principles which have validity and application apart from the authority of the groups or persons holding these principles and apart from the individual's own identification with these groups. This level again has two stages:

Stage 5: The social-contract legalistic orientation. Generally has utilitarian overtones. Right action tends to be defined in terms of general individual rights and in terms of standards which have been critically examined and agreed upon by the whole society. There is a clear awareness of the relativism of personal values and opinions and a corresponding emphasis upon procedural rules for reaching consensus. Aside from what is constitutionally and democratically agreed upon, the right is a matter of personal 'values' and 'opinion'. The result is an emphasis upon the 'legal point of view', but with an emphasis upon the possibility of changing law in terms of rational considerations of social utility (rather than freezing it in terms of Stage 4 'law and order'). Outside the legal realm, free agreement, and contract is the binding element of obligation. This is the 'official' morality of the American government and Constitution.

Stage 6: The universal ethical principle orientation. Right is defined by the decision of conscience in accord with self-chosen *ethical principles* appealing to logical comprehensiveness, universality, and consistency. These principles are abstract and ethical (the Golden Rule, the categorical imperative), they are not concrete moral rules such as the Ten Commandments. At heart, these are universal principles of *justice* of the *reciprocity* and *equality* of the human *rights* and of respect for the dignity of human beings as *individual persons*.

Using a similar technique McDonald (1963) found no correlation between the age of the child and the nature of his response and suggested that there was an intimate relationship between child-rearing techniques and the content of moral judgements. He was concerned with the type of reason given by the child for the moral judgements made and to explore this he told 780 children, between the ages of eight and fifteen, pairs of stories involving theft by a child. In one story of each pair the theft was from an individual and in the second from a public body. The child who had heard the story was then asked which thief 'did the worst thing'. The majority of the children saw both actions as equally bad because they were both stealing. McDonald says that this suggests that the children were taught in an undifferentiated and categorical way.

The relationship between judgement and action is less easy to study but Bull (1969) using a projective technique (see p. 235) did attempt this. He set out to discover what a child thought he would do in a given situation, not what he should do, and then followed this up with more detailed questions. His subjects ranged in age from seven to seventeen years and he used both written tests and personal interviews. For example a child would be shown a picture and told: 'Here is a picture of a boy about the same age as you. He is in the cloakroom at school. He is all alone. No one else is there to see what he does. Someone has left a briefcase in the cloakroom. It is open. Do you think the boy will take anything out of it and keep it?'

Five moral themes were explored: cruelty to animals, value of life, cheating, stealing and lying. He found four broad stages: first, 'anomy' or purely instinctive pre-moral behaviour; second, 'heteronomy' when the child acted in response to adult rewards or punishments; third, 'socionomy' during which the child responded more to social approval or disapproval rather than rewards and punishments; and, finally, 'autonomy' when the rules were internalized and the child became 'inner' rather than 'other' directed. Although in general maturity of moral judgement appeared to be more highly associated with intelligence than with socio-economic class this was more true for girls, and for boys there was a closer relation with socio-economic class.

Other experimenters (Grinder, 1964; Allinsmith, 1960; Grinder and McMichael, 1963; and Graham, 1968) have attempted to relate actual moral behaviour to the level of moral judgements expressed. For example, are pupils with high moral maturity scores less likely to cheat in an experimental situation? Results from investigations into this point are far from clear-cut, as in some cases (Grinder and McMichael, 1963) a partial relationship was found and in others none (Grinder, 1964; Allinsmith, 1960; Graham, 1968). Schwartz (1969) and his colleagues found that their subjects were not morally consistent. Development of moral thought was related to refraining from cheating and to helping others, and need for affiliation was also associated with helpfulness. Need for achievement, although it tended to be related to refraining from cheating, was not related to helpfulness.

Alternatively the same behaviour may represent different levels of moral judgements. When Berkeley students were deciding whether to stage a sit-in, Haan, Smith and Block (1968) tested 200 of them and found that those who were at the highest 'autonomous' level decided to sit in, those who were at the 'conventional' level decided against it and those who were at the lowest level *also* decided to sit in, but for an entirely different, and less 'moral' set of reasons.

Perhaps the most awkward question is that of motivation; how do children learn to *want* to do what they ought to do and are expected to do? Learning theorists put forward an apparently simple paradigm which says that the probability of an action of a certain kind being repeated is a function of the reinforcement that action has elicited in the past. Thus Eysenck (1957, 1960) argued that 'values develop through the usual process of learning and conditioning and that as some people are more easily conditioned than others their behaviour will be more "moral", thus conscience is a conditioned anxiety response to certain types of

situations and actions'. He supported this by quoting studies which
indicated that psychopaths, who were defined as exhibiting little
or no guilt, were difficult to condition (Lykken, 1957) whereas
people in anxiety states conditioned easily (Franks, 1956a and b,
1957). Introverts are seen as being more easily conditioned than
extraverts so that neurotic introverts develop personality problems
and neurotic extraverts conduct problems (i.e. the more easily conditioned introverts have more highly developed consciences and
hence are more likely to be deviant in socially acceptable ways).
Argyle (1965) disputed this saying that no British studies, using
Eysenck's own instrument 'The Maudsley Personality Inventory',
had found a high correlation between delinquency and extraversion.

Bandura (1969) brought together the ideas of modelling and
reinforcement and argued that there were two processes at work;
one, the perceptual or imaginal system by means of which the
child who has first seen a model behave in a certain way, is able
to re-imagine the sequence when the model is not present, and
a cerebral system which uses language as a mediator of the
model's behaviour. When the child models the adult behaviour
he either receives direct reinforcement or secondary reinforcement,
as hypothesized by Mowrer (see p. 194). Aronfreed (1969) developed the notion of verbal mediators and showed that if the child
was able to use language as an aid to labelling and hence to
discrimination, he was more able to respond to prohibitions
backed by punishment. If a child was forbidden to play with one
group of toys and permitted to play with another and if the toys
were clearly distinguishable the more severe punishment was more
effective, but if the toys were difficult to distinguish milder
punishment was more effective. It appeared that the anxiety
aroused by the anticipation of severe punishment interfered with
the cognitive task of distinguishing the toys, whereas if language
could help the child to label the toys the anxiety was diminished.
Thus behaviour is dependent on being able to discriminate
acceptable from unacceptable actions and cognition becomes as
salient as conditioning.

Stayton, Hogan and Ainsworth (1971) studied infant obedience
in relation to maternal behaviour and found that the mother's attitude was more important than her methods. Thus mothers who
were accepting, co-operative and sensitive had more obedient chil-

dren than those who were rejecting, interfering and insensitive regardless of the techniques used to ensure obedience.

Throughout childhood the individual is learning, whether by conditioning or a more complex process of internal mediation, to behave to a greater or lesser extent in accordance with the dictates both of his own social group and of the wider society; as he becomes older so his behaviour becomes more cognitively differentiated. In this context it becomes apparent that if a child belongs to a delinquent subculture and learns the values of that culture, there is nothing abnormal in his behaviour, his *learning* is totally and entirely adequate. The problem is that the wider society will dislike what he has learnt and will attempt to modify his behaviour, usually by punishment. As punishment is held to be less effective than reward, and if his early learning has been based on modelling, with rewarding secondary reinforcement, it is hardly surprising if attempts to 'reform' the child socialized into delinquency fail. Thus delinquency is not a single phenomenon as a 'born' delinquent is quite different from the child who rebels against his given value system and becomes delinquent.

Despite the apparent differences between thinkers such as Piaget who see the individual as interacting with his environment and Eysenck, who sees the individual as shaped by the environment, there is a measure of agreement in that while learning theory may indicate the mechanism whereby the individual comes to accept the values of his society, the description of developmental stages follows the sequence by which the individual comes to learn what these values are.

2.2 *The development of social concepts*

Moral development, however, is only one aspect of the child's social world in that whilst he is learning the values of his society he is also engaged in constructing his view of the characteristics of such a society. Although Piaget has explored the child's developing comprehension of the concepts of time, space, number, weight, etc., we have no comparable evidence as to how he develops his conception of social concepts such as power, class or status, and yet this knowledge is essential if we are to understand his social behaviour. There are a few studies worth considering, although the majority are mainly descriptive and seem to be more concerned with deficiencies in the child's knowledge rather than with exploring the nature of the child's social constructs.

The concept of authority.   A useful study is Kutnick's (1975) work on the development of the child's concept of authority. Kutnick studied 120 children aged four-and-a-half to eleven-and-a-half in London schools, using a projective technique which involved pictures of parental figures with children, a teacher in a classroom, and a group of children with one appearing to be saying something to the others. He found that there were no differences between the children's view of authority figures due to sex, class or religion but there were significant age differences. The youngest children only recognized parental authority, it took a year in the classroom for them to recognize the teacher as a teacher and they initially interacted with her as a mother figure. In the junior school the teacher was seen as a disciplinarian and the pupils recognized her as having knowledge and being able to solve problems. During the third year the children recognized other adults as having authority – for example – the police, doctors and nurses but it was not until the fourth year that the possibility of their peers having authority over them was acknowledged nor would they submit to peer leaders until the sixth year.

Political awareness.   The development of political awareness shows a movement from confusion concerning national identity, through an idealization of powerful personalities, authoritarianism, ethnocentrism plus jingoism and trust to a greater awareness of party allegiance and a more differentiated and critical approach to the nation and its leaders. Jahoda (1963a) showed that six-year-olds could not distinguish the town of Glasgow from the country of Scotland nor include Glasgow in Scotland and Scotland in Britain. During their years in primary schools the children gradually developed a notion of nationality (Jahoda, 1963b). In this period of identity development children appear to express heavily biased attitudes towards their own race and nation. Immigrants are viewed negatively particularly by those who live in multi-racial communities, and thus London children express more negative responses than do those from Lowestoft (Kawwa, 1968). When Tajfel (1966) asked children which country they preferred in each of the possible pairs of the four countries America, France,

Germany and Russia, two thirds of the seven-year-olds and 85 per cent of the eleven-year-olds placed America or France before Russia and Germany, and Litt (1963) found that between one fifth and one third of children in the Boston area in America could be classed as 'chauvinistic'.

Although children do identify with political parties in the middle years their focus is more on political personalities. The Queen is seen as more powerful than the Prime Minister and American children (Hess and Easton, 1960) express considerable respect and admiration for the President. (The extent to which a highly publicized incident such as Watergate will affect loyalty has not yet been reported but one could hypothesize that the concept of the 'President' will still tend to be positively valued while opprobrium will be cast on any particular incumbent who defaults. It is likely that the more highly the position is rated the more violent will be the reaction to a holder who publicly fails to live up to others' expectations.) However Jaros, Hirsh and Fleron's (1968) study of 'poor whites' in the Appalachian region of America found considerably less admiration expressed by children for politicians and the political system. Younger children and adolescents in general appear to have more authoritarian attitudes (Adelson and O'Neil, 1966), to be lacking in cynicism and to trust the political system (Jennings and Niemi, 1968).

During adolescence there is an increase in political discussion with peers (Hyman, 1969) and a decrease in trust in late adolescence. It is during this stage that the child begins to engage in 'formal' thought and hence is able to hypothesize alternative social systems, although the utopias of adolescents seem to show considerable similarity. Adelson and O'Neil (1966) used a similar technique to Kohlberg's (see p. 199) to elicit information on children's understanding of such concepts as community, law, and rights and found that before the age of thirteen children were authoritarian and were unable to relate social consequences to political actions; thirteen to fifteen was a period of transition and after that the idea of government being more of a social contract between government and governed developed.

Gallatin and Adelson (1971) conducted a cross-national survey of the development of political thought. The children were told to imagine that 1,000 people had moved to a Pacific island to form a new society and that they had to establish a political system.

They then questioned the children about such things as the nature of law and government, political forms and functions, the sources of crime and strategies of punishment. They found that the concept of individual freedom developed with age as did an increased understanding of the function of government. The American sample were more concerned with civil liberties and public welfare than were the British who seemed to see the relationship between the individual and the state as a business one. The British feared a strong central government whereas about one-third of the Germans, the majority of whom were democratic, were willing to accept more restrictive laws and showed a concern with being protected.

Tapp and Kohlberg (1971) found stages in thinking when the children were questioned on universal institutional structures like the law, the family and education, or on universal concepts such as justice, rule and responsibility. Each stage was found to represent 'a qualitatively different organization of thought not a set of specific beliefs'. At the pre-conventional level the importance of obeying rules was all important. At the conventional levels the maintenance of law and order was seen as the overriding aim with rules as instruments to this end, and at the post-conventional level man was seen as the maker of his own rules. With respect to educational level, primary children tended to be at the first level, pre-adolescents and college students at the conventional level with some college students giving post-conventional replies.

2.3   *Adolescent identity*

Adolescence does mark a fundamental change of orientation in that it is at this stage that the individual becomes concerned in a conscious way with himself as unique. Elkind (1967) underlines this by referring to the egocentricity of the adolescent as being characterized by 'the belief that others are preoccupied with his appearance and behaviour'. He does not appear to realize that others are not as keen as he is on the things he values. He is always constructing imaginary audiences whereas in actual social situations others are not usually his audience. When adolescents meet 'each is more concerned with being observed than with being the observer'. He also fails to distinguish what he 'believes to be attractive and what others admire' and believes that the emotions he feels are unique. Gradually, as formal operations become fully established, the adolescent replaces the imaginary audience with real people and the belief in his own uniqueness with empathy for others through interpersonal encounters.

Long, Ziller and Henderson (1968) have traced the development of the self-concept during adolescence. The younger girls, that is those in the first three years of secondary schooling, identified less with their mothers than did the older girls and less than boys of the same age, although the position was reversed in the higher forms. The boys identified more closely with their fathers until the middle of primary school, there was a decline at the top of primary school, after which there was no change until the sixth form when a further decline occurred. In general boys had more stable relationships with others throughout this period whereas girls tended to withdraw from social contact in early adolescence and then return. Fathers were given a higher status than either teachers or headmasters. Dependency decreased and self-esteem increased as adolescence progressed.

The adolescent therefore appears to pay less attention to constructing a picture of others or the social world and devotes his thought to his own self-concept. Although this stage is obviously dependent on what has gone before, it does require the youth to evaluate in a critical way where he stands and to move forward with less dependence on others, especially his parents, in order to form mature relationships outside his immediate family and peer group.

---

3 *Two approaches to adult personality*

As a result of the processes described thus far there develops an individual, a 'self', and any explanation of social behaviour has to take into account the unique contribution of each of the participating selves. How can the teacher find a way of bringing together the disparate findings on the nature of the self so that they can be of help to him in his work? Since this book has presented the classroom as a meeting point of discrete perceptions as well as a meaning-making environment, the following approaches may prove illuminating: the first is Kelly's (1955) theory of the nature of personality and the second Harré and Secord's (1972) attempt to elucidate social behaviour.

3.1 *Personal construct theory*

Kelly stated his theory formally beginning from the fundamental postulate that 'A person's processes are psychologically channelized by the ways in which he anticipates events'. By this he means that individuals build a hypothesis as to the nature of an event, prior to that event's occurrence, but in the light of previous events. The individual then tests out his hypothesis and, although the hypothesis may prove to be totally erroneous, its very existence affects the way in which he perceives the ensuing event. A 'construct' is an abstraction which the person uses to categorize events and thus make sense of them. Constructs are individualized and anticipatory rather than reactive, and any psychological response is the result of the act of construing an event in a certain way. To see people in this way leads the psychologist to attempt to understand people in *their own terms*, or in terms of their own constructs, and not in the psychologist's terms.

People view events by means of their personal construct system so that constructs become a way of actually conceptualizing events, and therefore two people who behave differently in what appears to a third person to be the same situation may, in fact, not see the situation as the same. Constructs are thought to be based on the mother's constructs, to develop throughout childhood, and then to be modified during adult life. If development is seen as the modification of constructs which prove inadequate, then failure in development may be due to overprotection causing the child to be unable to get beyond the parental constructs or it may be due to a failure to adapt the constructs already in existence.

A person's construct system is elicited by a repertory grid *technique*, not test. In its classic form this technique requires the psychologist to ask a person to write down twenty or thirty people who are important in his life – e.g. mother, father, sister, wife, employer, etc. The psychologist then groups all these cards into sets of three and asks the person to think of a way in which two are alike in contrast to the third. When the person has done this with many of the cards, the psychologists looks at, not which

person has been linked with which, but *the reasons given* for linking them, (thus one person may use limited factual constructs
'male/female' 'older/younger' and another affective ones 'likes
me/does not like me', etc.); and he will then note the extent to
which the constructs cluster.

Kelly was also concerned with 'self-characterization' which
involved simply asking the person to write about himself, since
he believed that asking a person what was wrong would yield
important information when his reply was carefully analysed. For
him anxiety meant that a person was unable to construe an event
or was unable to see all its implications, thus adulthood for the
adolescent or disease and death for all people are events likely to
cause anxiety.

Brierley (1967) elicited constructs from children aged seven, ten
and thirteen and divided them into six types:

1 Kinship; those in the family and those outside.
2 Social role; children v. adults.
3 Appearance; fat/thin.
4 Behaviour.
5 Personality; bossy or nosey.
6 Literal; people who have the same Christian name.

She found that usage varied over age (Table 8.5).

Table 8.5 *Percentage of six types of construct elicited from children in three
age groups*

Types of construct	% at age		
	7	10	13
Kinship	2.9	2.7	1.3
Social role	29.5	26.9	8.8
Appearance	32.3	30.6	8.9
Behaviour	24.3	31.0	41.3
Personality	9.8	18.4	39.7
Literal	0.2	0.0	0.0

(Brierley 1967, quoted in Bannister and Fransella, 1971)

Kelly's theory therefore

is not so much a theory about man as it is a theory of man.

Certainly this is no treatise to be studied by one who prefers
to be disidentified with the human race. It is, rather, part of
a psychologist's protracted effort to catch the sense of man going
about his business of being human ... our theme is the personal
adventure of the men we are and live with – the efforts, the
enterprises, the ontology of individuals so convinced that there
is something out there, really and truly, that they will not relent
no matter what befalls them, until they have seized it in their
own hands.

3.2 Man as a rule following agent

Harré and Secord (1972) take issue with the traditional method
of approach in the social sciences because, while it may have been
appropriate for the physical sciences (though they raise doubts
about this), they see it as certainly inappropriate for the social
sciences. Their argument, briefly, is as follows; they take as their
model the 'naturalistic conception of the human being as a rule
following agent' but argue that it is a mistake to believe that a
single biological organism has a single social self, rather: 'A normal
human biological individual is potentially associated with a whole
set of possible unitary social selves.' For this reason they give a
central place to personal reports concerning an individual's reasons,
intentions, and perceptions of others' expectations, in any explanation of social action. A person is defined, as an individual who
'is aware ... of what he is doing and capable of saying what he
was up to'.

Harré and Secord therefore concentrate on self-directed and self-
monitoring behaviour. Of special importance is their view that:

> Explaining behavioural phenomena involves identifying the
> generative 'mechanisms' that give rise to the behaviour. The
> discovery and identification of these 'mechanisms' we call
> *ethogeny*. We believe that the main process involved in them
> is self direction according to the meaning ascribed to the situ
> ation. At the heart of the explanation of social behaviour is the
> identification of the meanings that underlie it.

They analyse human interaction in terms of episodes paying par
ticular attention to 'rules' and 'roles'.

Rules are propositions and they guide actions, through the actor being aware of the rule and what it prescribes ... Rules are future directed: they not only guide actions but also determine expectations concerning the actions of other persons. The propositional nature of rules fits them to appear in accounts of and commentaries on action ... A role is that part of the act–action structure produced by the subset of the rules followed by *a particular category of individual*. A person's role, then, is the set of actions he is expected to take within the act–action structure of a certain kind of episode. Role expectations may be clear or they may be only dimly perceived.

Thus their system of explanation differs

... from explanations of physical phenomena in terms of causal mechanisms: the person offers accounts which (a) are subject to *post-hoc* modification, and (b) may be changed if the person can be persuaded that his account is wrong. There is no possibility of an absolutely objective, neutral account by which these ambiguities can be resolved.

Therefore meaning and man's ability to provide accounts of his actions are central. The ethogenist 'seeks the explanations of the *phenomena* he *observes* in the *accounts* he *elicits*. He proceeds always at two levels, the descriptive and the explanatory.'

Harré and Secord's emphasis on the accounts a person gives makes their theory similar to Kelly's although the latter stressed man as a maker of hypotheses while they stress that man monitors his behaviour. The explanation of social behaviour appears to be possible only if it takes into account the significance of individual differences, which may be the result of childhood experiences and influences, and which also give rise to adults who do not just react to the world but who also construe the world in various ways, monitor their behaviour and either adapt or fail to adapt when their constructs are invalidated. In this sense Sullivan is correct in seeing mental disorder as interpersonal disorder in that social interaction requires agents who construe each other's behaviour in such a way that the interaction becomes meaningful, and able to be understood, by all the participants.

How an individual behaves in a particular situation is a function of a multiplicity of competing forces, but some significant elements can be abstracted and interpreted. Those who work with other human beings need to be aware of the nature of some of these forces in others and in themselves so that they may be able to conduct their own interpersonal relationships aware both of the irreducible otherness of the other and of the behaviour they have in common as members of the same species.

Further reading

Bannister, D. and Fransella, F. (1971) *Inquiring Man*. Harmondsworth, Middlesex: Penguin.

Bowlby, J. (1969) *Attachment and Loss*. (Vol. 1) *Attachment*. London: Hogarth.

Bowlby, J. (1973) *Attachment and Loss*. (Vol. 2) *Separation*. London: Hogarth.

Conger, J. J. (1975) *Contemporary Issues in Adolescence*. London: Harper and Row.

Danziger, K. (1971) *Socialisation*. Harmondsworth, Middlesex: Penguin.

Harré, R. and Secord, P. F. (1972) *The Explanation of Social Behaviour*. Oxford: Basil Blackwell.

Evans, E. D. (ed.) (1970) *Adolescents: Readings in Behaviour and Development*. Illinois: Dryden Press.

Klein, M. (1960) *Our Adult World and its Roots in Infancy*. London: Tavistock.

Rutter, M. (1972) *Maternal Deprivation Reassessed*. Harmondsworth, Middlesex: Penguin.

Schaffer, H. R. (1971) *The Growth of Sociability*. Harmondsworth, Middlesex: Penguin.

[9]
Individual differences and learning

A child's capacity to learn can be affected by many factors besides intelligence. This chapter considers some of the influential personal factors, for example sex or position in the family, as well as personality variables such as anxiety level, academic motivation and cognitive style. To maximize achievement these individual dimensions need to be taken into account and instructional methods made sufficiently flexible. No teacher or school can be totally efficient with all of the children all of the time, but to succeed with all of the children some of the time would seem preferable to concentrating on some (i.e. either the most or the least intelligent) of the children most of the time.

---
1 *Sex differences*

To disentangle the influence of sex on learning is a most complex task as many studies appear to be contradictory. However, in general, it seems that there are sex differences in both ability and achievement and that not only do parents and teachers treat boys and girls differently but boys and girls, in their turn, respond differently to the same treatment.

1.1 *Differences in ability*

On the face of it boys appear to be better at tasks requiring spatial or mathematic abilities, girls at ones requiring verbal fluency, but it is possible that the matter is more complex. Girls learn to count at an earlier age than boys and differences between sexes are not apparent in primary school although during secondary schooling the boys draw ahead (Maccoby, 1966). Helson (1971) made a special study of women mathematicians in general and creative women mathematicians in particular, in America. Her first significant finding was that 'half of the creative subjects were born in Europe or Canada and almost half of the subjects born in the USA had at least one parent born in Europe'. Their personalities, however, did not differ from those of native-born Americans. The creative women had higher scores for flexibility, and lower scores for achievement via conformance (see p. 236) and communality, than the controls. Indeed their scores were 'the most extreme of any creative or comparison group studied at the Institute of Personality Assessment and Research'. In terms of personality the creative subjects did seem to have more psychological problems but to balance this they also had better resources for dealing with them. All the women mathematicians had strong symbolic interests and this was particularly true of the creatives. The creatives were more likely to have professional fathers than the others, whose fathers were mainly business men or skilled workers, and they were more likely to report childhood poverty or financial insecurity. In terms of ordinal position (see p. 222), while it was true that creative men mathematicians were more likely to be first-borns, for creative women the only factor of significance was that the majority did not have brothers. However, the creatives tended to have identified primarily with their fathers, although he was not perceived as a warm person. It would appear that, in general, it was personality rather than intellectual characteristics that distinguished the creative women mathematicians. They appeared independent and flexible and had achieved a simplified and integrated life.

Helson took up the point of the creative girls being closer to their fathers and contrasted this finding with the one for creative men who reported being closer to their mothers. She concluded that: 'In a sense, it would seem that respect for the mother encourages a cathexis of symbolic activity in the boy, whereas a lack of respect may engender it in the girl.' This finding complements the view that girls with high achievement motivation (see p. 234) were more likely to have 'hostile' (i.e. non-nurturant) mothers (Bardwick, 1971; Garai and Scheinfeld, 1968; Maccoby, 1966) so that maternal protectiveness seems to have a negative effect for girls' achievement but a positive one for boys'. Girls who had 'hostile' mothers were also found to be less likely to withdraw from a situation when it became difficult.

With respect to spatial abilities among very young children there appear to be no differences but by school age Witkin *et al.* (1954) found that boys scored higher on the embedded figures test and the rod and frame test (see p. 69). Maccoby *et al.* (1965), however, did not find any difference among four-year-old males and females on the embedded figures test.

1.2 *Difference in interests*

Girls and boys also seem to have different interests and to choose different play things. It is often argued that this is culturally determined in that girls are more likely to be given dolls to play with than are boys but Danziger (1971) queried this explanation saying

> ... the permanent effectiveness of social reinforcement in older children depends on what the child considers appropriate for himself; it presupposes a previous definition of oneself as a person who engages in such and such behaviour. Normal boys do not need much social reinforcement to adopt new forms of acceptable 'masculine' activity, but it is well nigh impossible to devise an effective reinforcement for actions that would be considered 'effeminate'.

He also pointed out that for adults having masculine or feminine interests does not correlate with a person's view of himself as strongly masculine or feminine. For children the adoption of sex-typed interests may happen many years before the acceptance of appropriate sexual identity; Danziger's example is the little girl who is quite content to play with dolls but who also says that she would prefer to be a boy.

1.3 *Patterns of achievement*

Boys and girls show very different patterns of achievement. Girls are more likely to achieve better grades than boys in the early years of school and score higher on IQ tests, but this position is reversed in the secondary school. They also achieve a similar standard in all subjects whereas boys, being more

Table 9.1 *Productivity measures: article and book publication, research grant and consulting, by field, sex and marital status*

Field, sex, and marital status	Per cent published at least one article (1)	Mean number of articles (2)	Per cent published at least one book (3)	Mean number of books (4)	Per cent received at least one grant (5)	Per cent consult (6)
Sciences						
Women						
Unmarried	83.3	5.8	10.1	1.1	35.9	14.2
Married	75.4	6.3	6.2	2.6	30.4	7.8
Married w/children	91.9	7.8	9.5	1.7	25.6	7.9
Men	88.8	6.1	10.2	1.5	36.7	15.5
Social Sciences						
Women						
Unmarried	59.3	4.0	23.1	1.8	23.4	34.1
Married	61.5	4.2	20.9	2.1	22.2	27.2
Married w/children	66.9	3.9	19.9	1.5	24.9	33.6
Men	55.9	4.6	30.3	1.8	35.4	31.5

Humanities

Women						
Unmarried	47.0	2.8	22.6	1.3	21.0	15.2
Married	69.7	3.7	22.9	1.6	28.2	10.3
Married w/children	69.7	3.4	32.8	1.6	18.6	14.4
Men	50.0	4.3	27.7	1.6	32.9	26.8

Education

Women						
Unmarried	51.2	3.5	23.5	1.6	15.3	42.6
Married	57.4	5.4	35.3	1.7	15.3	50.9
Married w/children	39.6	3.9	26.0	2.0	14.2	41.5
Men	44.2	5.1	22.2	1.8	14.2	44.4

Combined

Women						
Unmarried	57.9	4.1	21.1	1.6	21.9	30.6
Married	66.2	5.3	20.2	1.9	24.0	24.0
Married w/children	63.9	4.3	21.8	1.7	21.9	27.7
Men	57.5	5.2	23.1	1.7	28.2	32.2

(Simon, Clark and Galway, 1967)

autonomous and selective, do well in the subjects they like and badly in those they dislike. In general boys are more variable in that while more are 'gifted' so too more are subnormal. Boys who score highly between the ages of six and ten grow up to be intellectually more powerful adults than do girls who score highly at that age (Sontag and Kagan, 1967). Boys are more realistic when they judge their own performances whereas girls are more afraid of failure and often retreat from an intellectual challenge.

Despite girls' greater achievement at school it is often said that women, in adult life, are less achievement-oriented than men. However, in a study of women Ph.Ds (Simon, Clark and Galway, 1967), differences between the sexes were found to be negligible. Women academics were as likely to win fellowships and belong to learned societies as their male peers and in terms of publication married women were found to publish as much, or even more, than men, and unmarried women slightly less (Table 9.1). Their findings however gave some support to the belief that women were more likely to be engaged in teaching than in research, i.e. for the woman to be one who 'passes on an intellectual heritage' rather than one 'who helps create the heritage'. There were nevertheless some areas in which women still experienced difficulties, 'even on such simple daily activities as finding someone to have lunch or take a coffee break with, or finding someone with whom she can chew over an idea, or on larger issues such as finding a partner with whom she can share a research interest, the woman Ph.D. has a special and lower status'.

1.4 *Personality variables*

Maccoby (1966) considered personality variables in some detail. Perhaps the most important of these is the girls' greater dependency and need to affiliate (Oetzel, 1966; Walberg, 1969). If 'boys try to figure the task, girls try to figure the teacher' (Kagan, 1964). Girls achieve in order to get approval from the teacher rather than to gain intellectual mastery. Hoffman (1972) suggested that this is because the girl does not need to see herself as separate from her mother in the same way as a boy does and she is encouraged to be more dependent. Since girls need feedback from others to reassure them that they are doing the right thing they are also likely to become more anxious. It is possible that the less dependent girls are intellectually more able: Witkin *et al.* (1962) argued that the personality traits of dependency and conformity correlate with field dependency and difficulty in restructuring when solving problems. Maccoby (1966) expands this by saying that two possible reasons for this could be given. First, 'an individual who is dependent and conforming is oriented toward stimuli emanating from other people; perhaps he finds it difficult to ignore these stimuli in favour of internal thought processes'; second: 'The independent-conforming person is passive waiting to be acted upon by the environment. The independent person takes the initiative. Intellectual tasks differ in how much activity they require, so that the passive person is more at a disadvantage on some tasks than others.' This affiliative behaviour can help women however, since if they wish to fulfil others' expectations they are likely to be more amenable to achievement-oriented suggestions than men. When Carey (1955) attempted, through group discussion, to convince college students that ability to solve problems was socially acceptable she was successful in improving the problem solving scores of the women but had no such success with the men.

Such sex differences are often explained in terms of differential child-rearing practices or different expectations of children related to sex. Hoffman (1972) pointed out that developmentally girls are six weeks ahead of boys at birth and one year ahead by the time they enter school. (The boys' greater immaturity at school age may well cause them to have greater difficulty than the girls with starting to write or in doing up their shoe laces and hence find school more trying in the early days.) Girls also have better hearing than boys (Garai and Scheinfeld, 1968). Mothers appear to react more swiftly to their infant daughters' cries, and to spend more time talking to them (Kagan, 1969; Moss, 1967; Goldberg and Lewis, 1969) although they do not, in general, attend to the girls more than the boys. Even though girls are developmentally ahead, parents have been found to think that their daughters are more fragile (Garai and Scheinfeld, 1968) and to handle boys less gently (Moss, 1967). Boys' attempts to be independent are also more likely to be encouraged by parents than are similar attempts by girls.

As early as 1932 St. John was drawing attention to the deleterious effects on boys of the 'feminized' school saying that the boys' lower achievement was 'due chiefly to a maladjustment between the boys and their teachers which is the result of interests, attitudes, habits and general behaviour tendencies of boys to which the teachers fail to adjust themselves and their school procedures as well as they do to the personality traits of girls'. Although Davis and Slobodian (1967) did not find any support for the contention that teachers favour girls when teaching a class to read, Meyer and Thompson (1956) found that in the American sixth grade, boys received considerably more blame from their teachers than girls did, and although they also received more praise this did not outweigh the amount of blame. The boys and the girls both appeared aware of the fact that the boys were more likely to be blamed and the authors argue that women teachers may well dislike 'typically' masculine behaviour, especially when it is aggressive, and therefore the 'teacher attempts to socialise the male child by means of dominative counter-aggressive behaviour'.

The type of school may also influence the children as Minuchin (1964) found when she compared a 'modern' with a 'traditional' school. In the 'traditional' school there were more clearly marked sex differences in intellectual performance and more sex-appropriate activity in the playground.

---

2 The child's position in the family

Roe's (1952) finding in her study of eminent scientists that 72 per cent were actually, or effectively, first-borns confirmed Galton's (1874) observation that first-borns were over-represented among men who had achieved eminence. An extensive study of 7,000 London school children (Stewart, 1962) found first-borns over-represented in grammar schools and later-borns in secondary moderns at age eleven, with first-borns showing a greater tendency to stay at school beyond the minimum leaving age so that in the top forms of both kinds of school the ratio becomes greater than two to one. In a review of birth-order effects Adams (1972) concluded, 'the most consistent finding in this area has been the greater educational attainment, including college attendance, among first-borns (including onlies)'. He says, however, that few studies have found first-borns to be higher in achievement motivation (see p. 234). Rothbart (1971) did, nevertheless, find that mothers interacted differently with their first-born children in an achievement situation. In her experiment she studied mothers and five-year-old children, half of whom had a same sex sibling two years older and half a same sex sibling two years younger. The mothers were asked to supervise their children while they were performing five tasks. They were found to give more complex technical explanations to their first-borns, concerning, for example, the way in which a water tap works. They also pressed the first-borns to achieve and seemed more anxious and interfering with them, especially with respect to first-born girls. This result supports Cushna's (1970) finding that mothers were 'more supportive and cautious in directing their boys but more demanding, exacting and intrusive toward their first-born girls'.

Oberlander *et al.* (1970) found first-borns to have higher IQs than later-borns but, in general, the first-born effect was related to family size in that as family size decreased so did the relative superiority of the first-borns. Rosenberg and Sutton-Smith (1969) looked even closer at the evidence and argued that for boys cognitive activity was higher for first-borns if there was a large (over two years) age space between them and their siblings. For girls ordinal position, as such, did not seem to be significant but girls who had a same sex sibling close to them in age achieved higher scores. Their explanation was that 'close age spacing which maximises the opportunities for sex typical dependency in girls also facilitates their cognitive functioning, large age spacing which maximises the opportunities for sex typical independence in boys facilitates their cognitive functioning'. The authors also suggest that a larger age spacing causes less competition between male siblings and therefore helps second-born boys.

Terman (1925) had also found a similar link between birth order and IQ since in his sample of gifted children first-borns were over-represented followed by the youngest children. It may be however that birth order only relates to aptitude at the highest level. When competitors for the American national merit competition were studied no correlation between birth order and score was found, but 60 per cent of the finalists, and hence the highest scorers, were first-borns (Altus, 1966). Munroe and Munroe (1971) also report over-representation of first-borns in East African secondary schools. The more prestigious the school the more likely the first-borns were to be over-represented. But in another cross-cultural study (Amir and Sharan, 1968) clear birth-order effects were not found. Amir and Sharan argued that the job of an army officer would be unattractive to first-borns since it was anxiety provoking but gave little opportunity for affiliation. However middle-eastern families, with a different family structure, might not show the same birth-order effects, for example the preferential status awarded to first-borns in these families might make them generally less anxious. To test these ideas they looked at the frequency with which first-born soldiers in the Israeli defence forces would appear for officer training. Their hypotheses were: first, that first-born males, with preferential family status, from middle-eastern extended families would appear with greater than expected frequency; second, that first-born males, with preferential status from middle-eastern nuclear families would appear with expected frequency; and, finally, that first-born males from western nuclear families would appear with less than expected frequency. They therefore hoped, by testing these hypotheses, to compare the effects of birth order in different types of family structure. The results confirmed the first and second hypotheses thereby suggesting that the birth-order effect may be specific to a certain form of family pattern (which contradicts the Munroes' findings). Israeli-born eastern first-borns were also found to differ from Israeli-born western first-borns, even though both were in nuclear families, perhaps because of the preferential treatment given to the eastern first-borns. Hypothesis three was only confirmed for Israeli-born western males, those born abroad appeared with greater than expected frequency.

The reason for first-borns' greater intellectual achievements are not entirely clear since the relationship between birth order and personality is still in dispute, but it is possible that the first-borns, or some first-borns', greater need to affiliate and greater tendency to depend on adults may make them more amenable at school and more willing to internalize the achievement-oriented values of the school.

---

3 *Date of birth*

Unlike the controversies surrounding some aspects of birth order the findings on the effect of date of birth are clear. As early as

1938 Huntington, writing on the significance of the season or person's birth, remarked that those born early in the year were more vigorous and eminent. Pidgeon (1965) found that more of the retarded readers and children who were educationally backward were born in the summer and the summer-born children were also more likely to be in lower streams. This finding was confirmed by Sutton (1967) who showed that, although the 11 + examination was corrected for age, in the secondary modern schools in his sample there was a marked bias in streaming against summer-born children (Table 9.2). After analysing the records of over 8,000 children Freyman (1965) concluded that children born between May and August were educationally at a disadvantage, and that this disadvantage was exacerbated by streaming.

Table 9.2 *Streaming percentages by birth group*

	A	B	C	D
September–December	40	35	30	28
January–April	32	35	35	30
May–August	28	30	35	42
Total	100	100	100	100

(Sutton, 1967)

4 Anxiety

There appears to be some sex difference in anxiety rates but the whole topic of anxiety is so central to the educational situation and yet much less researched than, say, IQ, that it requires more extensive treatment. Holt (1964) remarked:

> For many years I have been asking myself why intelligent children act unintelligently in school. The simple answer is because they're scared ... Perhaps most people do not recognise fear in children when they see it. They can read the grossest signs of fear ... but the subtler signs of fear escape them. It is these signs, in children's faces, noises and gestures, in their movements

[225]

,orking, that tell me plainly that most children
,cared most of the time, many of them very scared.

, may be an overstatement it does appear that anxiety
,y to hinder school achievement than to facilitate it.
,actly is 'anxiety'? Several distinctions need to be made
to attempt to answer this question. First of all the trait
or , ,ty (A-trait) must be distinguished from specific states of
anxiety (A-state) (Spielberger *et al.*, 1970):

> State anxiety, like kinetic energy, refers to an empirical process
> or reaction taking place at a particular moment in time and at
> a given level of intensity. Trait anxiety, like potential energy,
> indicates differences in the state of a latent disposition to mani-
> fest a certain type of reaction. And where potential energy
> denotes differences between physical objects in the amount of
> kinetic energy which may be released if triggered by an ap-
> propriate force, trait anxiety implies differences between
> people in the disposition to respond to stressful situations with
> varying amounts of A-state.

A person who is likely to be anxious in a wide variety of situations has A-trait, that is anxiety is a characteristic form of response
for him. All people, however, will respond with anxiety in situations
which they believe to be dangerous, for example, being under fire,
balancing on a high ledge or taking final examinations. The person
with A-trait, however, is more likely to perceive neutral situations
as dangerous and hence generate many more A-states than non
A-trait persons. Also truly dangerous situations may arouse different levels of anxiety in different situations. Secondly 'stress'
needs to be distinguished from 'threat'. 'Stress' refers to changes
in the external situation which are related to an objective danger
whereas 'threat' refers to the individual's subjective internal ap-
praisal that a situation is dangerous. Thus the level of stress felt
by an individual will be a function of the degree of threat he
perceives to be present in any particular situation. Anxiety can
cause problems for the individual in two distinct ways: it can be
'free floating' when it is more like a disposition or A-trait, that
is the individual is always inclined to be anxious and will respond
with anxiety to a minimal stimulus, or he may merely feel anxious
but not be able to relate it to anything in particular; alternatively,

the individual may feel free of anxiety but this apparent freedom is illusory since it is achieved by means of defence mechanisms which repress the feeling. These mechanisms are themselves un-helpful since their maintenance uses up a considerable amount of energy and their presence makes the individual unaware of the problem which is generating the repressed anxiety and hence he cannot take steps to solve it.

There are three main ways of telling if a person is anxious, first by taking certain physiological measures such as sweating, trem-bling, blushing or vomiting as indicators; second, by observing a person's general behaviour so that if before a test a person is very restless, chain smokes or talks too loudly and too much, it could be assumed, if these are not normal characteristics for him, that he is anxious; third, by means of tests of anxiety which are the most frequent indicators used by psychologists. To investigate test anxiety Sarason *et al.* (1960) devised the Test Anxiety Scale for Children (TASC) which consists of a series of items as 'when the teacher says she is going to find out how much you have learned, does your heart begin to beat faster?' or 'when you are in bed at night do you sometimes worry about how you are going to do in class the next day?'. The more positive responses a child gives the higher his anxiety level is judged to be. As a complement to this Ruebush (1960) composed the Defensiveness Scale for Children (DSC) to find out which children defended themselves against anxious feelings. It was found that in general girls gained higher TASC scores than boys and that scores tended to increase into the number of years a child spent in school. Another well known, and similar scale is Taylor's (1953) Manifest Anxiety Scale (MAS) which also consists of a series of items positive responses to which are judged to indicate anxiety.

Higher levels of anxiety correlate with lower IQ, lower school achievement and low self-esteem but it must be remembered that correlation does *not* imply a causal connection. The relationship between anxiety and IQ is somewhat difficult to disentangle. Even though high TASC scores have a negative correlation with IQ, this may not show that low IQ children are more anxious so much as point to the difficulty of testing high-anxiety children, since if they see an IQ test as threatening their performance will be lowered. There is also some support for the view that for very high IQ subjects a high level of anxiety may actually improve their performance. Denny (1966) showed that in a concept attainment task there was a crossover effect in that high anxiety hindered the low IQ subjects but appeared to improve the scores of high IQs.

The correlations between anxiety and achievement are much more coherent than are those between intelligence and anxiety. In almost every instance anxiety can be seen to impair performance at both school and university level. Paul and Eriksen (1964) tested the effect of anxiety by giving a group of first-year girl students a traditional examination on their course one morning. They knew that the marks on this test would count towards their course work mark. Immediately afterwards they were asked to fill in a test anxiety questionnaire and were then given a parallel form of the examination they had previously taken but this time it was stressed that the marks would not count towards their grade and every attempt was made to reduce stress by the examiners being 'warm, permissive and understanding'. When the results were analysed, with those students who either had very low or very high intelligence excluded, it was found that the highly anxious students did better on the non-stressful examination and the low anxiety students performed better in the traditional condition. Lunneborg (1964) tested boys and girls in top primary and lower secondary classes on their reading and arithmetic achievement and found that in all cases there was a negative correlation between anxiety and achievement, that the correlation was higher for girls than boys and that it increased as the children grew older. Hill and Sarason's (1966) results on a longitudinal study confirmed that the negative effect of anxiety increased during the primary years and also showed that in the early years reading achievement was more affected by anxiety than was arithmetic but that this was reversed in the later years. They also demonstrated that children whose anxiety level dropped over the years did considerably better than those whose anxiety level rose. For example those whose anxiety diminished improved 37.8 months in reading age compared with an improvement of 25.2 months for those whose anxiety increased. A similar effect for college students was found by Spielberger (1962) when his data revealed that while only eight out of 138 low-anxious students dropped out of college because of academic failure, twenty-six out of 129 high-anxious students left for this reason.

During a test it appears that highly anxious subjects, who are more disturbed by failure, are more likely to be put off by failing an early item than are low-anxious subjects. Smith and Rockett (1958) found that if students were asked to write comments on items during a multiple choice test the high-anxiety students did better and the low-anxiety worse but in the 'no comment' condition the high-anxiety students did worse. These results support Waite *et al.*'s (1958) finding that when children were matched for IQ the anxious children would do as well at the start of a test as the others but they deteriorated and finally scored much lower, nor did they seem able to improve with practice.

Cox (1963) showed that children in lower streams exhibited more test anxiety than those in higher streams. This is possibly because the experience of failure may cause a subsequent increase in anxiety (Bradshaw and Gaudry, 1968) or streaming itself may increase anxiety (Cox, 1963), or because the more anxious children do less well on tests given to them to decide their stream and hence end up in lower streams. A longitudinal study by Levy, Gooch and Kellmer-Pringle (1969) gave some support to the third explanation. In their study they tested primary children while they were still in unstreamed classes and found that the average anxiety score for boys who were subsequently put in the 'A' stream was 7.3, while it was 11.0 for those who went into the 'B' stream and 11.9 for those later in the 'C' stream.

Loughlin *et al.* (1965) showed that girls were significantly more anxious than boys and that this difference was most marked for girls of average intelligence and achievement and least for girls of high intelligence and achievement. The girls' anxiety level was highest in the middle years of primary rather than in top primary or lower secondary classes but this may not indicate that they had become less anxious rather it may reflect the increasing anxiety of the boys as they grew older.

Anxious children in addition to showing lower achievement also appear to be much lower in self-esteem and to day dream more – perhaps as a form of compensation. They are therefore much more likely to do badly in 'important' examinations in which there is a considerable degree of ego-involvement (Sinclair, 1969). Teachers may not recognize the highly anxious child (Barnard, Zimbardo and Sarason, 1968) in the same way as they recognize the highly intelligent but they have also been found (Cowen *et al.* 1965) to assess highly anxious children more negatively. While it was difficult to pick out the highly anxious girls within the classroom, Sarason *et al.* (1958) found high TASC scores for boys to be 'associated with hiding emotions, difficulty in communication, submissiveness, caution, lack of ambition, underactivity, under-achievement, lack of attention and lack of responsibility' (Gaudry and Spielberger, 1971). Anxious children were also found to be less popular with their peers and to have fathers who rated them more negatively and mothers who were defensive about them.

Thus anxiety appears to be detrimental in all areas, both at home and at school; if these children are to fulfil their potential it seems essential for tests and examinations to be made less stressful for them, although it is also important to keep the more traditional examinations for the low-anxious children since they appear to perform better under conditions where some stress is involved.

---

5 *Learning, personality and cognitive style*

In addition to the variables already mentioned some people may achieve more in one situation rather than another purely because of their personality or cognitive style. Eysenck has made two important sets of distinctions as measured by the Junior Eysenck Personality Inventory (S. G. B. Eysenck, 1965); these are between extraversion and introversion, and between neuroticism (or emotionality) and stability. The extravert is one who seeks stimulation and hence likes parties, crowds, activity, bright colours, is outgoing and seeks social contacts; the introvert is the reverse. The neurotic or emotional person is moody, nervous, worrying and restless whereas the stable person's responses are, generally speaking, appropriate to the situation. There are therefore four 'ideal' types: (1) neurotic extraverts, (2) stable extraverts, (3) neurotic introverts, and (4) stable introverts. Eysenck and Cookson (1969) tested 4,000 eleven-year-old boys and girls to see the degree of relationship between personality variables and achievement in verbal reasoning, mathematics, English, reading and grammar school entrance. Their main findings were that:

1 Extraverts, both male and female, did better on all tests than did introverts.
2 Stable children did only slightly better than neurotic ones

and among the neurotics those with high or low scores did better than those with average neuroticism scores.

3 There was a sex-effect in that female neurotic extraverts did well but their male counterparts performed badly.

4 Stable extraverts were more likely to gain a place in a grammar school and neuroticism seemed to lower the girls' chances more than the boys'.

5 Extraversion seemed a more important determinant of girls' scores than boys'.

Entwistle and Cunningham (1968) had also found a negative relationship between neuroticism and school achievement in thirteen-year-olds but they differed from Eysenck and Cookson in finding that achievement was related to extraversion in girls and to introversion in boys. It may be that age is the important factor here since Warburton (1968) found that introverts were superior in higher education. Entwistle, Percy and Nisbet (1971) however argued that personality factors were related to the subject studied in that neurotic introverts were better engineers and were good at languages whereas stable introverts were superior in the pure sciences and history. In the social sciences no correlation was found between personality and achievement. An important question is whether the extraverted primary child becomes the introverted university student or whether the selective nature of the university sample would account for the apparently superior performance of the introverts.

Leith and Trown (1970) related teaching techniques to personality variables with twelve-year-old children. They argued that,

There is a growing tendency to ask: 'What significance have individual differences for *how* particular people learn and *what* they achieve?' The implication is that individuals may well differ in their manner of approaching learning tasks, that some methods of instruction may be suitable for a proportion but not for all pupils and that ideally we should match methods media and order of presentation, in teaching, to particular students' strategies and modes of learning, their previously acquired knowledge, skills and aptitudes and their experience of success and failure.

Accordingly the authors compared the performance of children in two learning conditions. Both groups completed a programme on vectors but in the first group the rules were given before the practice examples and in the second after the example. Extraverts were found to perform much more poorly in the 'rules before' conditions while there was no difference for introverts.

In a different, but related, study of university students Parlett (1969) was able to distinguish between the 'syllabus-bound' and the 'syllabus-free' student. These different types of student were each able to achieve high grades but only if their academic setting was supportive of their preferred style of working. The 'syllabus-bound' student liked to work to a syllabus, have clearly defined assignments and work for regular examinations which were marked, whereas the 'syllabus-free' student needed a more open atmosphere in which he could follow his own interests in his own time and not be forced to conform to an external timetable or schedule. The 'syllabus-bound' student was more likely to reply 'true' to:

1 If I were to go to graduate school it would not primarily be because I was really excited about finding things out.
2 Without the stimulus of exams I doubt whether I would do much effective studying.
3 If I think about the amount that has to be covered and learned in my course work I sometimes get harassed and anxious.

They were also more likely to reply 'false' to:

1 I spend too long on certain topics because I get very involved in them.
2 Every year for the past few years I have read a lot of books covering widely differing subjects.
3 I frequently think of experiments or issues I would like to tackle.

It would seem that the 'syllabus-bound' student was more concerned with doing what was required of him, and his learning was contingent on this, whereas the 'syllabus-free' student learnt by following those aspects of the subject which were of interest to him.

The dividing line between personality variables and cognitive style is somewhat hazy since there may well be an interaction between the two. Nevertheless, for convenience, being dependent on a syllabus is here seen as a facet of personality whereas being 'field-dependent' is seen as indicating a certain type of cognitive style. Wilkin (see p. 69) has worked for many years in this area and has made an important distinction between the 'field-dependent' and the 'independent' person. The 'dependent' person perceives more globally and has difficulty in separating himself from his surroundings. The independent person is more likely to abstract himself from his surroundings and to view those surroundings more analytically. Witkin, Goodenough and Karp (1967) showed that field independence was likely to increase up to age seventeen and then level off and that individuals showed consistency in their preferred styles, sometimes for as long as fourteen years. Corah (1965) found that boys' scores were significantly related to those of their fathers and girls' to those of their mothers and hypothesizes that if 'field dependence–independence' is related to the degree of autonomy granted to the child (Witken *et al.*, 1962) then 'the present results might indicate that it is the opposite-sexed parent who plays the important role in this process ... this process may be mediated by the efforts of the opposite-sexed parent to foster the appropriate sexual identification in the child'.

If the 'independent' person is, in some sense, 'flexible' then the syllabus-bound student or the field-dependent thinker is rigid. Cognitively the rigid subject will have difficulty in analysing a problem and find particular difficulty in changing his strategy if the problem demands it or in using familiar objects in unfamiliar ways. Frenkel-Brunswick (1948) related perceptual and conceptual rigidity to personality factors such as a dislike of ambiguity, and a tendency towards being prejudiced and authoritarian.

However the influence of the flexibility/rigidity dimension on learning needs to be very carefully scrutinized. Parloff *et al.* (1968) looked at the 'personality correlates which differentiate creative male adolescents and adults' and extracted four factors: (1) 'disciplined effectiveness' which described those who were 'disciplined, painstaking and reliable' – the creative adolescents were found to be higher on this than the non-creatives whereas the reverse was true for adults; (2) 'assertive self-assurance' which picks out the outgoing, socially assured person, and was positively related to creativity for both groups; (3) 'autonomy' which was also positively correlated with creativity; and (4) 'humanitarian conscience' which for adolescents was 'characterised by breadth of interests, sensitivity and conscientiousness' and, for adults, with 'a tendency to hold and express conventional ideas, to be dependable, resourceful, sensitive and efficient' – this factor was not related to creativity for either sample. The authors summarized their findings by saying:

> The creative individual recognises and identifies new relationships among phenomena, and, by virtue of his respect for his own capacity is willing to attempt new integrations. Such functioning is consistent with the factors of adaptive autonomy and assertive self-assurance. A creative product, however, must also be effective – a bizarre idea may be novel but not effective. To produce an effective idea the creative individual must have a thorough grasp of his field. This requires a high degree of competence, discipline and motivation. These attributes may be reflected in the factor of disciplined effectiveness.

---

6 *Academic motivation*

6.1 *Forms of motivation*

Achievement motivation. When Entwistle (1968) administered a self-rating inventory to 2,707 Aberdeen school children he found that academic motivation correlated more closely with school attainment than did reasoning ability. Results such as this have led educators to stress the importance of 'motivation', often grouping many different types of motivation under the umbrella term of 'achievement' motivation. There seems little doubt that people who are motivated to succeed are likely to do better than others, who, all things being equal, are not so motivated but it would be a mistake to equate all the different forms of motivation simply because they all have the same result of increasing achievement. This is an important point since people will often realize the importance of motivation without realizing that different people are motivated in different ways and hence need different forms of stimulation.

What motivates one child may in fact act as a disincentive to another.

McClelland's own study (1955) and that in conjunction with his colleagues (1955) have concentrated on 'achievement motivation' which refers to the desire to seek 'success in competition with some standard of excellence'. His research was based on Murray's (1943) Thematic Apperception Test (TAT). In this test subjects are shown pictures of people in ambiguous situations and asked to tell stories about them or answer questions about what is happening in the picture. It is therefore a 'projective technique' since it is based on the theory that people will 'project' their own wishes and aspirations on to the subject of the picture and hence really be talking about themselves rather than the picture. Subjects in this type of test would be given a task designed to arouse their achievement motivation, as, for example, asking them to solve anagrams and telling them that it was a test of leadership potential. Having done this the subjects were then shown four TAT cards and their responses were scored for achievement themes and imagery. For example, when subjects were shown a picture of a man standing in a doorway looking out at the view, they would get a high need to achieve (n. ach.) score if they said he was a 'son about to step out into the world of reality. He is thinking of the prospects of success ahead of him and the events he will have to face.' A person who said 'A young man is lingering lazily in a doorway in a daydreaming type of pose' would get a low one (Atkinson, 1958).

Ausubel (1968) argued that 'achievement motivation' as exhibited in school has at least three components. The first is 'cognitive drive' by which the learner finds the task intrinsically interesting or wishes to be competent in it; it is thus a form of intrinsic motivation. White (1959) also spoke of the 'competence drive' as a wishing to do things well as distinct from wishing to achieve a task. This drive has some of the elements of play in that the agent will persue an activity well for its own sake and seek to meet the highest standards in its execution. The second component consists of the 'ego-enhancing' aspect of achievement motivation whereby the person is motivated not by intrinsic interest but by the extrinsic rewards in terms of praise and status. Closely related to this is Ausubel's third motive of affiliation, whereby an individual attempts to gain the approval of those with whom he wishes to affiliate. This can cut both ways however in that if a child affiliates with a group that does not value academic achievement his level will drop.

Gough (1964a and b), using an inventory method in which a person would check statements as true or false, distinguished 'achievement through conformance', which picked out self-disciplined, hard-working, rule-bound achievers, from 'achievement through independence' on which people who liked to solve their own problems and work in their own way, scored high. Both types of motivation were found to correlate with high school achievement.

The willingness to delay gratification has been linked with achievement motivation. Mischel (1961) related a person's preference for immediate small reinforcements (Im R) as contrasted with delayed larger reinforcements (Del R) with achievement motivation in a study of another culture. He argued that Del R would be related to achievement since Metzner (1960) had shown that 'one of the crucial conditions that facilitates the ability to delay gratification is the acquired reward value of working itself' and 'Liking to work for its own sake is generally assumed to be a basic ingredient of the high *n achievement* pattern'. Mischel studied 112 Trinidadian children aged eleven to fourteen years in which Im R was represented by a small bar of candy available immediately as opposed to a large candy bar in a week's time (Del R), and achievement was measured by TAT cards and an open-ended question: 'Now let's pretend that the magic man who came along could change you into anything that you wanted to be, what would you want to be?' The results showed that the Del R subjects consistently expressed more need for achievement than did the Im R subjects.

Crandall and Battle (1970) made an important distinction between 'accademic achievement' and 'intellectual effort' and said that achievement motivation is more differentiated than is often thought. They defined achievement behaviour as 'behaviour directed towards attainment of positive reinforcement or avoidance of negative reinforcement (from oneself or others) specifically *for the competence (skill) of one's performance* in tasks where standards of excellence are applicable'. Intellectual effort, on the other hand, 'means behaviours which exercise, maintain, or increase knowledge or intellectual skills in activities which are not demanded by the individual's vocational, academic status, or other pragmatic demands of his life situation'. The importance of their distinction was that adults who sought the one rather than the other were found to have had different types of childhood experiences, especially in terms of their relationships with their parents. (See p. 241.)

Atkinson *et al.* (1960) found that high achievement-motivated subjects would set goals of moderate difficulty whereas those with low levels of achievement motivation would set very high or very low goals. Atkinson and Feather (1966) have developed a theory which says that the harder a goal is to obtain the more attractive it is but its attractiveness for most people is modified by their perception of their probability of success. Thus people with a high need for achievement will select goals that are difficult but which they think they will achieve whereas those with a low need will select either very easy goals or very difficult ones, because of the former's ease of attainment and the latter's inherent attractiveness.

Fear of failure. In addition to being motivated to achieve success people may also seek to avoid failure. Mahone (1960) contrasted achievement motivation with avoidance of failure motivation. Since these two sets of motives are independent he was able to divide his subjects into four groups: (1) high achievement motivation/high fear of failure; (2) high achievement/low fear of failure; (3) low achievement/high fear of failure; and (4) low achievement/low fear of failure. He found that subjects who had a high fear of failure, i.e. groups (1) and (3), were more unrealistic in their vocational aspirations than were groups (2) and (4). In group (2), 75 per cent of choices were realistic as against 25 per cent unrealistic, whereas in group (3), 39 per cent were realistic in contrast to 61 per cent unrealistic. In a similar way Damm (1968) compared the goal-setting behaviour of 'approach success' versus 'failure avoidant' subjects. The former were reasonably confident when competing with peers but if they were in a face to face situation with an experimenter who was evaluating them they seemed no more confident than the 'failure avoidant' subjects. The latter, when in the face to face evaluative situation, behaved like the 'approach success' subject in the non-evaluative condition. Damm explains this crossover effect by saying that the face to face situation also arouses affiliative needs and that the highly achievement-motivated person becomes over-aroused and/or is in a conflict situation. The 'failure avoidant' person on the other hand is prepared to take greater risks in order to win social approval.

Avoiding success. Although most studies have been concerned with motivation to achieve success or avoid failure it has been found that certain groups may be motivated to avoid success. Woodward (1969) argued that blacks may avoid achievement since they do not wish to deviate from the ghetto norm and become alienated from their peers. Horner (1970) showed that women have a 'motive to avoid success' which she distinguished from a 'will to fail'. She had found (1968) that when girls who had a motive to avoid success, had to compete against boys they performed significantly lower than when they had to carry out the same task in a non-competitive situation, when the only competition was with the girls' own standard and the requirements of the task itself; those who had no such motive performed better in the competitive study. Like McClelland, Horner used TAT cards to infer the motive to avoid success and judged it as being present if a subject dwelt on 'the negative consequences of success, conflict about success, denial of effort or responsibility for success or bizarre and inappropriate responses'. She also found that while fear of success was characteristic of white women it was more characteristic of black men than black women. Fear of success imagery appeared in 10 per cent of the white men's stories, 29 per cent of the black women's, 64 per cent of the white women's and 67 per cent of the black men's. College women who feared success, although they were doing well, were found to change their study course to make it more consonant with their image of women. One such student, who had changed from medicine to law, said: 'Law school is less ambitious, it doesn't take as long . . . is more flexible in terms of marriage and children. It is *less masculine* in that it is more accepted for girls to go to law school.'

6.2 *Foundations of academic motivation*

Parental values and aspirations. A person's achievement motivation is often seen to be related to their parents' values, and aspirations. Kahl (1953) showed that only working-class boys who had parents who viewed school as a way of achieving a better life than their own had been, actually took advantage of the opportunities offered by the school: 'Only sons who internalised such values were sufficiently motivated to overcome the obstacles which faced the common man boys in school; only they saw a good reason for good school performance and college aspirations.' Hyman (1953) argued that working-class values hindered mobility in that they did not stress high success goals but stressed the difficulties of achieving success, and did not emphasize the achievement of sub-goals which were instrumental for adult success. Similarly Rosen (1956) argued that values affect mobility by defining goals and by making the child aware of achievement, and thus help him to take the necessary steps to achieve. Katz (1964), found that 'success' had different connotations for different groups of adolescents. For the middle-class children success meant prestige through personal effort whereas for the working-class children success meant having possessions which were usually unobtainable.

Sewell and Shah (1968) looked at social class, parental encouragement and educational aspirations and found that parental encouragement was more important than either socio-economic status (SES) or intelligence for the college plans of their children, although SES was much more important than intelligence for girls.

Turner (1970) found that in all classes male adolescents with a high need for achievement came from homes in which the fathers had an entrepreneurial role in their jobs, and Swift (1964) showed that fathers in the lower middle class who were dissatisfied with their jobs were more likely to have children who passed the 11+ and to have values which were closer to those of the middle class. Swift concluded that:

> This second ideal type of academically successful family was one in which mobility pessimism was high, and discipline was 'traditional'. Commitment to education was 'high' but of a very different nature to the high commitment expressed in the ideal-type middle class family where it is valued for its liberating qualities for the individual. Instead (in the light of the 'traditional' discipline ethos) it was seen as a necessary aspect of certificate collecting which was, in turn, seen to be the major 'external' demand of the social environment.

Child-rearing techniques. In 1958, Winterbottom found that the mothers of high achievers expected their sons to master certain activities earlier than did the mothers of low-achieving sons; for example, a son was expected to know his way around the city, be active and energetic, try hard for things for himself, make his own friends and do well in competition. Since then researchers have been interested in the effect of early child-rearing practices on later achievement.

A classic study is that of Rosen and D'Andrade (1959). They tested forty boys aged between nine and eleven, half of whom had high achievement and half low achievement scores, in the presence of both parents. The boys had to perform four tasks – block stacking, anagrams, Kohl's block patterns and a ring-toss game. The parental behaviour was carefully monitored throughout and parents were asked to estimate how well they thought their child would do. The results were complex and interesting. Direct achievement training was more positively associated with achievement than was independence training, and parents of high achievers seem to be more competitive and take more pleasure in the experiments. The fathers tended 'to beckon from ahead rather than push from behind'. The mothers of high achievers were considerably more involved than were the mothers of low achievers since they were more likely to reward success with approval and punish failure with hostility. The parental profiles were different in that the boys did best with fathers who did not dominate and with mothers who did. The authors comment that this is '... possibly because she is perceived as *imposing her standards* on the boy, while a dominating father is perceived as *imposing himself* on the son'. Fathers of high achievers were less pushing, rejecting and dominant than average, mothers more so.

McClelland (1961) related the need for achievement in adults to child-rearing practices in which mothers expected their sons to be independent at an early age (Winterbottom, 1958) and argued that this type of training could be combined with Weber's (1930) theory of the protestant religion favouring an independent type of character who, in adulthood, caused the development of the modern industrial capitalist state:

> The Protestant Reformation might have led to earlier independence and mastery training, which led to greater n achievement, and in turn led to the rise of modern capitalism. Certainly Weber's description of the kind of personality type which the Protestant Reformation produced is startlingly similar to the

picture we have drawn of a person with high achievement motivation (Fig. 9.1).

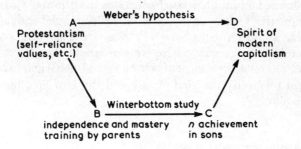

Fig. 9.1 *Parallels between Weber's hypothesis and Winterbottom's findings*
(McClelland, 1961)

Husted and Cervantes (1970) studied high school drop-outs and found that for these boys their mothers were the single most important influence on them and that their view of the value of academic achievement was primarily influenced by her. In addition the relationship between them was found to be limited, with little 'depth communication' and little 'companionship in pleasure'. After a lengthy and detailed study of the childhood experiences which lead to academic achievement on the one hand, and intellectual effort on the other, Crandall and Battle (1970) concluded that girls who were later achievers avoided achievement situations when aged three to five whereas boys who later achieved did so in early childhood. Both sexes showed that later achievers were dependent on adults and fearful of peers. The mothers of girls who later displayed intellectual effort did not support their daughter's dependency behaviour, unlike the mothers of academic achieving girls. The 'intellectual-effort' boys were independent and unruly and always resisted adult socializing attempts unlike the dependent adult-orientated boys who were alienated from their peers and later became the high academic achievers; these boys seemed to be particularly sensitive to adult socializing influences. The authors found that maternal independence training was related *only* to subsequent intellectual effort for males, and that childhood achievement effort did not relate to such effort in adulthood. They concluded:

> It would seem that the distinction made between effort in academic and in intellectual situations has allowed a more discriminating look at a number of factors associated with achievement approach behaviour ... We are past the point in achievement research where we can ignore the effects of the situation on achievement motivations and behaviour. We must begin to specify the *kind* of task and the *kind* of achievement situation.

6.3 *Increasing motivation*

Given that motivation is an extremely important determinant of academic achievement how can motivation be stimulated? Kolb (1965) ran an Achievement Motivation Training programme as part of a summer school programme, in which the boys were taught about the nature of achievement motivation, the nature of the behavioural changes they would need to make to achieve more and how people were likely to react to these. There was a deliberate attempt to get the boys to believe that they would, indeed, improve. All the boys showed improved school marks in follow-up studies, with those from higher SES homes improving most. The low SES subjects, in fact, improved less than the controls. All the experimental boys had a significant increase in achievement motivation but Kolb argued that the low SES boys were not able to capitalize upon this and turn it into good grades because their homes did not support them. The high SES boys, on the other hand, who had been failing, were able to use the techniques they had learned and let their behaviour become more consonant with the expectations of their parents, which led to a reduction in the tensions generated by their previous failures.

McClelland (1969) drew attention to the role educational technology, in terms of films, visual aids and recording apparatus, could play in developing achievement motivation; it could help convey information better, arouse attention, arouse and sustain achievement motivation, stimulate fantasy, encourage participation and make self-study easier. By using various media he was able to disseminate more widely tapes and films which had been found to be successful, and thereby aid teachers who, though willing to help their pupils, might have had neither the time nor the skill to produce their own materials.

Further reading

Adams, B. N. (1972) Birth order: A Critical Review. *Sociometry 35*(3): 411–39.

Atkinson, J. W. and Feather, N. T. (eds) (1966) *A Theory of Achievement Motivation.* New York: John Wiley.

Bardwick, J. M. (ed.) (1971) *The Psychology of Women: a Study in Biosocial Conflict.* New York: Harper and Row.

Bardwick, J. M. (ed.) (1972) *Readings on the Psychology of Women.* New York: Harper and Row.

Coopersmith, S. (1967) *The Antecedents of Self Esteem.* San Francisco: Freeman.

Crandall, V. C. and Battle, E. S. (1970) The Antecedents and Adult Correlates of Academic and Intellectual Achievement Effort. In John P. Hill (ed.) *Minnesota Symposia on Child Psychology.* University of Minnesota Press.

Gaudry, E. and Spielberger, C. D. (1971) *Anxiety and Educational Achievement.* Ryde, New South Wales: John Wiley.

Hobbs, N. (ed.) (1974) *Issues in the Classification of Children.* London: Dent.

Maccoby, E. E. (ed.) (1966) *The Development of Sex Differences.* London: Tavistock.

McClelland, D. C. (1961) *The Achieving Society.* Princeton, New Jersey: Van Nostrand.

Stott, D. H. and Neill, S. J. (1975) *Taxonomy of Behaviour Disturbance.* University of London Press.

Spielberger, C. (ed.) (1972) *Anxiety: Current Trends in Theory and Research.* New York: Academic Press.

Wolff, S. (1969) *Children Under Stress.* Harmondsworth, Middlesex: Penguin.

School achievement

The previous chapter was concerned with particular individual differences which affect learning, both positively and negatively. In this chapter more general factors which can affect school performance are considered, for example, extremes of intellectual capacity, language, home influence, type of school and teacher behaviour. A pupil's level of attainment is likely to be influenced by the interaction of personal and situational variables.

1 Exceptional children

1.1 The underachieving child

Probably the one topic that causes most concern to educationalists is that of underachievement, i.e. children who either appear not to fulfil their own potential or children whose performance is well outside the norms of the school, and falls below society's expectations. Shaw (1968) listed five definitions of underachievement:

1 A discrepancy model which utilizes the difference between attainment as reflected in grades and expected attainment as reflected in a measure of scholastic aptitude or intelligence.

2 A discrepancy model which utilizes the difference between attainment as reflected by achievement test scores and expected attainment as reflected in a measure of scholastic aptitude or intelligence.

3 A regression model which utilizes the interrelationship between achievement tests and tests of intelligence or scholastic aptitude.

4 A regression model which utilizes the relationship between

academic grades and objective measures of intelligence or scholastic aptitude.

5 A concept which utilizes only grades or an objective measure of achievement as an index of 'underachievement'.

These definitions are reasonably inclusive but, nevertheless, the larger variables of handicap, class and culture are also involved in descriptions of underachievement. Thus underachievement can mean 'those who do not do as well as expected' or 'those who do not do well'. It is also a relative definition since in one family failure to go to university may be seen as underachievement, in another failing to take 'O' levels.

Handicaps. School achievement is, fundamentally, a sign of adequate conceptual and, possibly, social development. It is often argued that conceptual development relies on perceptual development and therefore a person who has any perceptual inadequacies will show learning problems. Both Werner (1948) and Inhelder and Piaget (1964) maintained that children's original perceptions of objects are related to their actions towards that object, and subsequent conceptual development relies on adequate perceptual understanding through action. Keogh and Smith (1967) found that children who had low scores on the Bender Gestalt test (a test of visual/motor ability) in their first year at school also had low scores in reading and spelling in the junior school, and Snyder and Freud (1967) found a correlation between visual–perceptual measures and reading readiness measures from which they too concluded that children who have inadequate perceptual development when they enter school will have later reading problems. Spatial orientation skills were also found to be related to reading ability by Davol and Hastings (1967). Although correlations should not cause one to say that A causes B, it would seem sensible to combine perceptual-motor training with more direct teaching methods for all readers so that those children who are affected in this way will benefit while the rest will not be harmed.

Perceptual motor deficiencies however are not the only forms of handicap. Rutter and his co-workers (Rutter, Tizard and Whitmore, 1970; Rutter, Graham and Yule, 1970) studied a complete group (all children born between 1st September, 1953 and 31st August, 1965) living on the Isle of Wight in order to gain a picture of 'handicap' in a total school population. They concentrated on four areas of 'handicap': (1) subnormality of intelligence (2) backwardness in reading (3) maladjustment or psychiatric disorder and (4) physical handicap and neurological handicap. The numbers found were considerable and since the majority could not be placed in special schools primary teachers were expected to deal with children with single or multiple handicaps. Handicaps of the first and second kinds are particularly likely to affect educational achievement and so too may physical and neurological handicaps if they cause the child to have difficulties in attending or concentrating, or result in impoverished auditory or visual perception. Absences from school to attend hospital will affect the child's progress and he will be particularly likely to be retarded if his handicap affects the brain.

Maladjustment.   Maladjustment, although a handicap, is a very different problem. A child who is blind, deaf or brain-damaged may be maladjusted, a maladjusted child may have no specific handicap. The term 'mental illness' is somewhat misleading since it implies that the person has 'got something' like a virus, whereas 'maladjustment' is essentially an interactive concept; if a person is considered to be maladjusted, the implication is that he has fallen foul of a set of norms developed by others and it is the nature of these norms which defines his degree of maladjustment. Thus, like beauty, it is often to be found in the eye of the beholder rather than in the person himself.

Nevertheless if a child's behaviour is such that his family, teachers and peers find him unacceptable then in the child's own interests, some treatment is necessary. Ideally *all* parties should have some help so that the modification of behaviour is not all on the side of the maladjusted child but includes those who deal with him. Their greater insight into his perceptions will enable them to meet his needs with greater insight and understanding. To take a very simple example if a child needs reassurance he may make demands on the teacher for her attention which cannot be met in the time available. The child feels more anxious and demands more attention and a vicious circle is set up. Even if the teacher does meet his demands all he may learn is that attention seeking behaviour will be rewarded and so he continues to seek attention. The solution is to go one step further back and attempt to assuage the original anxiety so that attention seeking is no longer necessary. Sometimes group therapy is used (Ackerman, 1958), sometimes this may not be appropriate (Wolff, 1969). Behaviour therapy which concentrates on modifying behaviour, through positive and negative reinforcement has also had some success. Hewett (1967) concentrated on bringing the child's behaviour into line with what was required for him to be able to learn, and Haring and Phillips (1962) stressed the importance of a structured environment for emotionally disturbed children, so that they could gradually learn to be responsible, to learn effectively and to become more like 'normal' children. Whether psychotherapy or behaviour therapy is favoured as a method of treatment is, at present, rather an *ad hoc* decision since there is little evidence as to the relative efficacy of these two methods.

Personality and aspirations. Ironically underachievement may be the result of personal characteristics rather than specific handicaps or serious maladjustment. Shaw has carried out a series of studies based on a discrepancy model of underachievement, which point to personality differences between underachievers and achievers. In 1957 (Shaw and Brown, 1957) he studied first year American undergraduates and found that underachievers were rated as significantly more hostile on the social scale of the Bell Preference Inventory (1947). He followed this up in 1958 (Shaw and Grubb, 1958) and 1960 (Shaw and Black, 1960) and found more hostility exhibited by male underachievers in both studies. He then turned to the underachievers' self-concept and in a further series of studies (Shaw, Edson and Bell, 1960; Shaw, 1961) obtained consistent evidence of underachievers having a more negative self-concept than achievers, and having generalized feelings of inadequacy. His conclusions (Shaw, 1968) are important

> . . . it seems clear that these pupils manifest behaviour characteristics which cause negative social judgments to be made about them. Thus teachers' grades for these individuals reflect not what the underachievers *know* but rather the personal impact they have on their teachers. This should not be construed as a criticism of teachers. If, for example, a child fails to turn in required work, either because of a basic hostility or a fear of failure resulting from negative self-concept, the teacher may be

left without any basis on which to judge ... Underachievement viewed in this light appears to reflect *ineffective social behaviour* which results in generally negative social judgments by others. These negative social judgments include poor grades. Thus, the underachiever does not actually fail to learn but he fails to demonstrate that he did learn.

People have been found to differ in the extent to which they believe that they are able to control their environment and their life chances. Three researchers (Crandall, Katkovsky and Crandall, 1965) developed an Intellectual Achievement Responsibility (IAR) scale to see if belief in self-direction was related to academic achievement. The scale includes such items as: 'If the teacher passes you to the next grade, would it probably be (a) because she liked you, or (b) because of the work you did?' The respondent is forced to chose (a) or (b). McGhee and Crandall (1968) found that students who accepted responsibility for their own work did obtain higher grades and the boys who took responsibility for their own failures performed better on standardized tests of achievement. Coleman *et al.* (1960) found that disadvantaged children, in contrast to advantaged children, expressed much greater uncertainty concerning their ability to control their environment.

Frankel (1960) also found a series of differences between achieving and underachieving boys in secondary school, all of whom had high ability. Although matched for IQ, the underachievers had lower scores in mathematical and verbal aptitude tests; they were more interested in mechanical and artistic activities than in mathematical or scientific ones, but said 'Science' was their preferred school subject. Although reporting less health problems than the achievers the underachievers had more absences from school. The underachievers were less conforming and had a more negative attitude to school, but participated more in out of school activities such as social and athletic clubs and the Scouts than did the achievers.

Harrison (1964) looked at 'inconsistent' students, i.e. those who did better or worse than their socio-economic status would lead one to expect, and found that the attitudes of the 'disadvantaged successful' were more like those of the 'advantaged successful' and less like those of the other disadvantaged students. Similarly the attitudes of the 'advantaged unsuccessful' were unlike those of the other advantaged students being closer to those of the disadvantaged group. He analysed all the pupils' beliefs about man's ability to control his environment, their attitude to education, their membership of school groups, and the attitude of each particular pupil's peer group towards education. Both the 'advantaged successful' and the 'disadvantaged successful' had an optimistic approach to the future, had positive views of school groups and shared their peers' values but *all* groups had a positive view of education and this area did not distinguish between the successful and the unsuccessful students whether advantaged or not.

Hamachek (1968) argued that a pupil's self-concept would affect his level of achievement in that he will achieve what he thinks others expect him to achieve. The pupil's peer group can also have an important role since Grinder (1966) found that adolescents who are particularly interested in 'dating' and youth culture activities were likely to do less well in school. Ringness (1967) showed that one would be led to expect that students whose achievement was higher than their IQs, were less interested in the companionship of their peers than were pupils whose achievement was low compared to their IQs. In contrast Gecas' (1972) sample felt their self-esteem raised most when they were with their peers in comparison with the four other contexts of family, classroom, heterosexual relations and adults. Parental support was only found to raise their self-esteem when the adolescents were themselves using adult frames of reference. Sugarman (1968) showed that boys from homes with a low intellectual quality scored more highly for school adjustment than all other boys if they belonged to a group characterized by good achievement and good conduct. Although Wallen (1964) found peers to be no more motivating than teachers or the pupil himself, in general peer groups appear to reinforce home values.

In a British survey Marriott (1964) found that a boy's social background strongly influenced his career choice and that there was, at all levels, an equally strong tendency to aspire to a career either at, or slightly above, the parental level. In connection with ambition Turner (1964) made an important distinction between 'mobility ambition' and 'eminence ambition'. The former requires a person to move out of his own socio-economic class and adopt the values of the class he moves into, whereas the latter enables a person 'to get to the top' but remain within his original social class, i.e. rising, but within occupations linked to that class. Girls were more likely to have school friends from their own social class

and to adhere, in adult life, to their original values. They would
also turn to marriage as a way of improving their status rather
than seek to move upwards by their own work efforts. Turner argued
that an ambitious man puts all his investment in his career whereas
his wife would be more interested in the products of an occupation
rather than in the career itself.

1.2 The gifted child

Who are the gifted?   In many ways the gifted child is as much
of an enigma as is the underachieving child and some children
can be both gifted and underachieving. The Plowden report (1967)
drew attention to the suspicion which surrounds the whole concept
of 'giftedness'. One major problem is that of definition: a 'gifted
child' may be one who has an exceptionally high IQ, but this
depends on whether 'exceptionally high' means the top 1 per cent,
5 per cent or 30 per cent; it may mean a child who is exceptional
in one area – for example musical ability; or it could be based
on multiple criteria following Burt's (1962) suggestion of looking
at the child as a whole.

The Donnison report (1970) defined the gifted as the top 2 per
cent of the population (IQ 130+). Burt (1974) said he used the
term 'gifted' to mean 'the brightest three per cent in the general
population' since when he began work in London this percentage
and the IQ 130 borderline picked out those likely to obtain scholar-
ships to grammar schools. The National Child Development Study
(NCDS) (Hitchfield, 1973) which is following up all the children
born in England, Scotland and Wales in the week the 3rd to the
9th March, 1958 (17,000 births) used three separate criteria for
identifying children as 'gifted': first, the Goodenough 'Draw-a-
man' test; second, high attainment in reading and number work;
and third, parents' recommendations. IQ was not used for selecting
the gifted sample but all the children were given an individual
IQ test once they had been selected on the above criteria.

Once selected the 'gifted' children were also given tests of
propositional logic, general knowledge, understanding of concepts
such as responsibility, rules, equality, authority and causality, tests
of divergent thinking and the 'Barron-Welsh art scale', since this
had been found to distinguish 'artists' from 'non-artists' and
research scientists from other adult scientists. They were also given

a sentence completion test and a structured interview which covered school, teachers, interests, self and friends. The intelligence test showed that the boys' average IQ was 131 and the girls' 126. Parents were also found to be 'as effective in identifying intelligent children as other methods used'.

Hildreth (1966) summarized the various definitions of giftedness by listing five criteria which could be used to identify the gifted child:

1 He is superior to his age-mates in traits other than those capacities that are purely physical, physiological, or dependent primarily on muscular development.

2 He possesses the intellectual powers and qualities essential for success with advanced education and training in general or in his speciality.

3 His superior developmental maturation is reasonably consistent from the early years of life to maturity.

4 His unusual abilities may be general or specialized, his superior traits single or multiple.

5 The traits and abilities in which he shows superiority are those that predict unusual achievement or productivity in areas of high social value.

Characteristics of gifted children. Probably a broad definition of giftedness is wisest rather than one based purely on IQ. Although the NCDS found no justification for separating the 'creative' from the 'intelligent', it did identify several other characteristics which distinguished the gifted from the average children. At birth they were heavier than average, were more likely to be near the top of their families in birth order (see p. 222) and, surprisingly, had significantly more mothers over forty than did the other children born in the same week. At school three-quarters of the group were rated, both at age seven and eleven, by their teachers as being above average in reading, mathematics, oral ability and general knowledge. There was a strong social-class effect with middle-class children being over-represented (Table 10.1).

Terman (1925, 1930, 1947, 1959) has followed a gifted group through childhood and adulthood. He selected them in 1921 and all had IQs of 150+. One of his most interesting findings was that highly intelligent children were also more likely to be physically

Table 10.1 *Social class distribution of gifted children*

Registrar General's social class classification	Whole cohort (%)	Gifted group (%)
I	5	12
II	14	28
III	54	40
IV	17	13
V	6	5
No male head of household	3	2

(Hitchfield, 1973)

better developed than their peers and this physical superiority was maintained in adult life when they were found to be less likely to suffer from physical or mental illness than the general population and to have a lower incidence of alcoholism. They also appeared to be better adjusted than the average and have a considerably lower delinquency rate. The NCDS survey used the Bristol Social Adjustment Guide (Stott, 1963) and found that at age seven 67 per cent of the whole cohort were rated as 'stable', 21 per cent 'unsettled' and 12 per cent 'maladjusted', in the gifted group the percentages were 88 per cent 'stable' and only 3 per cent 'maladjusted'. The teachers also found the gifted children well integrated in school and were more likely to describe them as 'extraverts'. However, there was some indication that those with IQs over 130 found 'life "more difficult" than the others' and their parents reported that they tended to worry. The reason for this may be related to an interesting finding that came out of the children's interview in the NCDS and this was that the highly intelligent children may have philosophical difficulties. They reported being disturbed by the idea of infinity, some even saying they were frightened to think of it. When the researchers asked the children if they had discussed this with anybody they all replied that they had not.

Gallagher (1958) found that gifted children were exceptionally popular with peers of all intellectual levels and that they chose their friends from all intellectual levels. Gifted children in less academic schools were also popular but seemed to have more motivational problems which the author suggested could be because they were seeking peer acceptance to the detriment of their intellectual performance. There was a slight, but statistically non-significant, indication that the children with the highest scores had more social problems than those with slightly lower scores. Grace and Booth (1958) found that gifted children were more likely to be among the most popular children and were under-represented in the 'least popular' group. On the other hand under-achieving children were more likely to appear in the 'least popular' category and none appeared, in their sample in the 'most popular' group. The NCDS survey found the most intelligent to be self-appointed leaders and were likely to see themselves as 'self-assertive'. All of the children appeared to enjoy life with those with IQs under 130 accepting happily what came and those with IQs over 130 being concerned to achieve their ambitions in life – 'There's lots of chances but you have to take the chances when you get them.'

The NCDS interviews with parents found some class differences although all the parents showed greater interest in their children's education than did the general run of parents in the cohort. They were also ambitious for their children and although the children were still at primary school 60 per cent of the parents had already thought of the career they wanted their child to follow. Thirty per cent said they wanted them to go to university and a further 32 per cent agreed with this idea when it was suggested to them. Both the middle-class and working-class parents who had children with IQs of 130+, had had a longer than average education and 43 per cent of the middle-class and 19 per cent of the working-class mothers reported having previously worked with children, mainly as teachers. The vast majority of the parents were satisfied with their children's school but, if dissatisfied, it was the middle-class parents who were more likely to complain. In terms of secondary schooling the middle-class parents favoured grammar or indepen-dent schools whereas the working-class parents were prepared to accept what was offered to them. One clear class difference appeared when the parents were asked to sum up their child 'as a person'. The researchers categorized their replies as 'warm' if they stressed positive attributes and 'cold' if they were mainly critical; 'objective' if they referred to their child as a separate person and 'subjective' if they referred to their child with reference to themselves. When combined these replies gave four response categories: 'parents who speak warmly of their child, appreciate and value him as a person, WO because of qualities in his own personality which are seen to be valuable (objective), WS because of the closeness of identification with parents (subjective); parents who speak critically of their child, focus on faults more than virtues, CO because the qualities they see in him they judge rather harshly (objective), CS because their child does not come up to subjective demands' (Table 10.2). Parents were also found to undervalue their able girls.

Table 10.2 *Parents' descriptions of their child*

	WO	*WS*	*CO*	*CS*	*Total*
IQ 130+	54	26	14	20	114
IQ 129−	44	51	7	22	124
Total	98	77	21	42	238
Total %	41	32	9	18	100
Social Class					
Non-manual	64	26	16	22	128
Manual	34	51	5	20	110
Total	98	77	21	42	238
Total %	41	32	9	18	100

(Hitchfield, 1973)

Educational provision. Perhaps the most difficult question to answer is whether special educational provision should be made for gifted children. Although they appear to be happy and successful at school Armstrong (1967) showed that of the children admitted to West Riding grammar schools in 1956 and 1957 with IQs of 135+, twice as many middle-class children continued into full-time higher education even though both middle-class and working-class children exhibited a similar performance at 'O' and 'A' level. If the children are bored at school or not recognized as gifted there is an obvious problem but, when they are recognized, 'acceleration' may not be the answer since they will probably have to repeat a year at the end of primary school. 'Enrichment' is obviously helpful but it is to be hoped that primary schools are flexible enough to incorporate this into the daily activities rather than causing these children to be segregated in special schools. However, in the 1968 pamphlet 'Education of Gifted Children', the Department of Education and Science did support the Royal Ballet School and the Yehudi Menuhin School for children who needed specialist and intensive tuition which could not be provided in a local school.

There appears to be a tendency to deny the needs of 'gifted' children; Rowlands (1974) quotes a local authority spokesman who said to him in 1973:

> Gifted children – if they exist, that is, and I suppose they do to some extent – aren't a problem exactly. We've got lots of problems – we've got some kids who ought to be in an ESN School but aren't, we've got truancy, we've got a couple of real 'jungles'. In the older lot we've got gangs and too few teachers. There's a hell of a lot to work at without taking on extra responsibility. No, a gifted child – he's going to do very well, if he's ahead of the class he can always read on his own. And sometimes you get an opportunity to use them as teachers you know, they help the slower ones along. Teachers need a bit of help. What with the size of classes … we *have* had a kiddie or two who's been getting on badly but the head teachers got them seen by the psychologist. They turned out to be much brighter than anyone had thought – I don't know about *gifted*. Well, they seem to be getting on better now. But any teacher can make mistakes.

A National Association for Gifted Children (NAGC) was formed in 1964 which is a group of interested parents and teachers, represented at both national and local level. The Association aims to help identify the gifted, to run conferences on giftedness and to arrange special activities for the gifted and members of their families. It is to be hoped that their activities will help alert teachers and local authorities to these children's existence in order to avoid wastage particularly among those who underachieve or come from academically unstimulating homes.

2 *The role of language*

It is often said that 'language deficit' is responsible for educational underachievement and there seems to be at least three research strands contributing to this view. First there are the studies of the role of verbal mediation in mental development, second, studies of children who have difficulty in using language as a medium of communication in school, and third, studies of social-class differences in language usage. Great care, however, should be taken to keep these strands separate otherwise one can slip into an argument that runs: 'working-class children have difficulty in communicating; their language development is different from that of middle-class children; and, therefore, their cognitive development is inferior to that of middle-class children.' There may well be important half-truths contained in this but it is a gross over-simplification. In the first place *all children develop 'linguistic competence'*, i.e. they are all able to use, for example, verbs, nouns and adjectives appropriately and do not produce a form of jumbled syntax; *but* some children are more able to utilize their linguistic competence to communicate and hence differ in their 'communicative competence'. Secondly we should not assume that because a child does not use a certain linguistic form he does not have the underlying cognitive understanding. This is illustrated in Slobin's (1973) study of two girls who were bilingual in Hungarian and Serbo-Croatian. Before the age of two, when speaking Hungarian, the children were able to express notions of direction and position, e.g. 'into' 'out of' 'on top of', etc., but they did not express such notions in Serbo-Croatian. It happens that it is more complex, linguistically, to express direction and position in Serbo-Croatian than in Hungarian, and therefore we can see that it is possible for a child to have developed an idea cognitively but to be inhibited in its expression by linguistic complexity.

2.1 *Verbal mediation and cognitive development*

The relationship between language and thought has generated considerable controversy. Piaget (1949) argued that since language is a symbolic system it will show the limitation characteristic of all symbols, which is that since a symbol stands in place of the object it symbolizes, then it can only be interpreted if one *already knows* the object. Therefore symbols do not add anything new to an individual's knowledge, they merely enable him to formulate what he already knows in a different way. Nevertheless language can facilitate 'formal' thinking (see p. 24) since, by its very nature, it enables a person to transcend the here and now and is therefore concerned with possible rather than actual worlds and with the hypothetical rather than the verified. Thus language seems to be particularly important for certain cognitive tasks rather than under-lying cognitive ability in general. Jensen (1973) makes a useful distinction between 'developmental' and 'experiential' factors and points out that developmental factors may be relatively important in vocabulary acquisition in early childhood, while experiential factors may be of much greater importance for vocabulary acquisition in adolescence.

Verbal mediation theories refer to covert symbolic representation as 'standing between' the overt stimulus and the overt response. As Cassirer (1953) said: 'man has, as it were, discovered a new method of adapting himself to his environment. Between the receptor system and the effector system, which are to be found in all animal species, we find in man a third link which we may describe as the symbolic system.' Similarly Werner (1967) argued that human cognition represented a discontinuity with the animal world since the emergence of symbolic behaviour was man's means of going beyond the simple responses of other species

> ...at the post-neonatal human level, with the emergence of a basic directiveness towards knowing, man's hand and man's brain participate in the construction of tangible tools out of the properties of the environment and the construction of cognitive objects (percepts and concepts) which mediate between man and his physical milieu. It is primarily towards these objects that man's distinctive behaviour is orientated. It is in this context, ... that the most significant of man's instrumentalities, *the symbol* is formed.

Jensen (1973) quotes White's (1968) study which argued that 'adult mental organisation is hierarchical, consisting of two main "layers" (a) an associative level laid down early in development and following conventional associative principles [see p. 64] and (b) a "cognitive layer" laid down in later childhood'. He then lists some of the experimental studies which White used to illustrate the transposition, for example:

1 Narrow to broad transposition.
2 Easier non-reversal shifts to easier reversal shifts. (See p. 48.)
3 Growth of inference in problem-solving tasks.
4 Shift from 'near' receptors (tactual, kinesthetic, etc.) to 'distance' receptors (visual and auditory) in attending to environmental events.
5 Shift from colour to form–dominance in classifying objects.
6 Development of personal left–right sense.
7 Decrease in form, word, and letter reversals.
8 Ability to hold spatial information through disorientation.
9 Increasing predictability of adult IQ.
10 Internalization of speech.
11 Shift from syntagmatic (associations having a meaningful connection but not grammatical likeness) to paradigmatic (associations having the same grammatical form class) word associations.
12 Shift of verbalization towards a planning function in the child's activity.
14 A number of transitions involving conservation of number, length, space, volume, etc., shown in Piaget-type studies.

Jensen maintains that the shifts illustrated by White can be summarised in terms of four general transitions:

(a) from direct responses to stimuli to responses produced by mediated stimuli;
(b) emergence of the ability to induce invariance on the welter of phenomenal variability;
(c) the capacity to organize past experience to permit inference and prediction; and
(d) increased sensitivity to information yielded by distance as against near receptors.

Since these are significant cognitive changes differences in ability to use verbal mediation are almost certain to result in differences in academic achievement.

Luria and Yudovich (1959) investigated the role of symbolic mediation experimentally by following the progress of a pair of twins. Initially the twins, aged five, had a speech defect and did not appear to need speech to communicate with each other. The result of their linguistic impoverishment was, according to the researchers, that they showed mental retardation in that they did not use speech to organize their activities, nor were they able to classify in the most elementary way. Words for them only had meaning in a 'concrete-active situation'. The researchers then separated the twins by putting them in parallel kindergarten classes and began systematic speech training with twin A. Both twins showed both linguistic and mental improvement but this was particularly marked for twin A. For example when asked to find the difference between 'an egg' and 'a stone' twin A said 'A stone is black, an egg white' whereas twin B could not compare since she could do no more than mark similar features 'a white stone and a white egg'. Again when faced with an 'absurd' picture (presumably 'the cat and the fiddle') the twins reasoned thus:

Twin A

Experimenter:	Do you think this happens?
Twin A:	It does.
Experimenter:	What is the cat doing?
Twin A:	The cat is playing.
Experimenter:	Can a cat really play a violin?
Twin A:	No.
Experimenter:	Then does this happen?
Twin A:	No.

Twin B

Experimenter:	Is this drawing right?
Twin B:	It is.
Experimenter:	Can a cat really dance like this?
Twin B:	No.
Experimenter:	Then is this drawing right or not?
Twin B:	Right.
Experimenter:	Have you seen a cat play on a balalaika?
Twin B:	No.
Experimenter:	Then is the drawing right or not?
Twin B:	Right.
Experimenter:	But can a cat play a balalaika? etc., etc.

Luria and Yudovich concluded that their experimental study had demonstrated the role of speech in the mental processes of man.

Although words may act as mediators such research reports need to be treated with caution since other studies come to different conclusions. Take the case of deaf children; Vernon (1968) summarized her review of research by saying '. . . the research of the last fifty years which compares the IQ of the deaf with the hearing and of subgroups of deaf children indicates that when there are no complicating multiple handicaps the deaf and hard-of-hearing function at approximately the same IQ level on performance tests as do the hearing'. Furth (1964), who studied the cognitive abilities of deaf children, also concluded that: 'Deaf were found to perform similarly to hearing persons on tasks where verbal knowledge could have been assumed *a priori* to benefit the hearing. Such evidence appears to weaken a theoretical position which attributes to language a direct, general, or decisive influence on intellectual development.'

2.2 *Language in school*

'Experiential' and opposed to 'developmental' factors, however (see p. 257), may well influence a child's ability to use language as a vehicle of communication in school and hence affect his progress. Barnes (1969) looked at the use of language in school since he wished to investigate 'the interaction between the linguistic expectations (drawn from home and primary school experience) brought by pupils to their secondary school, and the linguistic demands set up (implicitly or explicitly) by the teachers in the classroom'. What he found was that teachers used a prescribed form of language which was not modified in response to the clear lack of understanding of the children. He gives many examples of this, one being of a teacher trying to explain the phrase 'city state' and in doing so using a whole set of equally complex forms as 'complete in themselves', 'ruled by themselves', 'supported themselves', 'communicate', 'tended to be'. Barnes commented: 'One set of counters is being substituted for another: words are being shown to be equivalent to words; and it is left to the pupils to summon up some kind of meaning for them ... Children whose home life does not support such language learning may feel themselves to be excluded from the conversation in the classroom.' This problem is one of considerable proportions, Creber (1972) reproduces

a list drawn up by seminar groups, of characteristics of disadvantaged children's linguistic behaviour:

'*Language Habits*'
1 Speaks in a very limited vocabulary.
2 Reproduces sounds inaccurately.
3 Misnames objects or omits naming them.
4 Speaks haltingly without physical defect.
5 Often speaks in monotone.
6 Indiscriminate in both noisy and quiet responses.
7 Seldom or never asks questions.
8 Constantly uses present tense.
9 Seldom uses modifiers.
10 Cause and effect relationships absent in speech.
11 Rarely engages in dialogue with adults.
12 Talks almost exclusively about things.
13 Avoids situations which require words.
14 Tells transparent lies.
15 Distrusts vocal people, especially those who use 'big' words.
16 Exhibits too ready agreement.
17 Cannot easily transfer abstract information into concrete
usage.
18 Unable to vary language with situation.
19 Reluctant to move from oral to written language.

2.3 *Language and social class*

How has this situation come about? One explanation is that the
mothers of the middle-class and the working-class children have
a different view of their role in communicating with their young
children. Tulkin and Kagan (1970), having observed that middle-
class mothers both spoke more and responded verbally more
quickly to their ten-month-old daughters, concluded:

It appeared that one source of variance in maternal behaviour
was the mother's conception of what her infant was like. Some
working class mothers did not believe that their infants possessed
the ability to feel adult like emotions or to communicate with
other people; hence, they felt it was futile to attempt to interact
with their infants. One working class mother who constantly

spoke to her daughter lamented that her friends chastised her for 'talking to the kid like she was three years old'. A common working class philosophy appeared to be that only after the child began to talk was it important for the mother to speak back.

Similarly Robinson (1972) found that middle-class mothers thought they had to teach their children to speak whereas working-class mothers believed that speech would come 'naturally' or 'automatically'.

'Developmentally' the working-class mothers appear to be correct since Dodd (1972) showed that when parents stimulated their children aged between nine and twelve months, vocal stimulating alone had no effect but vocal and social stimulations increased the quantity of babbling. It did not, however, alter the type of sounds the children made, in other words they did not imitate the sounds their parents made but merely increased quantitatively the production of their own sounds. Nor do children seem to imitate their parents directly. It may be that parental linguistic training is not what is important so much as the parents' ability to enable the child to use language as a vehicle for meaning. Robinson (1972) quotes an earlier study concerning mothers responses to 'wh' questions and found that middle-class mothers were more likely to give structured explanations implying cause and effect whereas the working-class child's question was either not answered or tended to be answered in a brief and unstructured way, and hence the child did not learn to *organize* his knowledge.

It is possible that the underachieving child does show linguistic deficit but that this deficit and his underachievement are both symptoms of a more basic difficulty caused by an early failure to learn that the environment is meaningful, organized, and, at least partially, controllable.

3 *The effect of the home*

Whether or not children are conceived equal need not detain us here but there is no doubt that within a very short time both developmental and experiential inequalities are evident and these inequalities will seriously affect the child's academic achievement.

The Summerfield report (1968) states that

> Family and school are the two main social environments in which
> a school child lives; it should be recognised even more widely
> than it is at present that when a child has special psychological
> needs and problems these involve an interaction in him of
> influences of both family and school, even though his difficulties
> may show themselves in only one setting or the other.

3.1 *Early stimulation*

All children are affected by the family especially during their early
years. Perhaps the earliest and certainly one of the most dramatic
studies of the 'family effect' was that of Skeels and his associates
(1939). They tested two infants and found them to have IQs of
46 and 35. Since their mothers were also retarded and in those
days IQ was thought to be inherited, they recommended that the
infants be put in an orphanage for the mentally retarded. However,
the orphanage was full and the babies were put in an adult institution for the subnormal. The children were tested again at two
and then had IQs of 77 and 87; a year later their IQs had risen
to 87 and 100. Apparently in the adult institution they had been
'adopted' by the women inmates and received a great deal of
attention and overt affection. Skeels and Dye (1939) then took
eleven more children and put them in the adult institution leaving
twelve in the orphanage as a control group. The same IQ rise
occurred in the institutionalized children. The original two children
plus nine of the eleven experimental children were then adopted
with the remaining two being returned to the orphanage. Two
years after adoption none of the children had an IQ of less than
90 whereas the children who had stayed in the orphanage had an
average IQ of 66. Asbell (1967) comments: 'thus while the retarded
children sent to the home for the feeble-minded had now become
normal, the near-normal children left in the orphanage had now
become slow or feeble-minded.' When followed up as adults
(Skeels, 1966) all the thirteen children placed in the adult institution were self-supporting whereas of those left in the orphanage
only six were not institutionalized and their jobs were of the most
menial kind – only one had achieved a skilled job and a secure
marriage.

his question of early stimulation seems to be crucial. Stimu-
on may, through poverty or institutional organization, be very
w (Dennis, 1960) or it may be plentiful but totally disorganized
(Wachs, 1967) or lacking in variety. The child cannot develop new
cognitive schemes if his environment does not provide him with
opportunities for finding that his present ones are inadequate.
Normal structures may not develop if they are not stimulated.
Rosenzweig (1966) found that rats reared in a stimulating environment had cortexes that weighed 4 per cent more than a contrast
group of rats raised in a non-stimulating environment. Cats, rats,
and mice were found to have less dendritic spines in their visual
cortexes when reared in the dark (Coleman and Riesen, 1968;
Valverde, 1967). While studies with animals may not be relevant
to humans we do have evidence that disadvantaged children are
more likely to have disorders of the central nervous system (Amante
et al., 1970) which will result in perceptual-motor problems which
will, in turn, affect school learning. Wolf (1964) found a correlation
of .69 between certain aspects of the home environment and the
child's IQ. The most important variables seemed to be the extent
to which opportunities for learning were provided within the home,
the opportunities for vocabularly enlargement, the expectations the
parents had concerning the child's intellectual development and
the amount of information the mother had on this factor.

3.2 *Parental attitudes*

Parents' attitudes towards their young children may engender in
them an approach to learning which will either facilitate or inhibit
subsequent learning. Katkovsky, Crandall and Good (1967) found
that children who had warm, nurturant and accepting parents were
more likely to have faith in their own ability to master their environment. Bronfenbrenner (1961) stressed the curvilinear shape of
parental control in that too much and too little may impede the
child's progress. Baumrind (1967) pointed out the value of
'authoritative' discipline by which a parent creates a structured,
reason-based environment which makes demands on the child but
is not unduly restrictive.

Pidgeon (1970) reported an interesting study on the effects of
parental encouragement. In this study the aim was to evaluate

mathematical achievement, and as part of it the scores of children at boarding school were compared with those at day schools. The results showed that although the boarding-school children tended to come originally from more favoured backgrounds and achieved higher scores in the early years, their proficiency declined the longer they remained at school (Table 10.3).

Table 10.3 *Means and standard deviations for total mathematics score for pupils attending boarding and non-boarding schools*

Population	Boarding		Non-boarding		Diff. of means[a]
	M.	S.D.	M.	S.D.	B.–N/B.
13-year-olds	41.30	11.48	34.31	12.68	*6.99*
15-year-olds	14.38	7.12	17.36	10.72	−2.98
'O' level cand.	21.92	4.44	24.48	6.25	−2.56
'A' level mathns.	36.24	5.57	42.15	9.06	*−5.91*

[a] Values in italics are statistically significant ($p < 0.01$).

(Pidgeon, 1970)

Pidgeon concluded that:

> It is the interest which parents will consistently show in their children's school progress, if not the actual help they may provide in explaining homework difficulties which will lead to better school work, not the fact that the parents have good jobs and are themselves well educated ... Boarding school pupils lack this intimate contact with the encouragement it provides, and hence, over the course of their secondary schooling their motivation for school work decreases and their performance falls.

Support for the significance of parents is given in Banks and Finlayson's (1973) finding that parents of successful or unsuccessful boys could be distinguished by the amount of pride and approval they expressed during the interview with the researchers (Table 10.4). It is not clear however whether disapproving parents are likely to have unsuccessful children or whether unsuccessful children evoke parental disapproval.

Table 10.4 *Parents' ratings for approval of boys: first and third year extreme groups*

Parent	Success category	1st year groups			3rd year groups		
		High rating	Intermediate rating	Low rating	High rating	Intermediate rating	Low rating
Mothers	S	12	21	0	17	11	1
	US	3	17	7	5	15	9
Fathers	S	12	21	0	17	9	3
	US	1	18	9	3	17	9

(Banks and Finlayson, 1973)

3.3 *The mother as teacher*

Wiseman (1968) pointed out that home factors are more important than neighbourhood factors and that parental attitude to education had more significance than either social class or parental occupation. He also asserted that 'backwardness' did not seem to be the opposite of 'brightness' when considered in terms of the effect of parental behaviour, since backwardness seemed to be related to the mother's attitude towards the child, whereas it was the parents' attitude to education which was correlated with brightness. Earlier Burt (1937) had made the forthright statement: 'If I had to single out one factor in the home which bore the closest relationship to a child's school progress, it would not be the economic or industrial status of the family but the efficiency of the mother.' Mothers, or mother substitutes, seem to have a particularly important role in teaching their children *how* to approach cognitive tasks and hence in enabling them to learn how to learn. Hess and Shipman (1967) explored the hypothesis that the effect of a mother's method of interaction with her child was to 'induce enduring forms of information processing in him'. They argued that

Social class has been a useful independent measure in research on social and mental behaviour, but it is too gross to be considered a variable. Rather social class is a statement of probability – expressing the likelihood that certain experiences have occurred or will occur in the life of the individual. It is these more specific experiences that the project attempted to identify and to study.

They were not concerned with the affective variables of love or control but with the cognitive variable of the mother as a teacher. They therefore stated that 'The questions central to our study are, what is the effect of a given type of maternal behaviour upon the cognitive processes of the child? What responses does it evoke and what learning styles are encouraged if the maternal behaviour is persistent?'

Hess and Shipman's sample consisted of black mothers and their four-year-old children from four socio-economic groups: (1) upper-middle-class professionals; (2) skilled workers; (3) semi-skilled or unskilled workers; (4) also unskilled or semi-skilled workers but the fathers were absent and the families were supported by the state. The mothers were required to teach three simple tasks to their children which they themselves, had previously been taught by the researchers. The mothers and children were alone during the teaching session but their speech was recorded and their behaviour observed through a one way mirror. Afterwards the child's performance on the experimental task was assessed. The mothers showed significant differences in their behaviour in that on all tasks the lower-class mothers failed to tell the child what he was expected to do and merely responded to the child's actions. From the child's point of view he was unable to see the point of the exercise and was working in the dark. The researchers concluded: '... in spite of the mother's good intentions, if she fails to inject sufficient cognitive meaning into her interactions with her child, she may structure the interactions so that he not only fails to learn but develops a negative response to the experience.'

Brophy (1970) followed up Hess and Shipman's 'meaning hypothesis' by observing the extent to which mothers structured, and hence made meaningful, a simple teaching task. All the subjects were black and the children were aged around three-and-a-half to four years. The children had to learn to sort blocks into piles of (1) tall blocks with an 'X' on, (2) tall blocks with an 'O',

(3) short blocks with an 'X', (4) short blocks with an 'O'. Two types of maternal behaviour were coded; first 'verbalisation of specific labels', for example, 'X' 'O' 'tall' or 'short' versus the non-specific usage 'that one there' 'this one'; and, second 'focusing', when the mother did more than give verbal labels by deliberately drawing the child's attention to the salient dimensions of the blocks. It was found that middle-class mothers spent more time on focusing and on explaining the task to the children whereas the working-class mothers 'attempted to teach through corrective feedback'.

Hertzig *et al.* (1968) performed a similar study by comparing middle-class white Americans with lower-class Puerto Ricans. The children were matched for IQ but the experimenters were concerned with how the children approached the IQ tasks. The children could work or not work and either talk about their activities or keep silent. The results showed significant differences between the groups. One particular difference was that the middle-class children were more likely to talk about their difficulties whereas the Puerto Ricans would either sit silent or substitute an irrelevant response: 'I want to get a drink of water.' The researchers attributed these differences to differences in the mothers' response to the children which they had observed in home visits. The middle-class mothers were much more inclined to encourage the children to do things for themselves whereas the Puerto-Rican mothers would do things for them saying 'If I do it for him, I get done faster'. In speech the middle-class mothers described the task to be done whereas the Puerto-Rican mothers' speech was 'social and affective'. When the child had a new toy the middle-class parents encouraged him to learn how to use it whereas the Puerto Ricans would solve the problem for him once he got into difficulties, but would not explain the toy to the child in the first place. The authors conclude that since we cannot expect cognitive styles to change educators may have to vary their methods in accordance with the expectations of the various ethnic groups.

Feschbach (1973) made a cross-cultural study of mothers' teaching styles with their four-year-old children with particular reference to their style of reinforcement. She selected four groups of mothers and children: middle-class whites, middle-class blacks, lower-class whites and lower-class blacks. First of all the four-year-olds were asked to teach a puzzle to three-year-olds and their use of positively and negatively reinforcing statements was tallied

Their mean frequency was, for positive reinforcement: middle-class white children 2.4, middle-class blacks .08, lower-class whites 1.9 and lower-class blacks .08. For negative reinforcement the mean was: middle-class whites 2.3, middle-class blacks .4, lower-class whites 2.6, lower-class blacks 1.6. The mothers were then asked to teach their children a more complex form of the puzzle. The mothers' mean use of positive reinforcement was: middle-class whites 6.5, middle-class blacks 4.7, lower-class whites 4.7, and lower-class blacks 4.8; and negative reinforcement: middle-class whites 1.4, middle-class blacks 2.0, lower-class whites 2.2 and lower-class blacks 5.4. The author concluded that the learning situation was more stressful for the lower-class black child. Next Feschbach looked at reinforcement styles in Israel and replicated the American study using western and eastern Israeli mothers and children, where the western were mainly middle-class and the eastern mainly lower-class. Middle-class four-year-olds had 1.8 positive reinforcements and lower-class children .6 but both groups used very few negative reinforcers. For positive reinforcement there was a significant difference on the mothers' scores with the middle-class mothers having a mean of 6.7 and the lower-class a mean of 4.3. However with negative reinforcement an interesting sex difference occurred; while both groups used about the same amount of negative reinforcement with their daughters, for sons the lower-class mean was 4.6 and the middle-class 2.2. Finally English children and their mothers were studied. The results for the children were similar and there was no difference between the middle-class and working-class mothers with respect to negative reinforcement nor with respect to the use of positive reinforcement towards their daughters, but when it came to the sons the middle-class mothers' mean of positive reinforcement was 6.1 and the working-class mean was 2.7. The author had thus found some interesting cross-cultural parallels and differences, and stressed that 'the way in which a child is taught may often be at least as important as what the child is taught'.

4 The effect of the school

4.1 School organization

Even when allowance has been made for individual differences and for varieties of family background, children's achievement may still vary due to their school and the behaviour of their teachers. That schools can seriously affect their pupils was shown by a study of delinquency in a London borough (Power, Benn and Morris, 1972). They found that schools had very different delinquency rates (Table 10.5) which could not be accounted for by any outside environment factors and the authors concluded that 'schools as social institutions and environments, have an important part to play in protecting their pupils from the risk of court appearances'. In the academic sphere Peaker (1967) found school effects to be responsible for 17 per cent of the variation in English attainment among primary school pupils and that this was mainly attributable to the length of experience and calibre of the teachers. A longitudinal study (Himmelweit and Swift, 1969) looked at the effects of different schools on boys with matched home backgrounds and the effect of the same schools on boys with contrasting home back-

Table 10.5 *First appearances before the courts (cases proved),*
1958/9–1967/8

Secondary schools in Tower Hamlets	Average annual first appearance rate per 1,000 boys aged 11–14		
	1958/9–1967/8	1958/9–1962/3	1963/4–1967/8
R	13	11	15
B	14	13	14
N	21	19	23
D	25	23	27
P	26	23	29
S	37	39	35
T	45	39	50
C	46	36	60
U	53	48	58
O	56	34	97
A	59	59	58
	36	31	42

(Power, Benn and Morris, 1972)

grounds. It was apparent that the school was a better predictor of the boys' attainment, attitude and subsequent career than was either his social background or his measured ability.

Pidgeon (1970) was able to take advantage of a situation which occurred naturally but which enabled him to compare the effects on similar children of two different types of school regime. One local authority administered, as usual, the Moray House tests of English, Arithmetic and Intelligence to all the pupils in their top primary classes in the Spring term. In the following September those who had 'passed' went to the grammar school and the others went to the secondary modern school. A small group who went to the secondary modern school took the 11 + again the next year as over-age candidates if their parents wished them to do so and if their teachers thought they had a reasonable chance of passing. But, in this particular year, the local authority decided to change the date of eligibility to sit the 11 + from August 1st to September 1st, so for that one year all the children born between August 1st and September 1st who had not gained grammar school places were allowed to stay on at primary school for another year and retake the examination there. Therefore Pidgeon was able to compare two groups of children all of whom had taken the same examination in the Spring term. Group A whose birthdays fell before August 1st went to a secondary modern school and retook the 11 + from there whereas group B, whose birthdays fell after August 1st, remained in their primary schools and retook the 11 + there. The results (Table 10.6) showed that while the primary group's scores rose in all areas the secondary modern group's fell.

Table 10.6 *Mean differences in standardised scores in tests given one year apart for primary and modern school children*
Standard errors are given in brackets. All differences are statistically significant.

Test	Primary	Modern
Arithmetic	+3.63 (0.43)	−5.14 (0.17)
English	+2.10 (0.94)	−1.47 (0.56)
Intelligence	+2.55 (0.42)	−2.79 (0.21)

(Pidgeon, 1970)

When these results were analysed in greater detail some further problems were revealed. The authority used a weighted system of allocation which was A + E + 2I (i.e. double weighting was given to the Intelligence test score) and the children were divided into three groups on the basis of their total score: (1) 440+ (2) 400 to 439 (3) below 399. When the children's scores were compared after they were divided into ability bands on the basis of the first testing, it was found that while in the primary group the brighter children tended to improve most, in the modern group the brightest children deteriorated most. Pidgeon points out the effect this could have on individual children:

> Consider two 'average' children, each with a score of 475 on the first year's testing, and thus both 'border-zone' children; one stays in the primary school and next year scores 490 – a clear grammar school place; the other, whose birthday may have been on July 31st, only one day older than the first child, goes to a modern school, and the next year scores 461 – a score which does not even entitle him to be considered a 'border-zone' candidate.

The reasons suggested for these results are the differences in the curricula and organization between the two types of school.

Comprehensive schools.   If school organization can have an effect on attainment parents will naturally be concerned about the effects on their child of going to a non-selective or a less well thought of selective school. Obviously it is impossible to make any general statement on this as children's individual needs vary so enormously and one factor which cannot be ignored is that parents' attitudes will influence their children. Therefore if the parents are happier with a certain type of school their children may well do better there. However some research findings are relevant and may help parents and teachers when considering the choice of secondary schooling for individual pupils. Christie and Griffin (1970) compared the 'O' and 'A' level results of five 'elite' schools with those of ninety-four other selective schools and concluded that 'given viable units and adequate facilities the sixth form need not be highly selective to safeguard the achievement of the most able pupils'. Griffin (1969) studied 568 fourteen to fifteen-year-old children, children from three comprehensive, three grammar and six secondary modern schools, and he too found that there was little difference in English attainment between the three types of school and that the children at the comprehensive schools had slightly more favourable attitudes than those in the other types of school.

In their detailed study of comprehensive schools Benn and Simon (1970) give some indication of the pattern of results but this again is difficult to assess since one cannot compare percentage figures. Any school is likely to achieve a 100 per cent pass rate by allowing only those pupils to sit an examination who are likely to pass it. The catchment area a school serves also affects its passes since they quote a school serving a working-class housing estate which only achieved 11 per cent of its pupils passing in more than five 'O' level subjects whereas an established London school gained 40 per cent pupil passes. One grammar school head reported no lowering of his pass rate and found that the ex-secondary modern pupils did better than those who had passed the 11+. Another ex-grammar school head reported that those pupils who had passed the 11+ thus entering his school when it was selective, and were then joined by secondary modern pupils did better than his previous all selective intake.

In terms of entry to higher education Benn and Simon only have figures for the years 1966–7, but at that time of the 312,000 leaving secondary modern schools 24,630 intended to continue their education mainly in the further education sector with 120 planning to go to university; of the 111,000 leaving grammar schools 51,730 were planning full-time higher education and of the 77,000 leaving comprehensives 2,260 intended to go to universities, a further 2,140 to colleges of education, and 4,130 to other forms of full-time further education.

Streaming.   Schools of the same type may have differential effects because of their internal organization particularly if they are streamed. In an early work Jackson (1964) pointed to the apparently superior performance of children in unstreamed as against streamed classes in primary school. He compared the reading age at the end of the first year in junior school, of 88 children in the streamed year and 101 in the unstreamed year of a recently unstreamed school (Table 10.7). He then chose a random sample from each group and matched the number in each category (Table 10.8) and tested this sample at the end of their second junior year.

Table 10.7   *Reading attainment at the end of the first junior school year*

Reading quotient	Children in streamed classes	Children in unstreamed classes
130+	18	19
120+	11	11
110+	14	13
100+	19	19
90+	13	25
80+	7	14
70+	0	0
70−	7	0
Total	88	101
Mean	109.1	108.9
Standard deviation	20.3	17.7

(Jackson, 1964)

Table 10.8   *Sample of 162 children at the end of their first junior school year*

Reading quotient	Children in streamed classes	Children in unstreamed classes
130+	18	18
120+	11	11
110+	13	13
100+	19	19
90+	13	13
80+	7	7
70+	0	0
70−	0	0
Total	81	81

(Jackson, 1964)

The results (Table 10.9) showed that in the unstreamed class the average had been raised whereas in the streamed there was movement up and down. Barker Lunn (1970) conducted a survey involving 5,500 children in seventy-two junior schools and found that streaming had a very slight effect on academic attainment but a considerable effect on the children's social and personal development.

Table 10.9 *Sample of 162 children at the end of their second junior school year*

Reading quotient	Children in streamed classes	Children in unstreamed classes
130+	18	26
120+	14	16
110+	13	14
100+	8	13
90+	16	7
80+	10	4
70+	2	1
70−	0	0
Total	81	81

(Jackson, 1964)

Banks and Finlayson (1973) report some interesting effects of streaming in the secondary school. In a comprehensive school in their sample there were six academic streams composed of various proportions of 11+ success and failures (Table 10.10). When the number of GCE passes were checked the results (Table 10.11) showed that while there was little difference in the rates between those who had passed or failed the 11+ within streams, the differences between streams was such that an 11+ failure in a top stream was much more likely to obtain a number of GCE passes than was an 11+ success who was put in a lower stream. The good academic performance of the children in the top stream however may have been at the expense of their perception of the school. The pupils' perception of the extent to which they felt the teachers were 'considerate' was assessed by a 'consideration' scale of sixteen items which the authors said 'refers to behaviour of teachers which demonstrates their awareness of the individual problems of pupils,

Table 10.10 *The third year school class of 11 + success and failures at the comprehensive school*

School class	11 + success	11 + failure	Total
L and M	22	5	27
N and O	16	11	27
P and Q	6	16	22
Total	44	32	74

(Banks and Finlayson, 1973)

Table 10.11 *Mean number of GCE passes by stream for 11 + successes and failures*

School class	11 + success	11 + failure	Total
L and M	3.36	3.80	3.44
N and O	1.19	0.73	0.96
P and Q	0.33	0.13	0.18

(Banks and Finlayson, 1973)

and their willingness to adapt their behaviour in the light of pupils' differences'. Considerable differences were found between the pupils in the comprehensive, the technical grammar school and the traditional grammar school (Fig. 10.1). Thus the least successful pupils in the comprehensive school saw their teachers as more considerate than did the most successful possibly because the successful group were being pressurized towards academic success. The authors comment:

At this time the school was under considerable constraint to demonstrate the success of the comprehensive experiment, particularly in academic terms. The resultant pressure on the top forms led, as we have seen, to a highly creditable performance at GCE but probably at the cost of a very great deal of hard work and the rigid enforcement of rules.

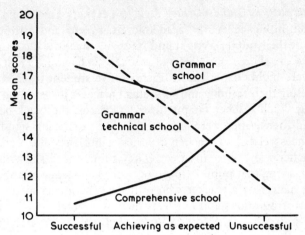

Fig. 10.1 *Mean score of the differentially successful groups on the consideration scale*
(Banks and Finlayson, 1973)

Pidgeon (1970) drew attention to England's position, relative to other countries, with respect to its spread of scores as shown by the 'standard deviation' which may be related to school organization. Five tests – non-verbal, mathematics, reading, geography and science – were administered to thirteen- to fourteen-year-old children in twelve countries – Belgium, England, Federal Republic of Germany, Finland, France, Israel, Poland, Scotland, Sweden, Switzerland, USA and Yugoslavia. England, closely followed by Scotland, had the greatest diversity of scores (i.e. the largest standard deviations) of all the countries (Fig. 10.2).

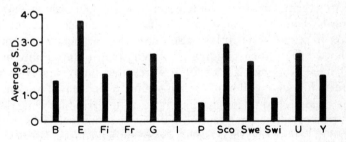

Fig. 10.2 *The average value of the standard deviations for five tests for each of twelve countries*
(Pidgeon, 1970)

Teachers' attitudes and teaching style.   Teachers can have a considerable influence on the academic attainment and attitude to school of their pupils. Wright and Nuthall (1970) did a controlled study of the short term effects of teachers' behaviour. Their subjects were highly experienced teachers, five student teachers just completing their training and six student teachers just starting their training. Each teacher taught three lessons on the black-backed gull and their pupils were then tested. They found no significant differences related to teacher experience but they did find that the teacher's style had an effect. They summarized their discussion by saying that pupils will gain greater knowledge of a specific subject matter by a teacher who provides a summary at the end, asks direct questions and redirects them to several pupils, thanks pupils and gives time for thorough revision at the end of the lesson.

Flanders (1963) argued that teacher efficiency is dependent on the use of direct and indirect influence. Contrary to what is often supposed he maintained that direct influence had a role, and did not set up undue dependency in children when the goals were relatively clear, particularly since it might stimulate the pupils to challenge the ideas and conclusions under discussion. Indirect influence would increase the pupils' independence and this was found to be particularly appropriate when the goals were unclear and when part of the pupils' task was to clarify them and discuss alternatives. Flanders' theory may explain Wright and Nuthall's results showing the superiority of the more direct method.

Davidson and Lang (1960) were concerned with the effect on pupils' achievement of their perceptions of their teachers' feelings towards them. Children who felt their teachers had positive views towards them were found to have better self-images and to do better in school. The authors also found that teachers were more inclined to rate their children favourably than unfavourably but that more working-class children were rated unfavourably than were middle-class children. In their sample 58 per cent of working-class children had their behaviour rated as 'undesirable' while this was true of only 20 per cent of middle-class children. Girls were found to believe that their teachers were more favourably disposed towards them than were the boys.

Yee (1968) looked carefully at teachers' attitudes to advantaged and disadvantaged pupils in a study of over 2,000 pupils in thirty schools. He found that middle-class teachers and their pupils had consistently more favourable attitudes towards each other than did lower-class pupils and their teachers. In addition the middle-class pupils had warmer, more sympathetic and more progressive teachers unlike the lower-class who had older and more punitive teachers. Those teachers who had over nine years experience of work with the lower-class pupils expressed particularly negative attitudes. Yee's study indicates a need to look carefully at the attitudes of *experienced* teachers, since inexperienced teachers, although originally viewed favourably by lower-class pupils were subsequently disliked, and, in general, lower-class pupils' attitudes declined as the teacher's years of experience increased. Middle-class pupils' attitudes were most positive towards teachers with moderate experience and most negative towards relatively new and older teachers. Strom's (1968) data revealed that successful pupils reported that their teachers' failure to provide support and encouragement was more of an obstacle to them than parental lack of interest. Teachers were found to be more encouraging to pupils who came from an educated background. Hargreaves (1972) in Britain, commented:

> Perhaps the most favourite topic for staffroom discussion is the pupils. They provide an endless source of amusement and outrage. Such informal conversations have two important effects. First, they pressure teachers into reaching a consensus about the 'goodness' or 'badness' of particular pupils or classes ... Second, teachers who have not met a particular class or pupil before cannot help but be influenced by these established reputations. One of the main functions of teachers' staffroom gossip is to create preconceptions and expectations in the new teacher's mind prior to an actual teacher interaction.

Rist (1970) found, in the American context, that within the first fortnight the middle-class children came to be more favourably perceived by their teachers and Passow (1966) considering American inner-city schools comments:

> The foregoing survey of literature gives a bleak montage of teachers and administrators who are blinded by their middle class orientations; prejudiced toward all pupils from lower class, racial, and ethnic minority groups; culturally shocked and either

immobilised or punitive in the classroom; and groping constantly for safer births where success, in terms of academic achievement, is more likely. Some, not all, teachers are hostile, vindictive, inept, or even neurotic, but many more are compassionate and skillful ... Many disadvantaged children *do* achieve; many *do* have healthy self images, high aspirations, and positive motivations; for many, the classroom is the most supportive element in their lives.

Staines (1958) made a detailed study of teacher behaviour and showed that teachers differed significantly in the extent to which they made references to the child in such a way as to enhance or reduce his self-image, for example 'Jack, you're tall; help me with this' as against 'You won't do for the queen – you're not tall enough'; or, with reference to performance: 'Good boy! Look at this everyone (class approves)'; versus: 'Wrong. Just look what Jack's done (class laughs).' Staines then asked a teacher (Teacher A), having seen the self-ratings of his class, to teach in such a way that some of these self-ratings would be changed, and gave no such instructions to Teacher B. Their classes were matched for age, intelligence and socio-economic class, but Teacher A had a larger number of children with low achievement scores. Teacher A was then helped to alter his methods in accordance with each child's relative concept of himself. At the end of the period the experimental class were found to place less cards in the 'not sure' category when being asked to rate themselves and hence the author concludes that they had become more certain 'as to what the self really was'. The experimental group's uncertainty scores were reduced, in all areas, between the first test and the second. Attainment was not adversely affected by the teachers stressing self-concept, indeed the experimental group showed a slightly greater gain in achievement scores than did the control group. Staines concluded:

> If it is objected that a teacher cannot spend his time teaching for an improved self-picture and better adjustment because of examination pressure, here is some evidence that at least equally good academic results may be got while improving adjustment. In other words it is possible for a teacher to conceive his educational goals in the wider terms of the self-picture and to secure these while attaining the necessary academic standards.

On the negative side it is likely that Teacher B, conceiving his goals in academic terms and ignorant of the concomitant outcomes, laid the child open to failure in the future because he failed to strengthen the child's self-picture.

While pictures of the prejudiced and the dedicated teacher may be too highly coloured one fact in all the research seems indubitable: *teachers do have power over the minds and feelings of their pupils.* It is to be hoped that their understanding of the complex interrelations of home, school and self which affects a child's achievement will enable them to use this power wisely and justly.

Further reading

Banks, C. and Finlayson, D. (1973) *Success and Failure in the Secondary School.* London: Methuen.

Barker Lunn, J. C. (1970) *Streaming in the Primary School.* Slough: National Foundation for Educational Research.

Burt, C. (1975) *The Gifted Child.* University of London Press.

Hitchfield, E. M. (1973) *In Search of Promise.* London: Longman.

Luria, A. R. (1961) *The Role of Speech in the Regulation of Normal and Abnormal Behaviour.* New York: Pergamon Press.

Pidgeon, D. (1970) *Expectation and Pupil Performance.* Slough: National Foundation for Educational Research.

Robinson, W. P. (1972) *Language and Social Behaviour.* Harmondsworth, Middlesex: Penguin.

References and
name index

Abercrombie, D. (1956) Gesture. *English Language Teaching 9.* *115*

Abercrombie, M. L. J. (1970) *Aims and Techniques of Group Teaching.* London: Society for Research into Higher Education. Monograph 2. *146*

Ackermann, N. W. (1958) *The Psychodynamics of Family Life.* New York: Basic Books. *247*

Adams, B. N. (1972) Birth Order: A Critical Review. *Sociometry 35*(3): 411–39. *222*

Adelson, J. and O'Neill, R. (1966) The Growth of Political Ideas in Adolescence: The Sense of Community. *Journal of Personality and Social Psychology 4*: 295–306. *207*

Adorno, T. W., Frenkel-Brunswik, E., Levinson, D. J. and Sanford, R. N. (1950) *The Authoritarian Personality.* New York: Harper and Row. *126*

Allinsmith, W. (1960) Moral Standards: 11. The Learning of Moral Standards. In D. R. Miller and G. C. Swanson *Inner Conflict and Defence.* New York: Holt. *203*

Altus, W. D. (1966) Birth Order and its Sequelae. *Science 151*: 44–9. *223*

Amante, D., Margules, P. H., Hartman, D. M., Storey, D. B. and Weber, L. F. (1970) The Epidemiological Distribution of CNS Dysfunction. *Journal of Social Issues 26*: 105–16. *264*

Amidon, E. J. and Hunter E. (1970) Categories for the Verbal Interaction Category System (VICS). In A. Simon and E. Boyer (eds) *Mirrors for Behaviour II. An Anthology of Observation Instruments* (2 Vols). Philadelphia: Classroom Interaction Newsletter in co-operation with Research for Better Schools. *165*

Amir, Y. and Sharan, S. (1968) Birth Order, Family Structure and Avoidance Behaviour. *Journal of Personality and Social Psychology 10*(3): 271–8. *224*

Archer, E. J. (1962) Concept Identification as a Function of Obviousness of Relevant and Irrelevant Information. *Journal of Experimental Psychology 63*: 616–20. *52*

Argyle, M. (1965) Eysenck's Theory of Conscience: a Reply. *British Journal of Psychology 56*: 309–10. *204*

Argyle, M. (1969) *Social Interaction.* London: Methuen. *132*

Armstrong, H. G. (1967) Wastage of Ability among the Intellectually Gifted. *British Journal of Educational Psychology 37*(2): 257–9. *254*

Aronfreed, J. (1969) The Concept of Internalisation. In D. Goslin (ed.) *Handbook of Socialisation Theory and Research.* Chicago: Rand McNally. *204*

Asbell, B. (1967) The Case of the Wandering IQs. *Redbook Magazine* (August). *263*

Asch, S. E. (1946) Forming Impressions of Personality. *Journal of Abnormal and Social Psychology 41*: 258–96. *119*

Asch, S. E. (1956) Studies of Independence and Conformity. A Minority of One against a Unanimous Majority. *Psychological Monographs 70*(9): 1–70. *106, 143, 154*

Atkinson, J. W. (ed.) (1958) *Motive in Fantasy, Action and Society.* Princeton, New Jersey: Van Nostrand. *235*

Atkinson, J. W., Bastian, J. R., Earl, R. W. and Litwin, G. H. (1960) The Achievement Motive, Goal Setting and Probability Preferences. *Journal of Abnormal and Social Psychology 60*: 27–36. *237*

Atkinson, J. W. and Feather, N. T. (eds.) (1966) *A Theory of Achievement Motivation.* New York: John Wiley. *237*

Ausubel, D. P. (1963) *The Psychology of Meaningful Verbal Learning: An Introduction to School Learning.* New York: Grune and Stratton. *55*

Ausubel, D. P. (1968) *Educational Psychology: a Cognitive View.* New York: Holt, Rinehart and Winston. *235*

Bakan, D. (1949) The Relationship between Alcoholism and Birth Rank. *Quarterly Journal of Studies in Alcoholism 10*: 434–40. *108*

Bales, R. F. (1951) *Interaction Process Analysis.* Cambridge, Mass.: Addison-Wesley. *144–5*

Bandura, A. (1969) Social Learning Theory of Identificatory Processes. In D. Goslin (ed.) *Handbook of Socialisation Theory and Research.* Chicago: Rand McNally. *204*

Bandura, A., Ross, D. and Ross, S. (1963) A Comparative Test of Status Envy, Social Power and Secondary Reinforcement Theories of Identificatory Learning. *Journal of Abnormal and Social Psychology 67*: 527–34. *194*

Banks, O. and Finlayson, D. (1973) *Success and Failure in the Secondary*

School: An Interdisciplinary Approach to School Achievement. London: Methuen. *265–6, 275–6*

Bannister, D. and Fransella, F. (1971) *Inquiring Man*. Harmondsworth, Middlesex: Penguin. *211*

Bardwick, J. M. (ed.) (1971) *The Psychology of Women: A Study of Biosocial Conflict*. New York: Harper and Row. *216*

Barker Lunn, J. C. (1970) *Streaming in the Primary School: Research Report*. London: National Foundation for Educational Research. *92–3, 275*

Barnard, J. W., Zimbardo, P. G. and Sarason, S. B. (1968) Teachers' Ratings of Student Personality Traits as They Relate to I.Q. and Social Desirability. *Journal of Educational Psychology 59*: 128–32. *229*

Barnes, D. (1969) Language in the Secondary Classroom. In D. Barnes, J. Britton, H. Rosen and the L.A.T.E. *Language the Learner and the School*. Harmondsworth, Middlesex: Penguin. *260*

Barron, F. (1955) The Disposition toward Originality. *Journal of Abnormal and Social Psychology 51*: 478–85. *84*

Barron, F. (1967) The Psychology of the Creative Writer. In R. L. Mooney and T. A. Razik (eds.) *Explorations in Creativity*. New York: Harper and Row. *80, 84*

Bartlett, Sir F. (1958) *Thinking: An Experimental Social Study*. London: George Allen and Unwin. *31, 32*

Baumrind, D. (1967) Effects of Authoritative Parental Control on Child Behaviour. *Child Development 38*: 888–907. *264*

Bavelas, A., Hastorf, A. H., Gross, A. E. and Kite, W. R. (1965) Experiments on the Alteration of Group Structure. *Journal of Experimental Social Psychology 1*: 55–70. *135*

Becker, S. W. and Carroll, J. (1962) Ordinal Position and Conformity. *Journal of Abnormal and Social Psychology 65*: 129–31. *153*

Becker, S. W., Lerner, M. J. and Carroll, J. (1964) Conformity as a Function of Birth Order, Pay-off and Type of Group Pressure. *Journal of Abnormal and Social Psychology 69*: 318–23. *153–4*

Becker, S. W., Lerner, M. J. and Carroll, J. (1966) Conformity as a Function of Birth Order and Type of Group Pressure, a Verification. *Journal of Personality and Social Psychology 3*: 242–4. *153–4*

Beez, W. V. (1970) Influence of Biased Psychological Reports on Teacher Behaviour and Pupil Performance. In M. W. Miles and W. W. Charters (eds.) *Learning in Social Settings*. Boston, Mass.: Allyn and Bacon. Reprinted in A. Morrison and D. McIntyre (eds) (1972) *Social Psychology of Teaching*. Harmondsworth, Middlesex: Penguin. *123*

Bell, C. (1956) *Old Friends: Personal Recollections*. London: Chatto and Windus. *31*

Bellack, A. A., Kliebard, H. M.; Hyman, R. T., Smith, F. L. Jr (1966)

The Language of the Classroom. New York: Teachers College Press. *180*

Beloff, H. (1958) Two Forms of Social Conformity: Acquiescence and Conventionality. *Journal of Abnormal and Social Psychology* 56: 99–104. *148, 152*

Benn, C. and Simon, B. (1970) *Half-way There*. London: McGraw-Hill. *273–4*

Berlyne, D. E. (1954) An Experimental Study of Human Curiosity. *British Journal of Psychology* 45: 256–65. *36*

Berlyne, D. E. (1965) *Structure and Direction in Thinking*. New York: John Wiley. *35, 37, 80*

Biddle, B. J. and Adams, R. S. (1967) Teacher Behaviour in the Classroom Context. In L. Siegal (ed.) *Instruction. Some Contemporary Viewpoints*. San Francisco: Chandler. *161*

Binet, A. *4–6, 8, 13, 21*

Birdwhistell, R. L. (1961) Para-Language Twenty-Five Years after Sapir. In H. G. Brosin (ed.) *Lectures in Experimental Psychiatry*. Pittsburg University Press. *115*

Birdwhistell, E. L. (1968) Kinesics. *International Encyclopedia of the Social Sciences* 8: 379–85. *115*

Blacke, R. R. and Brehm, J. W. (1954) The Use of Tape Recording to Simulate a Group Atmosphere. *Journal of Abnormal and Social Psychology* 49: 311–13. *107*

Blair, R. *7*

Bloomberg, M. (1967) An Inquiry into the Relationship between Field Independence – Dependence and Creativity. *Journal of Psychology* 67: 127–40. *69*

Bloomberg, M. (1971) Creativity as Related to Field Independence and Motility. *Journal Genetic Psychology* 118: 3–12. *69*

Borg, W. R. (1965) Ability Grouping in the Public Schools. *Journal of Experimental Education* 34(2): 1–97. *142*

Bourne, L. E., Ekstrand, B. R. and Dominowski, R. L. (1971) *The Psychology of Thinking*. Englewood Cliffs, New Jersey: Prentice-Hall. *52*

Bowlby, J. (1953) *Child Care and the Growth of Love*. Harmondsworth, Middlesex: Penguin. *189, 190*

Bowlby, J. (1969) *Attachment and Loss*. (Vol. 1) *Attachment*. London: The Hogarth Press. *190*

Bowlby, J. (1973) *Attachment and Loss*. (Vol. 2) *Separation, Anxiety and Anger*. London: The Hogarth Press. *190*

Bradshaw, G. D. and Gaudry, E. (1968) The Effect of a Single Experience of Success or Failure on Test Anxiety. *Australian Journal of Psychology* 20: 219–23. *229*

Brierley, D. W. (1967) The Use of Personal Constructs by Children of Three Different Ages. Unpublished Ph.D. thesis, University of London. *211*

Bronfenbrenner, W. (1961) Some Familiar Antecedents of Responsibility Leadership in Adolescents. In L. Petrullo and B. M. Bass (eds) *Leadership and Interpersonal Behaviour.* New York: Holt, Rinehart and Winston. *264*

Bronowski, J. (1973) *The Ascent of Man.* London: BBC Publications. *xi, xiii*

Brophy, J. E. (1970) Mothers as Teachers of their own Pre-school Children: the Influence of Socioeconomic Status and Task Structure on Teaching Specificity. *Child Development 41*(1): 79–94. *267*

Bruner, J. S. (1962) The Conditions of Creativity. In J. S. Bruner, *On Knowing: Essays for the Left Hand.* Cambridge, Mass.: The Belknap Press of Harvard University Press. *55, 56–7*

Bruner, J. S. (1973) The Growth of Representational Processes in Childhood. In J. Anglin and J. Bruner (eds) *Beyond the Information Given.* London: George Allen and Unwin. *27, 29*

Bruner, J. S., Goodnow, J. L. and Austin, G. A. (1956) *A Study of Thinking.* New York: John Wiley. *47, 50*

Bruner, J. S., Olver, R. R. and Greenfield, P. M. (1966) *Studies in Cognitive Growth.* New York: John Wiley.

Bruner, J. S., Shapiro, D. and Tagiuri, R. (1958) The Meaning of Traits in Isolation and Combination. In R. Tagiuri and L. Petrullo (eds) *Person Perception and Interpersonal Behaviour.* Stanford University Press. *125*

Bryant, P. (1974) *Perception and Understanding in Young Children.* London: Methuen. *23*

Bull, N. (1969) *Moral Judgment from Childhood to Adolescence.* London: Routledge and Kegan Paul. *202*

Burke, P. J. (1967) The Development of Task and Social Emotional Role Differentiation. *Sociometry 30*: 379–92. *141*

Burt, C. (1937) *The Backward Child.* University of London Press. *226*

Burt, C. (1952) Autobiography. In E. G. Boring (ed.) *A History of Psychology in Autobiography* (Vol. 4). New York: Russell and Russell. *6–7*

Burt, C. (1962) The Gifted Child. In *Year Book of Education.* London: Evans. *250*

Burt, C. (1968) Mental Capacity and its Critics. *British Psychological Society Bulletin 21*(7): 11–26. *4*

Burt, C. (1974) The Gifted Child. In M. K. Pringle and Varma (eds) *Advances in Educational Psychology* (Vol. 2). University of London Press. *250*

Burt, C. *5, 8, 13, 20*

Cameron, M. B. (1967) An Investigation of Cognitive Differences in First Year Arts and Science Students. M.Ed. thesis, University of Aberdeen. *78*
Carey, G. L. (1955) Reduction of Sex Differences in Problem Solving by Improvement of Attitude through Group Discussion. Unpublished doctoral dissertation, Stanford University. *221*
Carlsson, B. (1963) Vaxjoforsoken, Skoldifferentieringes inverkan på elevernas kunskapsprestationer – En experimentell undersökning. Upsala Universitet. *142*
Cassirer, E. (1953) *An Essay on Man*. New York: Doubleday. *257*
Cattell, R. B. (1963) The Personality and Motivation of the Researcher from Measurements of Contemporaries and from Biography. In Taylor and Barron (eds) *Scientific Creativity*. New York: John Wiley. *80*
Cattell, R. B. and Butcher, H. J. (1968) *The Prediction of Achievement and Creativity*. New York: Bobbs-Merrill. *86*
Cattell, J. M. and Drevdahl, J. E. R. (1955) Comparison of the Personality Profile (16PF) of Eminent Researchers with that of Eminent Teachers and Administrators, and of the General Population. *British Journal of Psychology 46*: 248–61. *82*
Chambers, J. A. (1964) Relating Personality and Biographical Factors to Scientific Creativity. *Psychological Monographs 78*: 584. *81*
Christie, T. and Griffin, A. (1970) The Examination Achievements of Highly Selective Schools. *Educational Research 12*(3): 202–8. *272*
Coleman, J. S. *et al.* (1960) *Equality of Educational Opportunity*. Documents Nos. F55. 238: 38001. US Office of Education. *248*
Coleman, P. O. and Riesen, A. H. (1968) Environmental Effects on Cortical Dendritic Fields 1, Rearing in the Dark. *Journal of Anatomy 102*: 363–74. *264*
Combs, A. W. and Snygg, D. (1959) *Individual Behaviour*. New York: Harper and Row. *126*
Cook, M. (1971) *Interpersonal Perception*. Harmondsworth, Middlesex: Penguin. *128*
Coopersmith, S. (1967) *The Antecedents of Self-Esteem*. San Francisco: Freeman. *127*
Corah, N. L. (1965) Differentiation in Children and their Parents. *Journal of Personality 33*: 300–8. *233*
Cornell, F. G., Lindvall, C. M. and Saupe, J. L. (1952) *An Exploratory Measurement of Individualities of Schools and Classrooms*. Urbana: Bureau of Educational Research, University of Illinois. *161*
Cowen, E. L., Zax, M., Klein, R., Izzo, L. D., and Trost, M. A. (1965)

The Relation of Anxiety in School Children to School Record, Achievement and Behavioural Measures. *Child Development 36*: 685–95. *229*

Cox, F. N. (1963) Educational Streaming and General Test Anxiety. *Child Development 33*: 381–90. *71, 229*

Craig, R. (1966) Trait Lists and Creativity. *Psychologica 9*: 107–10. *70*

Crandall, V. C. and Battle, E. S. (1970) The Antecedents and Adult Correlates of Academic and Intellectual Achievement Effort. In J. P. Hill (ed.) *Minnesota Symposia on Child Psychology* (Vol. 4). Minneapolis: University of Minnesota Press. *236, 241*

Crandall, V. C., Katkovsky, W. and Crandall, V. J. (1965) Children's Beliefs in their own Control of Reinforcements in Intellectual-Academic Achievement Situations. *Child Development 36*: 91–109. *248*

Creber, J. W. P. (1972) *Lost for Words, Language and Educational Failure*. Harmondsworth, Middlesex: Penguin. *260*

Cropley, A. J. (1967) *Creative Education Today*. London: Longman. *86*

Cross, P., Cattell, R. B. and Butcher, H. J. (1967) The Personality Pattern of Creative Artists. *British Journal of Educational Psychology 37*: 292–9. *84*

Crutchfield, R. S. (1965) Instructing the Individual in Creative Thinking. In *New Approaches to Individualising Instruction*. Princeton, New Jersey: Educational Testing Service. *99*

Cushna, C. B. (1970) Agency and Birth Order Differences in very Early Childhood. In B. Sutton-Smith and B. G. Rosenberg, *The Sibling*. New York: Holt, Rinehart and Winston. *223*

Dahllöff, U. S. (1971) *Ability Grouping Content Validity and Curriculum Process Analysis*. New York: Teachers College Press. *142*

Damm, J. (1968) Effects of Interpersonal Context on Relationships between Goal Setting Behaviour and Achievement Motivation. *Human Relations 21*(3): 213–26. *237*

Danziger, K. (1971) *Socialisation*. Harmondsworth, Middlesex: Penguin. *217*

Davidson, H. H. and Lang, G. (1960) Children's Perception of their Teachers' Feelings toward them Related to Self-Perception, School Achievement and Behaviour. *Journal of Experimental Education 29*: 107–18. *278*

Davis, G. A. (1966) Current Status of Research and Theory in Human Problem Solving. *Psychological Bulletin 66*(1): 36–54. *42*

Davis, J. H. (1969) *Group Performance*. Reading, Mass.: Addison-Wesley. *135–6*

Davis, Ol. Jr and Slobodian, J. J. (1967) Teacher Behaviour toward

Boys and Girls during First Grade Reading Instruction. *American Educational Research Journal 4*: 261–9. *222*

Davol, I. H. and Hastings, M. L. (1967) Effects of Sex, Age, Reading Ability, SES and Display Position on Measures of Spatial Relations in Children. *Perceptual and Motor Skills 24*: 375–87. *245*

Dawson, J. L. M. (1967) Cultural and Physiological Influences upon Spatial Perceptual Processes in West Africa, Parts 1 and 2. *International Journal of Psychology 2*: 115–28; 171–85. *89*

Delamont, S. (1976) Beyond Flanders' Fields. In M. Stubbs and S. Delamont (eds) *Explorations in Classroom Observation*. Chichester, Sussex: John Wiley. *173*

Dellas, M. and Gaier, E. L. (1970) Identification of Creativity: the Individual. *Psychological Bulletin 73*(1): 55–73. *80*

Dennis, W. (1960) Causes of Retardation among Institutional Children: Iran. *Journal of Genetic Psychology 96*: 47–59. *267*

Denny, J. P. (1966) Effects of Anxiety and Intelligence on Concept Formation. *Journal of Experimental Psychology 72*: 596–602. *228*

Department of Education and Science (1968) *Education of Gifted Children*. London: HMSO. *255*

Deutsch, M. and Gerard, H. (1955) A Study of Normative and Informational Social Influences upon Individual Judgment. *Journal of Abnormal and Social Psychology 51*: 629–36. *154*

Dodd, B. (1972) Effects of Social and Vocal Stimulation on Infant Babbling. *Development Psychology 7*: 80–3. *262*

Donnison Report (1970) *Report on Independent Day Schools and Direct Grant Grammar Schools*. Public Schools Commission. London: HMSO. *250*

Dornbush, S. M., Hastorf, A. H., Richardson, S. A., Muzzy, R. E. and Vreeland, R. S. (1965) The Perceiver and the Perceived: their Relative Influence on Categories of Interpersonal Perception. *Journal of Personality and Social Psychology 1*: 434–40. *120*

Dreistadt, R. (1969) The Use of Analogies and Incubation in Obtaining Insights in Creative Problem Solving. *Journal of Psychology 71*: 159–75. *58–61*

Drevdahl, J. E. and Cattell, R. B. (1958) Personality and Creativity in Artists and Writers. *Journal of Clinical Psychology 14*: 707–11. *83*

Duncan, O. D., Featherman, D. L. and Duncan, B. (1968) *Socio-economic Background and Occupational Achievement: Extension of a Basic Model*. Final Report, Project No. 5–0074 (EO–191) US Department of Health, Education and Welfare, Office of Education, Bureau of Research. *15*

Dunker, K. (1945) On Problem Solving. *Psychological Monographs 58* (whole No. 270, Chapters 1 and 3). Reproduced in P. C. Wason and

P. N. Johnson-Laird (eds) *Thinking and Reasoning*. Harmondsworth, Middlesex: Penguin. *40–1, 45*

Edwards, M. P. and Tyler, L. E. (1965) Intelligence, Creativity and Achievement in a Non-Selective Public Junior High School. *Journal of Educational Psychology 56*: 96–9. *74*

Ekman, P. and Friesen, W. V. (1969) Non-Verbal Leakage and Cues to Deception. *Psychiatry 32*: 88–105. In M. Argyle (ed.) (1973) *Social Encounters*. Harmondsworth, Middlesex: Penguin. *115, 116*

Eliot, T. S. (1971) The Love Song of J. Alfred Prufrock. London: Faber and Faber. *57*

Elkind, D. (1967) Egocentrism in Adolescence. *Child Development 38*: 1025–34. *208*

Entwistle, N. J. (1968) Academic Motivation and School Attainment. *British Journal of Educational Psychology 38*(2): 181–8. *234*

Entwistle, N. J. and Cunningham, S. (1968) Neuroticism and School Attainment – a Linear Relationship? *British Journal of Educational Psychology 38*: 123–32. *231*

Entwistle, N. J., Percy, K. A. and Nisbet, J. B. (1971) Educational Objectives and Academic Performance in Higher Education. Unpublished Report. Department of Educational Research, University of Lancaster. *231*

Ervin-Tripp, S. (1964) An Analysis of the Interaction of Language, Topic and Listener. *American Anthropologist 66*: 86–94. In M. Argyle, (ed.) (1973) *Social Encounters*. Harmondsworth, Middlesex: Penguin. *113*

Eysenck, H. J. (1957) *The Dynamics of Anxiety and Hysteria*. London: Routledge and Kegan Paul. *203*

Eysenck, H. J. (1960) The Development of Moral Values in Children: The Contribution of Learning Theory. *British Journal of Educational Psychology 30*: 11–21. *203–4, 205*

Eysenck, H. J. and Cookson, D. (1969) Personality in Primary School Children. Ability and Achievement. *British Journal of Educational Psychology 39*: 109–22. *230–1*

Eysenck, S. G. B. (1965) *Manual of the Junior Eysenck Personality Inventory*. University of London Press. *230*

Farber, I. E. and Spence, K. W. (1953) Complex Learning and Conditioning as a Function of Anxiety. *Journal of Experimental Psychology 45*: 120–5. *138*

Feshbach, N. D. (1973) Cross-Cultural Studies of Teaching Styles in Four-Year-Olds and their Mothers. In A. D. Pick (ed.) *Minnesota. Symposia on Child Psychology* (Vol. 7). Minneapolis: University of Minnesota Press. *268*

Festinger, L. (1957) *A Theory of Cognitive Dissonance*. New York: Harper and Row. *156*

Festinger, L. and Carlsmith, J. M. (1959) Cognitive Consequences of Forced Compliance. *Journal of Abnormal and Social Psychology 58*: 203–10. *157*

Festinger, L., Schachter, S. and Back, K. W. (1950) *Social Pressures in Informal groups*. New York: Harper and Row. *137*

Fiedler, F. E. (1967) *A Theory of Leadership Effectiveness*. New York: McGraw-Hill. *140–1*

Fiegenbaum, E. and Feldman, J. (eds) (1963) *Computers and Thought*. New York: McGraw-Hill. *44*

Fishbein, H. D., Haygood, R. C. and Frieson, D. (1970) Relevant and Irrelevant Saliency in Concept Learning. *American Journal of Psychology 83*: 544–53. *52*

Fisher, R. L. (1967) Social Schemes of Normal and Disturbed School Children. *Journal of Educational Psychology 58*: 88–93. *118*

Flanders, N. A. (1963) Teacher Influence in the Classroom. In A. A. Bellack (ed.) *Theory and Research in Teaching*. New York: Teachers College Press. *278*

Flanders, N. A. (1970a) *Analysing Teacher Behaviour*. Reading, Mass.: Addison-Wesley. *163–4, 171, 172, 175*

Flanders N. A. (1970b) 'Sub-Categories of Flanders' Expanded Category System'. In A. Simon and E. Boyer (eds) *Mirrors for Behaviour II. An Anthology of Observation Instruments* (2 Vols). Philadelphia: Classroom Interaction Newsletter in co-operation with Research for Better Schools. *165*

Flanders, N. and Havumaki, S. (1960) The Effect of Teacher–Pupil Contacts Involving Praise on the Sociometric Choices of Students. *Journal of Educational Psychology 51*: 65–8. *181*

Franks, C. M. (1956a) Conditioning and Personality: A Study of Normal and Neurotic Subjects. *Journal of Abnormal and Social Psychology 52*: 143–50. *204*

Franks, C. M. (1956b) Recidivism, Psychopathy and Personality. *British Journal of Delinquency 6*: 192–201. *204*

Franks, C. M. (1957) Personality Factors and the Rate of Conditioning. *British Journal of Psychology 48*: 119–26. *204*

Frankel, E. (1960) A Comparative Study of Achieving and Underachieving High School Boys of High Intellectual Ability. *Journal of Educational Research 53*: 172–80. *248*

Frenkel-Brunswick, E. (1948) A Study of Prejudice in Children. *Human Relations 1*: 295–306. *233*

Freud, A. (1937) *The Ego and the Mechanisms of Defence*. London: The Hogarth Press. *194*

Freud, S. (1908) Creative Writers and Day Dreaming. In J. Strachey (1958) (ed.) *Standard Edition of the Complete Psychological Works of Sigmund Freud* (Vol. 9). London: The Hogarth Press. *62–4*

Freud, S. (1920) *A General Introduction to Psychoanalysis*. London: Boni and Liveright. *70*

Freud, S. (1926) *Standard Edition of the Complete Psychological Works* (Vol. 20). *190, 195–6*

Freyman, R. (1965) Further Evidence on the Effect of Date of Birth on Subsequent School Performance. *Educational Research 8*(1): 58–64. *225*

Furth, H. G. (1964) Research with the Deaf: Implications for Language and Cognition. *Psychological Bulletin 62*: 145–64. *260*

Furth, H. G. and Wachs, H. (1974) *Thinking goes to School. Piaget's Theory in Practice*. New York: Oxford University Press. *30, 36, 38*

Gage, N. L. (1963a) Paradigms for Research on Teaching. In N. L. Gage (ed.) *Handbook of Research on Teaching*. Chicago: Rand McNally. *159*

Gage, N. L. (ed.) (1963b) *Handbook of Research on Teaching*. Chicago: Rand McNally. *162*

Gage, N. L. (1965) Desirable Behaviours in Teachers. *Urban Education 1*: 85–95. *159*

Gagné, R. M. (1966) Human Problem Solving: Internal and External Events. In B. Kleinmuntz (ed.) *Problem Solving: Research, Method and Theory*. New York: John Wiley. *39, 43*

Gagné, R. M. (1964) Problem Solving. In A. W. Melton (ed.) *Categories of Human Learning*. New York: Academic Press. *39, 42*

Gallagher, J. J. (1958) Peer Acceptance of Highly Gifted Children in Elementary School. *Elementary School Journal 58*: 465–70. *252*

Gallatin, J. and Adelson, J. (1971) Legal Guarantees of Individual Freedom: A Cross National Study of the Development of Political Thought. *Journal of Social Issues 27*(2): 93–108. *207*

Galton, F. (1870) *Hereditary Genius*. New York: Appleton-Century-Crofts. *4*

Galton, F. (1874) *English Men of Science: Their Nature and Nurture*. London: Macmillan. *222*

Galton, F. *5, 8, 13*

Garai, J. E. and Scheinfeld, A. (1968) Sex Differences in Mental and Behavioural Traits. *Genetic Psychology Monographs 77*: 169–299. *216, 221*

Gardner, R. W. (1961) Cognitive Controls of Attention Deployment as Determinants of Visual Illusions. *Journal of Abnormal and Social Psychology 62*: 120–7. *69*

Garfinkel, H. (1964) Studies of the Routine Grounds of Everyday Activities. *Social Problems 11*: 225–50. *118*

Gaudry, E. and Spielberger, C. D. (1971) *Anxiety and Educational Achievement*. Ryde, New South Wales: John Wiley.

Gecas, V. (1972) Parental Behaviour and Contextual Variations in Adolescent Self-Esteem. *Sociometry 2*: 332–45. *249*

Getzels, J. W. and Jackson, P. W. (1961) Family Environment and Cognitive style: A Study of the Sources of Highly Intelligent and Highly Creative Adolescents. *American Sociological Review 3*: 351–9. *89*

Getzels, J. W. and Jackson, P. W. (1962) *Creativity and Intelligence*. New York: John Wiley. *72–5, 77, 78, 90*

Getzels, J. W. and Thelen, H. A. (1960) The Classroom Group as a Unique Social System. In N. B. Henry (ed.) *The Dynamics of Instructional Groups*. 59th Yearbook of the National Society for the Study of Education, (Part 2). *145–6*

Gibb, J. R. (1972) Managing for Creativity in the Organisation. In C. W. Taylor (ed.) *Climate for Creativity*. New York: Pergamon Press. *96–7*

Giles, H. (1971) Patterns of Evaluation to R.P., South Welsh and Somerset Accented Speech. *British Journal of Social and Clinical Psychology 10*(3): 280–1. *114*

Giles, H. (1976) *International Journal of the Sociology of Language*. *114*

Goffman, E. (1956) *The Presentation of Self in Everyday Life*. Edinburgh University Press. *133*

Goffman, E. (1971) *Relations in Public*. Harmondsworth, Middlesex: Penguin. *112*

Goldberg, S. and Lewis, M. (1969) Play Behaviour in the Year Old Infant: Early Sex Differences. *Child Development 40*: 21–31. *221*

Gordon, G. (1972) The Identification and Use of Creative Abilities in Scientific Organisations. In C. Taylor (ed.) *Climate for Creativity*. New York: Pergamon Press. *93–4*

Gordon, G., Marquis, S. and Anderson, O. (1962) Freedom and Control in Four Types of Scientific Settings. *American Behavioural Scientist*: 39–42. *98*

Gordon, W. J. J. (1961) *Synetics*. New York: Harper and Row. *101*

Gough, H. G. (1964a) A Cross-Cultural Study of Achievement Motivation. *Journal of Applied Psychology 48*: 191–6. *236*

Gough, H. G. (1964b) Academic Achievement in High School as Predicted from the California Psychological Inventory. *Journal of Educational Psychology 55*: 174–80. *236*

Grace, H. A. and Booth, N. L. (1958) Is the Gifted Child a Social Isolate? *Peabody Journal of Education 35*: 195–6. *253*

Graham, D. (1968) Children's Moral Development. In Butcher, H. J. (ed.) *Educational Research in Britain*. University of London Press. *203*

Greeno, J. G. (1973) The Structure of Memory and the Process of Solving Problems. In R. L. Solso (ed.) *Contemporary Issues in Cognitive Psychology: The Loyala Symposium*. Washington D.C.: W. H. Winston. *39*

Griffin, A. (1969) Selective and Non-Selective Secondary Schools: Their Relative Effects on Ability, Attainment and Attitudes. *Research in Education 1*(1): 1–20.   *272*

Grinder, R. E. (1964) Relations between Behavioural and Cognitive Dimensions of Conscience in Middle Childhood. *Child Development* 35: 881–91.   *203*

Grinder, R. E. (1966) Relations of Social Dating Attractions to Academic Orientation and Peer Relations. *Journal of Educational Psychology 57*: 27–34.   *249*

Grinder, R. E. and McMichael, R. E. (1963) Cultural Influence on Conscience Development: Resistance to Temptation and Guilt among Samoans and American Caucasians. *Journal of Abnormal and Social Psychology 66*: 503–7.   *203*

Gross, N. and Herriott, R. (1965) *Staff Leadership in Public Schools*. New York: John Wiley.   *159*

Guilford, J. P. (1950) Creativity. *American Psychologist 5*: 444–54.   *55, 65, 70*

Guilford, J. P. (1956) The Structure of Intellect. *Psychological Bulletin 53*: 267–93.   *11, 168, 172*

Guilford, J. P. (1959) Traits in Creativity. In H. H. Anderson (ed.) *Creativity and its Cultivation*. New York: Harper Bros.   *55, 66, 71, 102*

Guilford, J. P. (1962) Factors that Aid and Hinder Creativity. *Teachers College Record 63*: 380–92.   *55–6*

Guilford, J. P.   *8, 13*

Gump, P. B. (1964) Environmental Guidance of Classroom Behavioral System. In B. J. Biddle and W. J. Ellena (eds) *Contemporary Research on Teacher Effectiveness*. New York: Holt, Rinehart and Winston. *161*

Haan, N., Smith, M. B. and Block, J. (1968) Political, Family and Personality Correlates of Adolescent Moral Judgment. *Journal of Personality and Social Psychology 10*: 183–201.   *203*

Haddon, F. A. and Lytton, H. (1968) Teaching Approach and the Development of Divergent Thinking Abilities in Primary Schools. *British Journal of Educational Psychology 38*: 171–80.   *92–3*

Hamachek, D. E. (1968) Motivation in Teaching and Learning. *What*

Research says to the Teacher, No. 34: 5–9. Washington, D.C. Association of Classroom teachers, a Department of the National Education Association. *249*

Hargreaves, D. (1972) *Interpersonal Relations and Education.* London: Routledge and Kegan Paul. *279*

Haring, N. G. and Phillips, E. L. (1962) *Educating Emotionally Disturbed Children.* New York: McGraw-Hill. *247*

Harlow, H. F. and Zimmermann, R. R. (1959) Affectional Response in the Infant Monkey. *Science 130:* 421–32. *189*

Harré, R. and Secord, P. F. (1972) *The Explanation of Social Behaviour.* Oxford: Blackwell. *210, 212–3*

Harrison, F. I. (1964) Relationship between Home Background, School Success, and Adolescent Attitudes. *Merrill-Palmer Quarterly 14:* 331–44. *248*

Hasan, P. and Butcher, H. J. (1966) Creativity and Intelligence. A Partial Replication with Scottish Children of Getzels' and Jackson's study. *British Journal of Psychology 57:* 129–35. *77*

Hastorf, A. N., Schneider, D. J. and Polefka, J. (1970) *Person Perception.* Reading, Mass.: Addison-Wesley. *125*

Heider, F. (1958) *The Psychology of Interpersonal Behaviour.* New York: John Wiley. *121, 126*

Heist, P. (1967) College Transients. In P. Heist (ed.) *Education for Creativity in the American College.* University of California: Centre for Research and Development in Higher Education. *95*

Helmholtz, H. Von. *58*

Helson, R. (1971) Women Mathematicians and the Creative Personality. *Journal of Consulting and Clinical Psychology 36(2):* 210–20. *216*

Henry, J. (1966) *Culture Against Man.* London: Tavistock. *147, 199*

Herbert, J. (1967) *A System for Analysing Lessons.* New York: Teachers College Press. *170–1*

Hertzig, M. E., Birch, H. G., Thomas, A. and Mendez, O. A. (1968) Class and Ethnic Differences in the Responsiveness of Pre-School Children to Cognitive Demands. *Monographs of the Society for Research in Child Development 117.* *268*

Heshka, S. and Nelson, Y. (1972) Interpersonal Speaking Distance as a Function of Age, Sex and Relationship. *Sociometry 35(4):* 491–8. *117*

Hess, R. D. and Easton, D. (1960) The Child's Changing Image of the President. *Public Opinion Quarterly 24:* 632–44. *207*

Hess, D. and Shipman, V. C. (1967) Cognitive Elements in Maternal Behaviour. In J. P. Hill (ed.) *Minnesota Symposia on Child Psychology* (Vol. 1). Minneapolis: University of Minnesota Press. *266–7*

Hewett, F. M. (1967) Educational Engineering with Emotionally Disturbed Children. *Exceptional children 33:* 459–67. *247*

Hildreth, G. H. (1966) *Introduction to the Gifted.* New York: McGraw-Hill. *251*

Hill, K. T. and Sarason, S. B. (1966) The Relation of Test Anxiety and Defensiveness to Test and School Performance over the Elementary School Years: A Further Longitudinal Study. *Monographs of the Society for Research in Child Development 31*(2) No. 104. *228*

Himmelweit, H. T. and Swift, B. (1969) A Model for the Understanding of School as a Socialising Agent. In P. Mussen *et al.* (eds) *Trends and Issues in Developmental Psychology.* New York: Holt, Rinehart and Winston. *270*

Hitchfield, E. M. (1973) *In Search of Promise.* London: Longman in association with The National Children's Bureau. *250–4*

Hoffman, L. W. (1972) Early Childhood Experiences and Women's Achievement Motives. *Journal of Social Issues 28*(2): 129–54. *220–1*

Hoggart, R. (1957) *The Use of Literacy.* London: Chatto and Windus. *114*

Hollander, E. P. (1958) Conformity, Status and Idiosyncrasy Credit. *Psychological Review 65*: 117–27. *132*

Hollander, E. P. (1960) Competence and Conformity in the Acceptance of Influence. *Journal of Abnormal and Social Psychology 61*: 365–9. *132*

Hollander, E. P. and Julian, J. W. (1969) Contemporary Trends in the Analysis of Leadership Processes. *Psychological Bulletin 71*: 387–97. Reprinted in A. H. Yee (ed.) *Social Interaction in Educational Settings.* Englewood Cliffs, New Jersey: Prentice-Hall. *141–2*

Hollander, E. P. and Willis, R. H. (1967) Some Current Issues in the Psychology of Conformity and Non-Conformity. *Psychological Bulletin 68*: 62–76. *148*

Holt, J. (1964) *How Children Fail.* New York: Pitman. *225*

Homans, G. C. (1961) *Social Behaviour: Its Elementary Forms.* New York: Harcourt Brace Jovanovich. *135*

Horner, M. (1968) Sex Differences in Achievement Motivation and Performance in Competitive and Non-Competitive Situations. Unpublished doctoral dissertation, University of Michigan. *238*

Horner, M. (1970) The Motive to Avoid Success and Changing Aspirations of College Women. *Women on Campus, 1970 a Symposium*: 12–23. Reprinted in J. Bardwick (ed.) (1972) *Readings on the Psychology of Women.* New York, Harper and Row. *238*

Hudson, L. (1966) *Contrary Imaginations.* London: Methuen. *78, 91*

Hudson, L. (1971) Intelligence, Race and the Selection of Data. *Race 12*(3): 283–92. *14, 16*

Hunt, E. B. (1968) Computer Simulation: Artificial Intelligence Studies and their Relevance to Psychology. *Annual Review of Psychology 19*: 135–8. *44*

Huntington, E. (1938) *Season of Birth*. London: John Wiley. *225*

Husted, G. P. and Cervantes, L. F. (1970) The Psycho-Social Origins of Academic Achievement and the Maternal Role in Autonomy. In E. D. Evans (ed.) *Adolescents, Readings in Behaviour and Development*. Illinois: The Dryden Press. *241*

Hutt, C. and Vaizey, J. (1966) Differential Effects of Group Density on Social Behaviour. *Nature 209*: 1371–2. *118*

Hyman, H. H. (1953) The Value Systems of Different Classes. In R. Bendix and S. Lipset (eds) *Class Status and Power*. Glencoe, Illinois: The Free Press. *239*

Hyman, H. (1969) *Political Socialisation*. Glencoe, Illinois: The Free Press. *207*

Inhelder, B. and Piaget, J. (1964) *The Early Growth of Logic in the Child*. New York: Harper and Row. *245*

Izzett, R. R. and Leginski, W. (1972) Impression Formation as a Function of Self Versus Other as a Source of the Information. *Journal of Social Psychology 87*: 229–33. *120*

Jackson, B. (1964) *Streaming: an Education System in Miniature*. London: Routledge and Kegan Paul. *133, 273–5*

Jackson, P. S. and Messick, S. (1965) The Person, the Product, and the Response: Conceptual Problems in the Assessment of Creativity. *Journal of Personality 33*: 309–29. *56–7*

Jahoda, G. (1963a) The Development of Children's Ideas about Country and Nationality, Part 1. The Conceptual Framework. *British Journal of Educational Psychology 33*: 143–53. *206*

Jahoda, G. (1963b) The Development of Children's Ideas about Country and Nationality, Part 2. National Symbols and Themes. *British Journal of Educational Psychology 33*: 143–53.

Jahoda, M. (1959) Conformity and Independence. *Human Relations 12*: 99–120. *155–6*

James, W. (1890) *The Principles of Psychology*. New York: Holt, Rinehart and Winston. *59*

Jaros, D., Hirsch, H. and Fleron, F. J. Jr (1968) The Malevolent Leader: Political Socialisation in an American Sub-Culture. *American Political Science Review 62*: 564–75. *207*

Jecker, J. D., Maccoby, N. and Breitrose, H. S. (1965) Improving Accuracy in Interpreting Non-Verbal Cues of Comprehension. *Psychology of the Schools 2*: 239–44. *128*

Jenkins, D. H. and Lippitt, R. (1951) *Interpersonal Perceptions of Teachers, Students and Parents*. Washington, D.C.: Division of Adult Education, National Educational Association. *160*

Jennings, M. K. and Niemi, R. G. (1968) Patterns of Political Learning. *Harvard Educational Review 38*: 443–63. *207*

Jensen, A. R. (1969) How much can we Boost I.Q. and Scholastic Achievement? *Harvard Educational Review 39*: 1–123. *14, 15, 28*

Jensen, A. R. (1973) *Educational Differences*. London: Methuen. *257–8*

Johnson, T. J., Feigenbaum, R. and Weibey, M. (1964) Some Determinants and Consequences of the Teacher's Perception of Causality. *Journal of Educational Psychology 55*: 237–46. *122*

Jones, F. E. (1964) Predictor Variables for Creativity in Industrial Science. *Journal of Applied Psychology 48*: 134–6. *81*

Jones, E. E., Roch, L., Shaver, K. G., Goethals, G. R. and Ward, L. M. (1968) Pattern Performance and Ability Attribution: an Unexpected Primacy Effect. *Journal of Personality and Social Psychology 10*: 317–41. *121*

Jung, C. G. *85*

Kagan, J. (1964) Acquisition and Significance of Sex-Typing and Sex-Role Identity. In M. L. Hoffman and L. W. Hoffman (eds) *Review of Child Development Research*. New York: Russell Sage. *220*

Kagan, J. (1969) On the Meaning of Behaviour: Illustrations from the Infant. *Child Development 40*: 1121–34. *221*

Kahl, J. A. (1953) Educational and Occupational Aspirations of 'Common Man' Boys. *Harvard Educational Review 23*: 186–203. *238*

Kahn, R. L. (1964) *Organisational Stress. Studies in Role Conflict and Ambiguity*. New York: John Wiley. *133–4*

Katkovsky, V. C., Crandall, V. C. and Good, S. (1967) Parental Antecedents of Children's Beliefs in Internal–External Control of Reinforcements in Intellectual Achievement Situations. *Child Development 38*: 765–76. *262*

Katz, F. M. (1964) The Meaning of Success. Some Differences in Value Systems of Social Classes. *Journal of Social Psychology 62*: 141–8. *239*

Kawwa, T. (1968) A Survey of Ethnic Attitudes of Some British Secondary School Pupils. *British Journal of Social and Clinical Psychology 7*: 161–8. *206*

Keating, *7*

Kelly, G. A. (1955) *A Theory of Personality. The Psychology of Personal Constructs* (2 Vols). New York: Norton. *178, 210–11, 213*

Kelley, H. H. (1950) The Warm-Cold Variable in First Impressions of Persons. *Journal of Personality 18*: 431–9. *119–20*

Kelman, H. C. (1958) Compliance, Identification and Internalisation. Three Processes of Attitude Change. *Journal of Conflict Resolution 2*: 51–60. *152*

Kendler, H. H. and Tracy, S. (1962) Vertical and Horizontal Processes in Problem Solving. *Psychological Review 69*: 1–16. *41, 45*

Kendon, A. (1964) Progress Report of an Investigation into Aspects of the Structure and Function of Social Performance. Appendix II to First Annual Report to the Department of Scientific and Industrial Research of the Social Skills Project, Institute of Experimental Psychology, Oxford University. *115*

Kendon, A. (1967) Some Functions of Gaze-Direction in Social Interactions. *Acta Psychologica 26*: 27–47. Reprinted in M. Argyle (ed.) (1973) *Social Encounters*. Harmondsworth, Middlesex: Penguin. *116*

Kennedy, W. A., Vega, M. (1965) Negro Children's Performance on a Discrimination Task as a Function of Examiner Race and Verbal Incentive. *Journal of Personality and Social Psychology 2*: 839–43. *127*

Keogh, B. F. and Smith, C. E. (1967) Visual-Motor Ability and School Prediction: A Seven Year Study. *Perceptual and Motor Skills 25*: 101–10. *245*

Klausmeier, H. J., Ghatala, E. S. and Frayer, D. A. (1974) *Conceptual Learning and Development: A Cognitive View*. New York: Academic Press. *30, 51*

Klausmeier, H. J. and Meinke, D. L. (1968) Concept Attainment as a Function of Instructions Concerning the Stimulus Material, a Strategy and a Principle for Securing Information. *Journal of Educational Psychology 59*: 215–22. *30, 51*

Klein, M. (1960) *Our Adult World and its Roots in Infancy*. London: Tavistock. *197*

Kleinmuntz, B. (1966) *Problem Solving: Research, Method and Theory*. New York: John Wiley. *43*

Koestler, A. (1964) *The Act of Creation*. London: Hutchinson. *65*

Kohlberg, L. (1963) The Development of Children's Orientation towards a Moral Order. 1. Sequence in the Development of Moral Thought. *Vita Humana 6*: 11–33. *199–200, 207*

Kohler, W. (1927) *The Mentality of Apes*. London: Methuen. *40*

Kohn, M. (1966) The Child as a Determinant of his Peer's Approach to Him. *Journal of Genetic Psychology 109*: 91–100. *181*

Kolb, D. A. (1965) Achievement Motivation Training for Underachieving High-School Boys. *Journal of Personality and Social Psychology 2*: 783–92. *242*

Kounin, J. S. (1970) *Discipline and Group Management in Classrooms*. New York: Holt, Rinehart and Winston. *108, 162*

Kris, E. (1953) *Psycho-analytic Explorations in Art*. London: Georg Allen and Unwin. *63*

Krout, M. H. (1954) An Experimental Attempt to Determine th Significance of Unconscious Manual Symbolic Movements. *Journa of General Psychology 51*: 121–52. *116*

Kutnick, P. (1975) The Inception of Social Authority; A comparativ study of Samples of Children aged 4–12 in England and Midwester United States. Unpublished Ph.D. dissertation, University of London *206*

Laing, R. D. and Esterson, A. (1964) *Sanity, Madness and the Family* London: Tavistock. *109–10*

Lambert, W. E. (1967) A Social Psychology of Bilingualism. *Journal o Social Issues 23*: 91–109. *114*

Laver, J. (1963) Voice Quality and Indexical Information. *British Journa of Disorders of Communication 3*: 43–54. In J. Laver and S. Hutchinso (eds) (1972) *Communication in Face to Face Interaction*. Harmonds worth, Middlesex: Penguin. *114*

Leith, G. O. M. and Trown, E. A. (1970) The Influence of Personalit and Task Conditions on Learning and Transfer. *Programmed Learnin 7*: 181–8. *231*

Lenneberg, E. H. (1967) *Biological Foundations of Language*. New York John Wiley. *188*

Levy, P., Gooch, S. and Kellmer-Pringle, M. K. (1969) A Longitudina Study of the Relationship between Anxiety and Streaming in a Pro gressive and a Traditional Junior School. *British Journal of Education Psychology 39*: 166–73. *229*

Lippitt, R. and White, R. R. (1943) The 'Social Climate' of Children Groups. In R. G. Barker, J. S. Kounin and H. F. Wright (eds) *Chi Behaviour and Development*. New York: McGraw-Hill. *139*

Lipmann, W. *125*

Litt, E. (1963) Civic Education, Community Norms, and Politic Indoctrination. *American Sociological Review 28*: 69–75. *207*

Long, B. H., Ziller, R. C. and Henderson, E. H. (1968) Development Changes in the Self-Concept during Adolescence. *The School Revie 76*: 210–30. *117*

Lott, A. J. and Lott, B. E. (1966) Group Cohesiveness and Individu Learning. *Journal of Educational Psychology 57*: 61–73. *138*

Lott, D. F. and Sommer, R. (1967) Seating Arrangements and Statu *Journal of Personality and Social Psychology 7*: 90–5. *117*

Loughlin, L. J., O'Connor, H. A., Powell, M. and Parsley, K. M. (1965) An Investigation of Sex Differences by Intelligence, Subjec Matter Area, Grade and Achievement Level on Three Anxiety State

Journal of Genetic Psychology 106: 207–15. *229*

Lovell, K. and Shields, J. B. (1967) Some Aspects of a Study of the Gifted Child. *British Journal of Educational Psychology 37*: 201–8. *78*

Lowes, J. L. (1930) *The Road to Xanadu. A Study in the Ways of the Imagination.* Boston: Houghton Mifflin. *64*

Lunneborg, P. W. (1964) Relations among Social Desirability, Achievement and Anxiety Measures in Children. *Child Development 35*: 169–82. *228*

Luria, A. R. (1961) *The Role of Speech in the Regulation of Normal and Abnormal Behaviour.* New York: Pergamon Press. *17–18*

Luria, A. R. and Yudovich, F. la. (1959) *Speech and the Development of Mental Processes in the Child.* London: Staples Press (First published in the USSR, 1956). *258–9*

Lykken, D. T. A. (1957) A study of Anxiety in the Sociopathic Personality. *Journal of Abnormal and Social Psychology 55*: 6–10. *204*

Lytton, H. and Cotton, A. C. (1969) Divergent Thinking Abilities in Secondary Schools. *British Journal of Educational Psychology 39*: 188–90. *92*

Maccoby, E. E. (1966) Sex Differences in Intellectual Functioning. In E. E. Maccoby (ed.) *The Development of Sex Differences.* London: Tavistock. *216, 220–1*

Maccoby, E. E., Dowley, E. M., Degerman, J. W. and Degerman, R. (1965) Activity Level and Intellectual Functioning in Normal Pre-School Children. *Child Development 36*: 761–70 *217*

Mackinnon, D. W. (1960) The Highly Effective Individual. *Teacher's College Record 61*(7): 367–78. *84*

Mackinnon, D. W. (1962a) The Personality Correlates of Creativity: a Study of American Architects. *Proceedings of the Fourteenth Congress on Applied Psychology.* Vol. 2, Munksgaard: 11–39. *84–6, 87*

Mackinnon, D. W. (1962b) The Nature and Nurture of Creative Talent. *American Psychologist 17*: 484–95. *84, 87, 95*

Mackinnon, D. W. (1963) Creativity and Images of Self. In R. W. White (ed.) *The Study of Lives.* Englewood Cliffs, New Jersey: Prentice-Hall. *84*

Mahone, C. H. (1960) Fear of Failure and Unrealistic Vocational Aspiration. *Journal of Abnormal and Social Psychology 60*: 253–61. *237*

Marriott, S. (1964) Aspiration and Determination of the Career Choice of Adolescent Boys. *Educational Review 21*(2): 138–46. *249*

Maslow, A. H. (1962) Emotional Blocks to Creativity. In S. J. Parnes and H. F. Harding (eds) *A Source Book for Creative Thinking.* New York: Charles Scribner's Sons. *96*

Maslow, A. H. (1972) A Holistic Approach to Creativity. In C. W. Taylor (ed.) *Climate for Creativity*. New York: Pergamon Press. *70*

McClelland, D. C. (ed.) (1955) *Studies in Motivation*. New York Appleton-Century-Crofts. *235*

McClelland, D. C. (1961) *The Achieving Society*. Princeton, New Jersey Van Nostrand. *240–1*

McClelland, D. C. (1962) On the Psychodynamics of Creative Physica Scientists. In H. E. Gruber, G. Terrell and M. Wertheimer (eds) *Contemporary Approaches to Creative Thinking*. Englewood Cliffs New Jersey: Prentice-Hall. *81–3, 84, 87*

McClelland, D. (1969) The Role of Educational Technology in Developing Achievement Motivation. *Affective Domain* (October): 9–16. *24*

McClelland, D. C., Atkinson, J. W., Clark, J. W. and Lowell, E. (1955) *The Achievement Motive*. New York: Appleton-Century-Crofts. *235* *238*

McDonald, F. J. (1963) Children's Judgements of Theft from Individual and Corporate Owners. *Child Development 34*: 141–50. *202*

McElvain, J. L., Fretwell, L. N. and Lewis, R. B. (1963) Relationship between Creativity and Teacher Variability. *Psychological Reports 13* 186. *90*

McGhee, P. E. and Crandall, V. C. (1968) Beliefs in Internal–External Control of Reinforcements and Academic Performance. *Child Development 39*: 91–102. *248*

McGuire, C. (1967) Creativity and Emotionality. In R. L. Mooney, and T. A. Razik (eds) *Explorations in Creativity*. New York: Harper and Row. *79–80*

McIntyre, D., Morrison, A. and Sutherland, J. (1966) Social and Educational Variables relating to Teacher's Assessments of Primary School Pupils. *British Journal of Educational Psychology 36*: 272–9. *90, 177*

McWhinnie, H. J. (1967) Some Relationships between Creativity and Perception in Sixth Grade Children. *Perceptual and Motor Skills 25* 979–80. *69*

McWhinnie, H. J. (1969) Some Relationships between Creativity and Perception in Fourth Grade Children. *Acta Psychologica 31*: 169–75 *69*

Mead, M. (1962) Where Education Fits In. *Think*: 21. *89–90*

Medley, D. M. and Mitzel, H. E. (1958) A Technique for Measuring Classroom Behaviour. *Journal of Educational Psychology 49*: 86–92 *161*

Medley, D. M. and Mitzel, H. E. (1959) Some Behavioural Correlates of Teacher Effectiveness. *Journal of Educational Psychology 50*: 239–46 *161*

Medley, D. M. and Mitzel, H. E. (1963) Measuring Classroom Behaviour by Systematic Observation. In Gage, N. (ed.) *Handbook of Educational Research*. Chicago: Rand McNally. *161*

Mednick, S. A. (1962) The Associative Basis of the Creative Process. *Psychological Review* 69: 220–32. *64–5, 71, 96*

Mehrabian, A. (1968) Influence of Attitudes from the Posture, Orientation and Distance of a Communicator. *Journal of Consulting and Clinical Psychology* 32: 296–308. Reprinted in Argyle M. (ed.) (1973) *Social Encounters*. Harmondsworth, Middlesex: Penguin. *116*

Mehrabian, A. (1969) Significance of Posture and Position in the Communication of Attitude and Status Relationships. *Psychological Bulletin* 71: 359–72. *117*

Mendelsohn, G. A. and Griswold, B. B. (1964) Differential Use of Incidental Stimuli in Problem Solving as a Function of Creativity. *Journal of Abnormal and Social Psychology* 68: 431–6. *65*

Merei, F. (1949) Group Leadership and Institutionalisation. *Human Relations* 2: 23–39. *142*

Merton, R. (1957) *Social Theory and Social Structure*. Glencoe, Illinois: Free Press. *118*

Metzner, R. (1960) Preference for Delayed Reinforcement: Some Complications. Harvard Psychological Clinic. *236*

Meyer, W. J. and Thompson, G. G. (1956) Sex Differences in the Distribution of Teacher Approval and Disapproval among Sixth-Grade Children. *Journal of Educational Psychology* 47: 385–96. *222*

Milgram, S. (1963) Behavioural Study of Obedience. *Journal of Abnormal and Social Psychology* 67: 371–8. *149–50*

Milgram, S. (1964) Group Pressure and Action against a Person. *Journal of Abnormal and Social Psychology* 69(2): 137–43. *149–51*

Milgram, S. (1965a) Liberating Effects of Group Pressure. *Journal of Personality and Social Psychology* 1: 137–4. *149, 151*

Milgram, S. (1965b) Some Conditions of Obedience and Disobedience to Authority. *Human Relations* 18: 57–76. *149, 154–5*

Milgram, S. (1974) *Obedience to Authority*. London: Tavistock. *149*

Mill, J. S. *71*

Miller, G. A., Galanter, E. and Pribram, K. H. (1960) *Plans and the Structure of Behaviour*. New York: Holt, Rinehart and Winston. *44*

Miller, N. E. and Dollard, J. (1941) *Social Learning and Imitation*. Yale University Press. *194*

Minuchin, P. (1964) Sex Role Concepts and Sex Typing in Childhood as a Function of School and Home Environments. Paper presented at the American Orthopsychiatric Association, Chicago. *222*

Mischel, W. (1961) Delay of Gratification, Need for Achievement and Acquiescence in Another Culture. *Journal of Abnormal and Social Psychology* 62: 543–52. *236*

Moreno, J. L. (1934) *Who Shall Survive?* Washington Nervous and Mental Disease Publ. 10. *143*

Morrison, A. and Hallworth, H. J. (1966) The Perception of Peer Personality by Adolescent Girls. *British Journal of Educational Psychology* 36(3): 241–7. *120, 181*

Moscovici, S., Faucheux, C. (1972) Social Influence, Conformity Bias, and the Study of Active Minorities. In L. Berkowitz, (ed.) *Advances in Experimental Social Psychology* (Vol. 6). New York: Academic Press. *155–6*

Moss, H. A. (1967) Sex, Age, and State as Determinants of Mother – Infant Interaction. *Merril-Palmer Quarterly 13*: 19–36.

Mowrer, O. H. (1950) *Learning Theory and Personality Dynamics. Selected Papers.* New York: The Ronald Press. *194, 204*

Munroe, R. L. and Munroe, R. H. (1971) Over Representation of First Borns in East African Secondary Schools. *Journal of Social Psychology 84*: 151–2. *223–4*

Murray, H. A. (1943) *Thematic Apperception Test Manual.* Harvard University Press. *235*

Myers, R. E. and Torrance, E. P. (1961) Can Teachers Encourage Creative Thinking? *Educational Leadership 19*: 156–9. *98*

Nash, R. (1976) Pupils' Expectations of their Teachers. In M. Stubbs and S. Delamont (eds) *Explorations in Classroom Observation.* London: John Wiley. *178*

Neisser, U. (1966) *Cognitive Psychology.* New York: Appleton-Century-Crofts. *13, 26*

Newcomb, T. M. (1943) *Personality and Social Change: Attitude Formation in a Student Community.* New York: Holt, Rinehart and Winston. *153*

Newall, A., Shaw, J. C. and Simon, H. A., (1958) Elements of a Theory of Human Problem Solving. *Psychological Review 65*(13): 151–66. *44*

Newell, A., Shaw. J. C. and Simon, H. A. (1959) A Report on a General Problem-Solving Program. *Proceedings of the International Conference on Information Processing.* New York: UNESCO. *45*

Newell, A., and Simon, H. A. (1961) Computer Simulation of Human Thinking. *Science 134*: 2011–7. *45*

Newell, A. and Simon, H. A. (1963) G.P.S. a Program that Simulates Human Thought. In E. A. Feigenbaum, and J. Feldman (eds) *Computers and Thought.* New York: McGraw-Hill. *45*

Nilsen, T. R. (1954) Some Assumptions that Impede Communication. *General Semantics Bulletin 14* and *15*. Reprinted in Arthur N. Turner and George F. Lombard, *Interpersonal Behaviour and Administration.* New York: Free Press/London: Collier Macmillan. *128*

Nord, W. R. (1969) Social Exchange Theory: an Integrative Approach to Social Conformity. *Psychological Bulletin 71*: 174–208. *157*

Oberlander, M., Jenkin, N., Houliman, K. and Jackson, J. (1970) Family Size and Birth Order as Determinants of Scholastic Aptitude and Achievement in a Sample of Eighth Graders. *Journal of Consulting and Clinical Psychology 34*: 19–21. *223*

Oetzel, R. M. (1966) Annotated Bibliography and Classified Summary of Research in Sex Differences. In E. E. Maccoby (ed.) *The Development of Sex Differences*. London: Tavistock. *220*

Olson, R. M. (1966) On Conceptual Strategies. In J. S. Bruner, R. R. Olver and P. M. Greenfield, *Studies in Cognitive Growth*. New York: John Wiley. *27*

Olton, R. M. and Crutchfield, R. S. (1969) Developing the Skills of Productive Thinking. In P. Mussen, J. Langer and M. V. Covington (eds) *Trends and Issues in Development Psychology*. New York: Holt, Rinehart and Winston. *100*

Orne, M. T. and Scheibe K. E. (1964) The Contribution of Non-Deprivation Factors in the Production of Sensory Deprivation Effects: The Psychology of the 'Panic Button'. *Journal of Abnormal and Social Psychology 68*: 3–12. *110*

Osborn, A. F. (1957) *Applied Imagination*. New York: Charles Scribner's Sons. *101*

Paramanova, N. P. (1956) On the Formation of the Interaction of the Two Signal Systems in the Normal Child. In A. R. Luria (ed.) *Problems of Higher Nervous Activity of the Normal and Anomalous Child* (Vol. 1). Moscow: Academy of Pedagogic Sciences. *17, 19*

Parlett, M. P. (1969) The Syllabus-bound Student. Research report, Education Research Centre, Massachusetts Institute of Technology. Reprinted in L. Hudson (ed.) (1970) *The Ecology of Human Intelligence*. Harmondsworth, Middlesex: Penguin. *232*

Parloff, M. B., Datta, L., Kleman, M. and Handlon, J. H. (1968) Personality Characteristics which Differentiate Creative Male Adolescents and Adults. *Journal of Personality 36*: 528–52. *233*

Parnes, S. J. (1961) Effects of Extended Effort in Creative Problem Solving. *Journal of Educational Psychology 52*: 148–52. *101*

Parnes, S. J. and Brunelle, E. A. (1967) The Literature of Creativity (Part 1). *Journal of Creative Behaviour 1*: 52–109. *91*

Parnes, S. J. and Meadow, A. (1959) Effects of Brainstorming Instructions on Creative Problem Solving by Trained and Untrained Subjects. *Journal of Educational Psychology 50*: 171–6. *101*

Parnes, S. J. and Meadow, A. (1960) Evaluation of Persistence of Effects

Produced by a Creative Problem Solving Course. *Journal of Educational Psychology* 7: 357–61. *101*

Parsons, M. J. (1971) White and Black Creativity. *British Journal of Educational Studies 19*: 5–16. *55*

Passow, A. H. (1966) Diminishing Teacher Prejudice. In R. D. Strom (ed.) *The Inner-City Classroom: Teacher Behaviours*. Columbus, Ohio: Merrill Books. *279*

Patrick, J. (1973) *A Glasgow Gang Observed*. London: Eyre Methuen. *109*

Paul, G. L. and Eriksen, C. W. (1964) Effects of Test Anxiety on 'Real Life' Examinations. *Journal of Personality 32*: 480–94. *228*

Pavlov, I. P. (1927) *Conditioned Reflexes*. Oxford: Clarendon Press. *18–19, 22, 29*

Pavlov, I. P. (1941) *Conditioned Reflexes and Psychiatry*. New York: International Publishers. *17, 18*

Peaker, G. F. (1967) The Regression Analysis of the National Survey. In *Children and their Primary Schools*. Plowden Report. London: HMSO. *270*

Peel, E. A. (1960) *The Pupil's Thinking*. London: Oldbourne. *32*

Peltz, D. C. and Andrews, F. M. (1966) *Scientists in Organisation: Productive Climates for Research and Development*. New York: John Wiley. *98*

Perry, R. P. and Boyd, J. E. (1972) Communicating Impressions of People: a Methodological Study of Person Perception. *Journal of Social Psychology 86*: 95–103. *118*

Piaget, J. (1932) *The Moral Judgment of the Child*. London: Routledge and Kegan Paul. *199–200*

Piaget, J. (1949) *La Formation du Symbole*. Neuchâtel: Delachaux et Nièstle. *256*

Piaget, J. (1950) *The Psychology of Intelligence*. London: Routledge and Kegan Paul. *14, 22, 26, 29*

Piaget, J. (1952) Autobiography. In E. G. Boring (ed.) *A History of Psychology in Autobiography* (Vol. 4). New York: Russell and Russell. *20*

Piaget, J. (1953) *The Origin of Intelligence in the Child*. London: Routledge and Kegan Paul. *25*

Piaget, J. (1964) *The Early Growth of Logic*. London: Routledge and Kegan Paul. *24*

Piaget, J. (1971) The Theory of Stages in Logical Development. In D. R. Green, M. P. Ford and G. B. Flames (eds) *Measurement and Piaget*. New York: McGraw-Hill. *25*

Piaget, J. and Inhelder, B. (1958) *The Growth of Logical Thinking*. London: Routledge and Kegan Paul. *23–4*

Pidgeon, D. A. (1965) Date of Birth and Scholastic Performance. *Educational Research* 8(1): 3–7. *225*

Pidgeon, D. (1970) *Expectation and Pupil Performance*. Slough, Bucks: National Foundation for Education Research. *264–5, 271–2, 277*

Plato, *4*

Plowden Report (1967) *Children and their Primary Schools*. London: HMSO. *250*

Poincaré, H. (1924) *The Foundations of Science*. Translated by G. B. Halstead. Science Press. *54, 62, 64*

Polya, G. (1945) *How to Solve it*. Princeton University Press. *45, 46*

Popper, K. (1945) *The Open Society and its Enemies*. (Vol. 1) *The Spell of Plato*. London: Routledge and Kegan Paul. *3, 8*

Power, M. J., Benn, R. T. and Morris, J. N. (1972) Neighbourhood, School and Juveniles before the Courts. *British Journal of Criminology* *12*(2): 111–31. *270*

Pretchtl, H. F. R. and Lenard, H. G. (1967) A Study of Eye Movements in Sleeping New Born Infants. *Brain Research* 5: 477–93. *189*

Quetelet, *4*

Reed, H. B. and Dick, R. D. (1968) The Learning and Generalization of Abstract and Concrete Concepts. *Journal of Verbal Learning and Verbal Behaviour* 7: 486–90. *52*

Rees, H. W. and Parnes, S. J. (1970) Programming Creative Behaviour. *Child Development* *41*: 413–23. *100*

Reeves, J. W. (1965) *Thinking about Thinking*. London: Secker and Warburg. *5*

Rheingold, H. L., Gerwitz, J. L. and Ross, H. W. (1959) Social Conditioning of Vocalisations in the Infant. *Journal of Comparative and Physiological Psychology* *52*: 68–73. *193*

Richardson, E. (1967) *Group Study for Teachers*. London: Routledge and Kegan Paul. *145*

Ringness, T. A. (1967) Identification Patterns, Motivation and School Achievement of Bright Junior High School Boys. *Journal of Educational Psychology* *58*: 93–102. *249*

Ripple, R. E. and May, F. B. (1962) Caution in Comparing Creativity and I.Q. *Psychological Reports* *10*: 229–30. *74*

Rist, R. C. (1970) Student Social Class and Teacher Expectations: a Self-Fulfilling Prophecy in Ghetto Education. *Harvard Educational Review* *40*: 411–51. *279*

Robinson, W. P. (1972) *Language and Social Behaviour*. Harmondsworth, Middlesex: Penguin. *262*

Roe, A. (1951) A Psychological Study of Eminent Biologists. *Psychological Monographs* 65(14).   *87*

Roe, A. (1952) *The Making of a Scientist*. New York: Dodd Mead.   *81, 86, 90, 222*

Rogers, C. R. (1954) Toward a Theory of Creativity. *ETC: a Review of General Semantics* 2: 249–60.   *70, 80*

Rosen, B. C. (1956) The Achievement Syndrome: a Psycho-Cultural Dimension of Social Stratification. *American Sociological Review 21*: 203–11.   *239*

Rosen, B. C., and D'Andrade, R. (1959) The Psychosocial Origins of Achievement Motivation. *Sociometry 22*: 185–218.   *240*

Rosenberg, B. G. and Sutton-Smith, B. (1969) Sibling Age, Spacing Effects upon Cognition. *Development Psychology 1*: 661–8.   *223*

Rosenhan, D. L. (1973) On Being Sane in Insane Places. *Science 179*: (19th January): 251–7.   *124*

Rosenthal, R. (1966) *Experimenter Effects in Behavioural Research*. New York: Appleton-Century-Crofts.   *111, 124*

Rosenthal, R. (1967) Covert Communication in the Psychological Experiment. *Psychological Bulletin 67*: 356–67.   *111*

Rosenthal, R. and Jacobson, L. (1968) *Pygmalion in the Classroom. Teacher Expectation and Pupils' Intellectual Development*. New York: Holt, Rinehart and Winston.   *124*

Rosenthal, R., Kohn, P., Greenfield, P. and Carota, N. (1965) Psychology of the Scientist: XIV. Experimenters' Hypothesis-Confirmation and Mood as Determinants of Experimental Results. *Perceptual and Motor Skills 20*: 1237–52.   *111*

Rosenthal, R. and Rosnow, R. L. (eds) (1969) *Antifact in Behavioural Research*. New York: Academic Press.   *111, 124*

Rosenzweig, M. R. (1966) Environmental Complexity, Cerebral Change and Behaviour. *American Psychologist 21*: 321–32.   *264*

Rothbart, M. K. (1971) Birth Order and Mother Child Interaction in an Achievement Situation. *Journal of Personality and Social Psychology 17*: 113–20.   *222*

Rowlands, P. (1974) *Gifted Children and Their Problems*. London: Dent.   *225*

Ruebush, B. K. (1960) Children's Behaviour as a Function of Anxiety and Defensiveness. Unpublished doctoral dissertation, Yale University.   *227*

Runkel, P. J. (1965) Cognitive Similarity in Facilitating Communication. *Sociometry 19*: 175–91. Reproduced in Yee, A. H. (ed.) (1971) *Social Interaction in Educational Settings*. Englewood Cliffs, New Jersey: Prentice-Hall.   *113*

Rutter, M. (1972) *Maternal Deprivation Reassessed*. Harmondsworth,

Middlesex: Penguin. *190*

Rutter, M., Graham, P. and Yule, W. (1970) A Neuropsychiatric Study in Childhood. *Clinics in Developmental Medicine 35* and *36*. London: Spastics Society and Heinemann. *245*

Rutter, M., Tizard, J. and Whitmore, K. (1970) *Education, Health and Behaviour*. London: Longmans. *245*

Ryans, D. G. (1960) *Characteristics of Teachers*. Washington D.C.: American Council on Education. *159–60*

Ryle, G. (1949) *The Concept of Mind*. London: Hutchinson. *12, 14*

Salmon, P. (1969) Differential Conforming as a Developmental Process. *British Journal of Social and Clinical Psychology 8*: 22–31. *155*

Sarason, S. B., Davidson, K. S., Lighthall, F. F. and Waite, R. R. (1958) Classroom Observations of High and Low Anxious Children. *Child Development 29*: 287–95. *230*

Sarason, S. B., Davidson, K. S., Lighthall, F. F., Waite, R. R. and Ruebush, B. K. (1960) *Anxiety in Elementary School Children*. New York: John Wiley. *227*

Sartre, J. P. (1956) *Being and Nothingness*. Translated by H. E. Barnes. New York: Philosophical Library. *126*

Schachter, S. (1959) The Psychology of Affiliation. Stanford University Press. *107–8*

Schaffer, H. R. (1971) *The Growth of Sociability*. Harmondsworth, Middlesex: Penguin. *193, 194*

Schegloff, E. A. (1968) Sequencing in Conversational Openings. *American Anthropologist 70*: 1075–95. *112*

Schiller, P. H. (1952) Innate Constituents of Complex Responses in Primates. *Psychological Review 59*: 177–91. Reproduced in A. J. Riopelle (ed.) (1967) *Animal Problem Solving*. Harmondsworth, Middlesex: Penguin. *40*

Schmuck, R. (1963) Some Relationships of Peer Liking Patterns in the Classroom to Pupil Attitudes and Achievement. *School Review 71*: 337–59. *181*

Schmuck, R. A. (1966) Some Aspects of Classroom Social Climate. *Psychology of the Schools 3*: 59–65. *161*

Schmuck, R., Chesler, M. and Lippitt, R. (1966) *Problem Solving to Improve Classroom Learning*. Chicago: Science Research Associates. *147*

Schwartz, S. H., Feldman, K. A., Brown, M. E. and Heingartner, A. (1969) Some Personality Correlates of Conduct in Two Situations of Moral Conflict. *Journal of Personality 37*: 41–57. *203*

Sewell, W. H. and Shah, V. P. (1968) Social Class, Parental Encouragement, and Educational Aspirations. *American Journal of Sociology 73*: 559–72. *239*

Shaw, M. C. (1961) The Interrelationship of Selected Personality Factors in High Ability Underachieving School Children. Final Report, Project 58–M–1. California State Department Public Health. *247*

Shaw, M. C. (1968) Underachievement: Useful Construct or Misleading Illusion. *Psychology in the Schools* 5: 41–6. *244, 247*

Shaw, M. C. and Black, M. D. (1960) The Reaction to Frustration of Bright High School Underachievers. *California Journal of Educational Research 11*: 120–4. *247*

Shaw, M. C. and Brown, P. J. (1957) Scholastic Underachievement of Bright College Students. *Personnel and Guidance Journal 36*: 195–9. *247*

Shaw, M. C., Edson, K. C. and Bell, H. M. (1960) Self-Concepts of Bright Underachieving High School Students as Revealed by an Adjective Check List. *Personnel and Guidance Journal 39*: 193–6. *247*

Shaw, M. C. and Grubb, J. (1958) Hostility and Able High School Under-achievers. *Journal of Counselling Psychology 5*: 263–6. *247*

Sherif, M. and Sherif, C. (1969) *Social Psychology*. New York: Harper and Row. Original edition 1948. *112*

Shouksmith, G. (1970) *Intelligence, Creativity and Cognitive Style*. London: Batsford. *56*

Simon, A. and Boyer, E. G. (eds) (1970) *Mirrors for Behaviour II. An Anthology of Observation Instruments* (2 Vols). Philadelphia: Classroom Interaction Newsletter in co-operation with Research for Better Schools. *164, 168, 170*

Simon, R. J., Clark, S. M. and Galway, K. (1967) The Woman Ph.D., a Recent Profile. *Social Problems 15*(2): 221–36. *219, 220*

Simon, T. *20*

Sinclair, K. E. (1969) The Influence of Anxiety on Several Measures of Classroom Performance. *Australian Journal of Education 13*: 296–307. *229*

Singer, J. E. (1964) The Use of Manipulative Strategies: Machiavellianism and Attractiveness. *Sociometry 27*: 128–50. Reprinted in Argyle M. (ed.) (1973) *Social Encounters*. Harmondsworth, Middlesex: Penguin. *123*

Skeels, H. M. (1966) Adult Status of Children with Contrasting Early Life Experiences: a Follow-up Study. *Monographs of the Society for Research in Child Development 31*(3) (whole No. 105). *263*

Skeels, H. M. and Dye, H. B. (1939) A Study of the Effects of Differential Stimulation on Mentally Retarded Children. *Proceedings of the American Association for Mental Deficiency 44*: 114–36. *263*

Skinner, B. F. (1966) An Operant Analysis of Problem Solving. In Kleinmuntz (ed.) *Problem Solving: Research Methods and Theory*. New York: John Wiley. *42*

Slobin, D. I. (1973) Cognitive Pre-Requisites for the Development of Grammar. In C. A. Ferguson and D. I. Slobin (eds) *Studies of Child Language Development*. New York: Holt, Rinehart and Winston. *256*

Smith, P. B. (1969) Improving Skills in Working with People: the T-Group. Department of Employment and Productivity Training Information Paper 4. London: HMSO. *131*

Smith, W. F. and Rockett (1958) Test Performance as a Function of Anxiety, Instructor, and Instructions. *Journal of Educational Research* 52: 138–41. *229*

Smith, W. R. (1959) Favorable and Unfavorable Working Conditions Reported by Scientists at Two Research Centres. In C. W. Taylor (ed.) *The Third (1959) University of Utah Research Conference on the Identification of Creative Scientific Talent*: 250–67. *98*

Snyder, B. (1969) Creative Students in Science and Engineering. *Universities Quarterly 21*(2): 205–18. *94*

Snyder, R. T. and Freud, S. L. (1967) Reading Readiness and its Relation to Maturational Unreadiness as Measured by the Spiral after Effect and Visual-Perceptual Techniques. *Perceptual and Motor Skills* 25: 841–54. *245*

Sontag, L. W. and Kagan, J. (1967) The Emergency of Intellectual Achievement Motives. *American Journal of Orthopsychiatry 37*: 8–21. *220*

Soskin, W. F. (1953) Some Aspects of Communication and Interpretation in Psychotherapy. Paper read at the American Psychological Association, Cleveland. *114*

Spearman, C. E. (1904) 'General Intelligence' Objectively Determined and Measured. *American Journal of Psychology 15*: 72–101. *8, 10, 11, 13, 16*

Spearman, C. E. (1927) *The Abilities of Man*. London: Macmillan. *10*

Spender, S. (1954) The Making of a Poem. In B. Ghiselin (ed.) *The Creative Process: A Symposium*. Berkeley: University of California Press. *6*

Spielberger, C. D. (1962) The Effects of Manifest Anxiety on the Academic Achievement of College Students. *Mental Hygiene 46*: 420–6. *228*

Spielberger, C. D., Gorsuch, R. L. and Lushene, R. E. (1970) *The State-Trait Anxiety (S.T.A.I.) Test Manual for Form X*. Palo Alto: Consulting Psychologists Press. *226*

Sprott, W. J. H. (1958) *Human Groups*. Harmondsworth, Middlesex: Penguin. *145*

Staines, J. W. (1958) The Self Picture as a Factor in the Classroom. *British Journal of Educational Psychology 28*: 97–111. *280*

Stayton, D. J., Hogan, R. and Ainsworth, M. D. S. (1971) Infant Obedience and Maternal Behaviour: The Origins of Socialisation Reconsidered. *Child Development* 42: 1057–69. *204*

Stewart, M. (1962) *The Success of the First Born Child*. London: Worker's Educational Association. *222*

St. John, C. E. (1932) The Maladjustment of Boys in Elementary Grades. *Educational Administration and Supervision 18*: 649–72. *221*

Stott, D. H. (1963) *The Social Adjustment of Children. Manual to the Bristol Social Adjustment Guides*. University of London Press. *252*

Strom, R. D. (1968) Recognising Problems of the Successful. *The High School Journal* (April): 301–17. *279*

Stubbs, M. (1976) Keeping in Touch: Some Functions of Teacher Talk. In M. Stubbs and S. Delamont *Explorations in Classroom Observation*. London: John Wiley. *179*

Sugarman, B. (1968) Social Norm in Teenage Boys' Peer Groups. *Human Relations 21*(1): 41–58. *182, 249*

Sullivan, H. S. (1955a) *Conceptions of Modern Psychiatry*. London: Tavistock. *198*

Sullivan, H. S. (1955b) *The Interpersonal Theory of Psychiatry*. London: Tavistock.

Summerfield Report (1968) *Psychologists in Education Services*. London: HMSO. *198–9, 213*

Sutton, P. (1967) Correlation between Streaming and Season of Birth in Secondary Schools. *British Journal of Educational Psychology 37*(4): 300–4. *225*

Svennson, N. E. (1962) *Ability Grouping and Scholastic Achievement. Report on a Five Year Follow-up Study in Stockholm*. Stockholm: Almqvist and Wiksell. *142*

Swift, D. F. (1964) Who Passes the 11+? *New Society* (5th March): 6–9. *239*

Taine, H. *5*

Tajfel, H. (1966) Children and Nationalism. *New Society. 7*(196): 9–11. *206*

Tapp, J. L. and Kohlberg, L. (1971) Developing Senses of Law and Legal Justice. *Journal of Social Issues 27*(2): 65–91. *208*

Taylor, C. W. and Barron, F. (eds) (1963) *Scientific Creativity: its Recognition and Development*. New York: John Wiley. *82*

Taylor, C. W., Berry, P. C. and Block, C. H. (1958) Does Group Participation when Using Brainstorming Facilitate or Inhibit Creative Thinking? *Administrative Science Quarterly 3*: 23–47. *102*

Taylor, C. W., Smith, W. R. and Ghiselin, B. (1963) The Creative and Other Contributions of One Sample of Research Scientists. In C. W. Taylor and F. Barron (eds) *Scientific Creativity: Its Recognition and*

Development. New York: John Wiley. *98*

Taylor, J. A. (1953) A Personality Scale of Manifest Anxiety. *Journal of Abnormal and Social Psychology 48*: 285–90. *227*

Taylor, J. A. (1956) Drive Theory and Manifest Anxiety. *Psychological Bulletin 53*: 303–20. *138*

Terman, L. M. (1925) *Genetic Studies of Genius*. (Vol. 1) *The Mental and Physical Traits of a Thousand Gifted Children*. Stanford University Press. *223, 251*

Terman, L. M. (1947) Psychological Approaches to the Study of Genius. *Papers on Eugenics 4*: 3–20. *71*

Terman, L. M. (1954) Scientists and Nonscientists in a Group of 800 Gifted Men. *Psychological Monographs 68*(7): 44. *82, 87*

Terman, L. M., Burks, B. S. and Jensen, D. W. F. (1930) *The Promise of Youth. Genetic Studies of Genius* (Vol. 3). Stanford University Press. *251*

Terman, L. M. and Oden, M. H. (1959) The Gifted Group in Mid-Life. *Genetic Studies of Genius* (Vol. 4). Stanford University Press. *251*

Terman, L. M. and Oden, M. H. (1959) *The Gifted Group in Mid-Life. Genetic Studies of Genius* (Vol. 5). Stanford University Press. *251*

Thelen, H. A. (1967) *Classroom Grouping for Teachability*. New York: John Wiley. *176–7*

Thibaut, J. (1968) The Development of Contractual Norms in Bargaining: Replication and Variation. *Journal of Conflict Resolution 12*: 102–12. Reprinted in P. B. Smith (1970) (ed.) *Group Processes*. Harmondsworth, Middlesex: Penguin. *132*

Thibaut, J. W. and Kelley, H. H. (1959) *The Social Psychology of Groups*. New York: John Wiley. *157*

Thomas, D. *57*

Thorndike, R. L. (1963) The Measurement of Creativity. *Teachers College Record 64*: 422–4. *71*

Thorndike, R. L. *16*

Thurstone, L. L. (1938) Primary Mental Abilities. *Psychometric Monograph 1*. *8, 10–11, 13*

Tonkey, J. C. (1972) Role Perception and the Relative Influence of the Perceiver and the Perceived. *Journal of Social Psychology 87*: 213–7. *120*

Torrance, E. P. (1961) Priming Creative Thinking in Primary Grades. *Elementary School Journal 42*: 34–41. *102*

Torrance, E. P. (1962a) *Guiding Creative Talent*. Englewood Cliffs, New Jersey: Prentice-Hall. *67, 90, 100*

Torrance, E. P. (1962b) Developing Creative Thinking Through School Experience. In S. J. Parnes and H. F. Harding (eds) *A Source Book for Creative Thinking*. New York: Charles Scribner's Sons. *67, 91, 99*

Torrance, E. P. (1963a) *Education and the Creative Potential*. Minneapolis: University of Minnesota Press. *95*

Torrance, E. P. (1963b) Toward the More Humane Education of Gifted Children. *Gifted Child Quarterly 7*: 135–45. *98*

Torrance, E. P. (1965) *Rewarding Creative Behaviour*. Englewood Cliffs, New Jersey: Prentice-Hall. *67–8, 91–2, 100*

Torrance, E. P. *65, 70*

Trabasso, T. (1973) Stimulus Emphasis and All-or-None Learning of Concept Identification. *Journal of Experimental Psychology 65*: 395–406. *52*

Treffinger, D. and Ripple, R. E. (1965) Developing Creative Problem Solving Abilities and Related Attitudes through Programmed Instruction. *Journal of Creative Behaviour 3*: 105–10. *100*

Triandis, H. C. and Fishbein, M. (1963) Cognitive Interaction in Person Perception. *Journal of Abnormal and Social Psychology 67*: 446–57. *125*

Tuckman, B. W. (1965) Developmental Sequence in Small Groups. *Psychological Bulletin 63*: 384–99. *136–7*

Tulkin, S. R. and Kagan, J. (1970) Mother-Child Interaction: Social Class Differences in the First Year of Life. Paper presented at the Annual Convention of the American Psychological Association, Miami Beach, Florida. *261*

Tumin, M. (1962) Obstacles to Creativity. In S. J. Parnes and H. F. Harding (eds) *A Source Book for Creative Thinking*. New York: Charles Scribner's Sons. *96, 101*

Turner, A. N. and Lombard, F. F. (1969) *Interpersonal Behaviour and Administration*. New York: Free Press. *139*

Turner, J. H. (1970) Entrepreneurial Environments and the Emergency of Achievement Motivation in Adolescent Males. *Sociometry 33*: 147–65. *239*

Turner, R. H. (1964) *The Social Context of Ambition*. San Francisco: Chandler. *249*

Valverde, F. (1967) Apical Dendrite Spines of the Visual Cortex and Light Deprivation in the Mouse. *Experimental Brain Research 3*: 337–52. *264*

Vernon, M. (1968) Fifty Years of Research on the Intelligence of Deaf and Hard-of-hearing Children: a Review of Literature and Discussions of Implications. *Journal of Rehabilitation of the Deaf 1*: 1–12. *260*

Vernon, P. E. (1965) Abilities and Attainments in the Western Isles. *Scottish Educational Journal 48*: 948–50. *95*

Vernon, P. E. (1966) Educational and Intellectual Development among Canadian Indians and Eskimos. *Educational Review 18*: 79–91. *95*

Videbeck, R. (1960) Self Conception and the Reactions of Others. *Sociometry 23*: 351–9. Reprinted in M. Argyle (ed.) (1973) *Social Encounters*. Harmondsworth, Middlesex: Penguin. *127*

Wachs, T. D. (1967) Environmental Stimulation and Early Intellectual Development: a Broader Look at a One-sided Problem. Paper presented to Indiana Psychological Association, West Lafayette. *264*

Waite, R. R., Sarason, S. B., Lighthall, F. F. and Davidson, K. S. (1958) A Study of Anxiety and Learning in Children. *Journal of Abnormal and Social Psychology 57*: 267–70. *229*

Walberg, H. J. (1969) Physics, Femininity and Creativity. *Developmental Psychology 1*: 47–54. *220*

Walker, R. and Adelman, C. (1976) Strawberries. In M. Stubbs and S. Delamont (eds) *Explorations in Classroom observation*. London: John Wiley. *179*

Walker, W. J. (1967) Creativity and High School Climate (Abstract and Summary). In J. C. Gowan, G. D. Demos and E. P. Torrance *Creativity: Its Educational Implications*. New York: John Wiley. *91*

Wallach, M. A. and Kogan, N. (1965) *Modes of Thinking in Young Children*. New York: Holt, Rinehart and Winston. *75, 77, 80*

Wallas, G. (1926) *The Art of Thought*. London: Jonathan Cape. *57–9, 61–2, 70*

Walster, E. (1966) The Assignment of Responsibility for an Accident. *Journal of Personality and Social Psychology 5*: 508–16. *121*

Warburton, F. W. (1968) The Relationship between Personality Factors and Scholastic Attainment. Unpublished Report. Department of Education, University of Manchester. *231*

Ward, W. C. (1969) Creativity and Environmental Cues in Nursery School Children. *Development Psychology 1*: 543–7. *69*

Warner, F. (1890) *Mental Faculty*. Cambridge University Press. *7*

Washburne, C. and Heil, L. M. (1960) What Characteristics of Teachers Affect Children's Growth. *School Review 68*: 420–8. *175*

Watson, J. B. (1928) *Psychological Care of Infant and Child*. New York: Norton. *188*

Watson, O. M. and Graves, T. D. (1966) Quantitative Research in Proxemic Behaviour. *American Anthropologist 68*: 971–85. Reprinted in M. Argyle (ed.) (1973) *Social Encounters*. Harmondsworth, Middlesex: Penguin. *117*

Weber, M. (1930) *The Protestant Ethic and the Spirit of Capitalism*. New York: Charles Scribner's Sons. *240–1*

Weinstein, E. A. and Crowdus, S. E. (1968) The Effects of Positive and Negative Information on Person Perception. *Human Relations 21*(4): 383–92. *119*

Weisberg, P. S. and Springer, K. J. (1961) Environmental Factors in Creative Function. *Archives of General Psychiatry 5*: 64–74. *88*

Wells, R. *132*

Werner, H. (1948) *Comparative Psychology of Mental Development.* New York: International Universities Press. *245*

Werner, H. and Kaplan, B. (1967) *Symbol Formation: An Organismic-Developmental Approach to Language and the Expression of Thought.* New York: John Wiley. *257*

Wertheimer, M. (1945) *Productive Thinking.* New York: Harper Bros. Enlarged edition 1959. *12, 13–14, 30, 33–5*

Weschler, I. R., Kahone, M. and Tannenbaum, R. (1961) Assessing Organisational Effectiveness: Job Satisfaction, Productivity and Morale. In I. R. Tannenbaum, I. R. Weschler and F. Massarik (eds) *Leadership and Organisation: a Behavioural Science Approach.* New York: McGraw-Hill. *139*

White, J. P. (1968) Creativity and Education: A Philosophical Analysis. *British Journal of Educational Studies 16*(2): 123–7. *55*

White, R. W. (1959) Motivation Reconsidered: The Concept of Competence. *Psychological Review 66*: 297–333. *235*

White, S. H. (1968) Evidence for a Hierarchical Arrangement of Learning Processes. In L. R. Lipsitt and C. C. Spiker (eds) *Advances in Child Development and Behaviour* (Vol. 2). New York: Academic Press. *257–8*

Wiener, M., Carpenter, J. and Carpenter, B. (1956) External Validation of a Measure of Conformity Behaviour. *Journal of Abnormal and Social Psychology 52*: 421–2. *152*

Willard, D. and Strodbeck, F. L. (1972) Latency of Verbal Response and Participation in Small Groups. *Sociometry 35*(1): 161–75. *135*

Williams, F. (1967) The Mystique of Unconscious Creation. In J. Kagan (ed.) *Creativity and Learning.* Boston: Houghton Mifflin. *62*

Winterbottom, M. R. (1958) The Relation of Need for Achievement to Learning Experiences in Independence and Mastery. In J. W. Atkinson (ed.) *Motives in Fantasy, Action and Society.* Princeton, New Jersey: Van Nostrand. *239–41*

Wiseman, S. (1968) Social Deprivation and Education. In H. J. Butcher and H. B. Pont (eds) *Educational Research in Britain* (Vol. 1). University of London Press. *266*

Withall, J. (1949) Development of a Technique for the Measurement of Socio-Emotional Climate in Classrooms. *Journal of Experimental Education 17*: 347–61. *160*

Withall, J. (1951) The Development of a Climate Index. *Journal of Educational Research 45*: 93–9. *160*

Witkin, H. A., Dyk, R. B., Faterson, H. F., Goodenough, D. R. and

Karp, S. A. (1962) *Psychological Differentiation*. New York: John Wiley. *69, 89, 221, 233*

Witkin, H., Goodenough, D. and Karp, S. (1967) Stability of Cognitive Style from Childhood to Young Adulthood. *Journal of Personality and Social Psychology 7*: 291–300. *233*

Witkin, H. A., Lewis, H. B., Hertzman, M., Machover, K., Meissner, P. B. and Wapner, S. (1954) *Personality through Perception*. New York: Harper and Row. *69, 217*

Wiviott, S. P. (1970) *Bases of Classification of Geometric Concepts Used by Children of Varying Characteristics*. Technical Report No. 143. Madison, Wisconsin Research and Development Centre for Cognitive Learning. *51*

Wolf, R. M. (1964) The Identification and Measurement of Environmental Process Variables Related to Intelligence. Unpublished doctoral dissertation, University of Chicago. *264*

Wolff, P. H. (1967) The Role of Biological Rhythms in Early Psychological Development. *Bull Menninger Clinic 31*: 197–218. *189*

Wolff, S. (1969) *Children under Stress*. Harmondsworth, Middlesex: Penguin. *247*

Woodard, S. L. (1969) Black Power and Achievement Motivation. *The Clearing House 44*: 72–5. *238*

Woodworth, R. S. and Schlosberg, H. (1954) *Experimental Psychology*. New York: Holt, Rinehart and Winston. *59*

Wright, H. F., Barker, R. G., Nall, J. and Schoggen, P. (1951) Towards a Psychological Ecology of the Classroom. *Journal of Educational Research 45*: 187–200. *173*

Wright, C. J. and Nuthall, G. (1970) The Relationship between Teacher Behaviour and Pupil Achievement and Three Experimental Science Lessons. *American Educational Research Journal 7*: 477–91. *278*

Yamamoto, K. (1963) Relationships between Creative Thinking Abilities of Teachers and Achievement and Adjustment of Pupils. *Journal of Experimental Education 32*: 2–25. *91*

Yamamoto, K. (1965) Effects of Restriction of Range and Test Unreliability on Correlation between Measures of Intelligence and Creative Thinking. *British Journal of Educational Psychology 35*: 300–5. *74*

Yamamoto, K. (1966) Mental Health, Creative Thinking and Values·. *Elementary School Journal 66*: 361–7. *90*

Yarrow, L. J., Goodwin, M. S., Manheimer, H. and Milowe, I. D. (1974) Infancy Experiences and Cognitive and Personality Development at Ten Years. In J. L. Stone, H. T. Smith and L. B. Murphy (eds) *The Competent Infant*. London: Tavistock. *191–2*

Yee, A. H. (1968) Interpersonal Attitudes of Teachers and Advantaged and Disadvantaged Pupils. *Journal of Human Resources 3*: 327–45. *278–9*

Zaporozhets, A. V. (1965) The Development of Perception in the Pre-School Child. In P. H. Mussen (ed.) *Society for Research in Child Development Monograph 30*(2). *17, 19*

Subject index

ability 5, 8, 10–11, 29, 55, 74, 77, 105, 121–4, 127–8, 146, 215, 234, 248, 271
abstract concepts 52
academic achievement xii, 3, 8, 93, 127, 236, 241–2, 258, 262, 280; failure xii, 228; motivation 234, 216, 238; performance 127; success xii
accommodation 25
achievement 74, 76, 77, 159, 182, 191, 192, 215–7, 220–2, 226, 229, 231, 233, 239, 249, 251, 270, 272, 278, 280–1; motivation 234–7, 238, 241–2; tests 244, 248; through conformance 216, 236; through independence 263
acquiescence 148, 152–3
adaptation 25
adolescence xi, 199, 207–9, 257
adolescent(s) 208, 209, 211, 239, 249
advantaged children 248, 278
affiliation 107, 108, 203, 235
affiliative behaviour 221
age 112, 206; chronological 6, 71; mental 6, 71
aggression 82, 87
ambition 249
American national merit competition 223
anxiety 75, 76, 80–1, 84, 86, 107–8, 111, 127, 133, 190,

196–7, 203–4, 211, 215, 220, 224, 225–30, 247
arithmetic 228
artificial intelligence 44
artistic thinking 30–1
A-state 226
Ask and Guess Test 67
assimilation 25
associations 32, 41, 64, 75, 258
associationist approach 62, 64
associative level 257; principles 257; theories 47–9
A-trait 226
attachment 189, 190
attainment 3, 8, 143, 222, 234, 244, 271, 275, 278
attention-seeking 246, 247
attribution of ability 121–3, 125; of intention 121, 250; of responsibility 121
authoritarianism 152, 206
authoritarian personality 126
authority 206
autonomy 187, 203, 233
avoiding success 238

backwardness 266
Bales Interaction Analysis Schedule 144–5
Barr Scale 15–16
behaviour therapy 247
Binet–Simon Intelligence Scale 7
birth order 88, 108, 153–4, 222–4, 251